**Race among Nations:
A Conceptual Approach**

This book is published for the Center
on International Race Relations in
their *Race and Nations Series.* The
Center seeks the wider recognition of
the role of race in international affairs,
and through its research and teaching
programs develops a systematic analysis
of race in American foreign
relations.

Race among Nations: A Conceptual Approach

Edited by

George W. Shepherd, Jr.
Tilden J. LeMelle
University of Denver

with the assistance of

Gail S. Schoettler
Cynthia Kahn

Heath Lexington Books
D. C. Heath and Company
Lexington, Massachusetts

GN
320
R 27

Contents

List of Tables

Foreword

Three years after the first Pan-African Congress, held in London in 1900, W.E.B. DuBois uttered his now prophetic observation: "The problem of the Twentieth Century is the problem of the colour line—the relation of the darker to the lighter races of men in Asia and Africa, in America and the islands of the sea." When DuBois spoke these prophetic words, there was little, if any, attention paid to them outside the small circle of black men who three years earlier had come together in a common bond of color to organize and participate in the Pan-African Congress. Where was the color problem DuBois spoke of? Europeans had by that time successfully extended white hegemony over most of the nonwhite world. The fate of the black man in his own birthplace had already been decided some fifteen years before at a conference table in Berlin, where the continent of Africa had been carved up arbitrarily by white men and distributed among them for political domination and economic exploitation. By 1903, white European control was already firmly established in Africa. For nearly twenty-five years in the United States, the other bastion of white control, Jim Crowism had successfully reversed the short-lived Reconstruction experiment in multiracial democracy. Moreover, animated by Social Darwinism, the United States was already involved in its own adventures in the "imperialism of righteousness." Indeed, if there was a problem in terms of color, beyond that small group of Pan-Africanists, it was perceived as the problem of extending *white civilization* to the "backward" *colored* peoples of the world—as the problem of the "white man's burden."

Today, almost seventy years after DuBois' prophetic utterance, one still looks almost in vain for a serious public concern about the "problem of colour" in the world. Of the abundant literature on international relations in the United States, only one book-length study, Robert Browne's *Race in International Affairs* (Public Affairs Press, 1961), comes to grips directly with the fact of race. Browne's work received little attention in academic or popular literature despite the fact that 1960 was the great year of the Revolution of Color in Africa and the beginning of America's New Frontier image in international relations. Again, in the late 1960s, despite the greater involvement of peoples of color in international relations, and the growing tensions between the "have not" colored and the "have" non-colored peoples of the world, the study of the "colour line" in world affairs received little more attention. Ronald Segal's *The Race War,* which is more an analysis of the values and interests of the four major racially dominant areas of the world than a study of race per se, has only been the second book-length treatment of racial conflict in international affairs. Add Harold Isaacs' "Color in World Affairs" (*Foreign Affairs,* January 1969), and Robert Gardiner's "Race and Color in International Relations" (*Daedalus,* vol. 96, Spring 1966), and the list is complete. What characterizes all of these works is that they were written by men who must be considered more as scholarly observors of international relations than as scholarly pacesetters in the field. Moreover, the two articles listed appeared in popular intellectual journals rather than in the learned professional journals. Briefly, the academic standardbearers—the modelbuilders, theoreticians, and textbook writers—have almost totally disregarded the role of race in international relations (see James Rosenau's essay below, Chapter Three, note 4).

Why this persistent and virtual disregard of race as a factor in international relations? Most certainly students of international relations have not been unaware of race in world affairs. Even if they ignored the disconcerting treatises of a black DuBois, whose protests against international racism spanned almost one hundred years, they could not have been unaware of the concerns of so respectable an authority as Arnold Toynbee ("Is a 'Race War' Shaping Up?" *New York Times Magazine,* September 29, 1963).

It is perhaps in the realm of national ideology that race has played its most important role in modern international relations. As a conscious ideology—as a means for justifying national policies—race developed hand in hand with the eighteenth- and nineteenth-century expansionist thrust of Europe into other parts of the world. It provided some justification for the effort by European colonizers to maintain their supremacy in those lands that fell subject to European imperialism. Paradoxically, this era of expansionism occurred simultaneously with the period that produced Western Europe's and America's greatest and most noble pronouncements on the equality of man. Yet this same period produced what some consider to be one of the darkest chapters in the history of man's inhumanity to man.

It was not, however, until the latter part of the nineteenth century that the arguments in support of the inequality of races were systematized into what might be called an official ideology. In the United States this occurred as a result of the attempt to justify slavery and of the post-1876 discriminatory laws designed to reduce the American black man to his former position of subservience. Endless were the claims that the black American was of a naturally inferior race, suited only for servitude. A pseudoscientific base was sought in the concepts of Charles Darwin. Social Darwinism equated the principle of the survival of the fittest with the right of the fittest to rule. Naturally the white man was the fittest. His enslavement and conquest of other peoples proved his racial superiority. Governor J.H. Hammond of South Carolina brought the ideology to an extreme in his "mud sill" theory, which argued that in all societies there must be a class to do the menial tasks. The class at the bottom of the political, socioeconomic ladder (if on it at all) was necessary for the progress of the upper classes. To him, of course, that class was the Afro-American. The Civil War decided the issue of slavery, but racism remained as a part of the American ideology.

In Europe, again as a means for justifying imperialism in Asia and Africa, racism developed as an inherent part of national ideologies. Through the early efforts of ethnologists to classify peoples of the world according to biological characteristics, there developed among social scientists (who were even then concerned about their lack of a "scientific" frame of reference) a tendency to view "race" as the all-pervasive explanation for social behavior and institutions. The racist implications of anthropological terms such as brachycephalic (broad-skulled) and dolichocephalic (narrow-skulled), or the attempt to attribute the assumed sexual and athletic prowess of the black man to racial traits, are products of the attempt to systematize and intellectually legitimize racist ideology. The effects of these efforts persist today in some of the popular literature of the West.

Extremely influential in the modern development of racism as ideology was Count Arthur de Gobineau (1816-1882), French aristocrat, litterateur, and diplomat. It was he who first formulated the Aryan myth—the idea that all human characteristics were determined by race and that the white man descended from a superior race, the Aryas. The Aryas, he contended, were no longer pure, but some of their miscegenated descendants still carried enough Aryan blood to claim the right to rule. These descendants were the aristocrats of the white nations. Thus social superiority was to be determined in terms of whiteness and, after going through the various shades and hues of white, there was not much of value left for the brown or yellow or the black man who, again, was at the bottom of the scale.

De Gobineau's ideas were especially welcomed by such Nordic racists as Nietzsche and Schopenhauer and the composer Richard Wagner. It took the Englishman Houston Stewart Chamberlain, however, to crystallize the ideas for use in German nationalism. Since he and Hitler were very close friends and he married Wagner's daughter, one can imagine the mutually satisfactory conversations that must have taken place between them on the subject of race. The culmination of racist ideology in Europe in the oral and written ravings of Hitler is common knowledge. Hitler, however, was but the Frankenstein monster turned upon its creator.

Buoyed up by his assumption of superior rights based upon his assumption of racial superiority, the European set out to impose white rule over the whole world. Although he was seeking primarily political and economic gain, he justified his conquest of the nonwhite peoples of the world in terms of nature and religion. The result was what has come to be known as the color line in the colonial situation. Many attempts have been made to distinguish between French and British colonial policies, in particular, but the facts do not support a significant difference on the question of race. Both policies assumed the inherent racial inferiority of the nonwhite. The official French policy of assimilation or identity provided that the nonwhite colonized peoples could become black, brown, or yellow Frenchmen provided they rose above their own racially inferior culture and assimilated the universally superior civilization of the French. Among the British, the same policy was expressed through Cecil Rhodes' famous slogan: "Equal rights for all *civilized* men." Neither policy worked. The French, after a brief experiment in Senegal, could not bring themselves to accept the logic of practical assimilation—racial equality; the bloody consequences of racism in Cecil Rhodes' southern African empire are all too well known. All European powers resorted to what has been called the policy of association: the nonwhite could associate with the European as a "hewer of wood" but never as an equal. The contradiction of actual and *de facto* segregation in the United States and of South Africa's apartheid is that they are in fact nothing more or less than association on an unequal basis.

The same assumptions of the racial inferiority of nonwhites underlay the League of Nations mandate system that gave formal international legitimacy to the colonial situation. The ABC mandate system legally established the white nations of the world as the arbiters until the nonwhite peoples were considered sufficiently civilized to govern themselves. The irony, of course, is that these peoples had governed themselves quite well before the European intrusion. The mandate system was interesting in that the categories it projected conformed to the colonialist and De Gobineau assumptions of gradations in racial inferiority. Representative of this is the statement of Georges Hardy, one-time director of the French Ecole Coloniale. Speaking of the need to adjust colonial policy to the degree of backwardness of a country he says, "Differences in [the colonial] situations demand differences in approach: one does not handle a literate Vietnamese or Moroccan as he would a savage of Central Africa or Australia." That is, all nonwhites are inferior beings, but the black African is even more inferior—at the bottom of the human scale.

It is not difficult to understand the racist assumptions behind the mandate system when one considers the strong opposition to and eventual rejection of Japan's proposal for unreserved acceptance by the Western powers of the principle of racial equality. Great Britain and France especially regarded Japan's request as a challenge to the white man's superiority, and America's President Wilson, even though he supported Japan for a while, found that he could not buck racism in the United States, and rejected Japan's proposal. Thus, not only in the mandate system but in their refusal to support the principle of racial equality, the white European powers of the League of Nations and the United States sanctioned racism in international relations. The principle of self-determination enunciated in the Fourteen Points meant that the white powers would decide when the nonwhite peoples of the world could be free to direct their own lives.

It is no wonder, then, that Hitler's racial policies were so successful; or that South Africa today can defy the world in pursuing its racist policies not only at home but in Southwest Africa (Namibia); or that Rhodesia can openly flaunt the authority of Great Britain in the name of white supremacy.

Racism has manifested itself internationally not only through colonialism and in international organizations but also in immigration policies, where an entire nation pits itself against an individual on racist grounds. The 1870 immigration law of the United States discriminating against Chinese and Koreans, the 1906 Gentlemen's Agreement and the 1924 Johnson Immigration Act directed against the Japanese, the general discrimination against the Mediterranean darker-skinned European—all represent the noisome poison of racism and color prejudice. One might also cite Australia's 1901 law against those who could not write a European language or Canada's 1908 law restricting Japanese immigration or South Africa's current restrictions against non-Europeans.

Race as ideology in international relations has not only served to justify past European imperialism. Of grave concern to the student of international relations is the response of people still being oppressed in the name of white supremacy. The ideology of white imperialism has meant the further awakening of race consciousness among people everywhere, especially those who have been the direct victims of racism. It has meant the emergence of new states in Asia and Africa—created as part of the world reaction to racialism. It has meant the development of other ideologies in terms of race. The concepts of Negritude, African Personality, Afro-Asian solidarity, Pan-Arabism, Pan-Africanism—all are in large measure still more a consciousness of race than racism in reverse, but this is a consciousness that could develop into destructive racism of the Hitler type. Racism in international relations has meant that the originators of modern racism—the Europeans and Americans—are almost always distrusted in their dealings with the nonwhite world. It has meant that Mainland China, in its yet unsuccessful attempts to win over the peoples of Asia and Africa in opposition to the West and the Soviet Union, could speak to a receptive audience at the Bandung Conference in 1955 in terms of the colored peoples of the world uniting against the white, an imperialistic minority in a predominantly nonwhite world. In the Pan-African movement it meant that those nations forming the Monrovia-Brazzaville group could be accused of fostering neocolonialism because of their close association with the former colonial powers. It means that the United States if often portrayed in the Vietnam War as a great white power bullying a weak but determined little yellow nation, especially when Secretary of State Dean Rusk raised images of the "yellow peril" in his defense of United States policy in Vietnam. It means that the United States symbolizes to many the West's historical obsession with the yellow peril in its cold war with China. The United States is able to provide little moral leadership in international politics when its representatives have to talk with tongue in cheek in discussing questions of human equality or when pointing to violations of human rights.

The poison of modern racialism—the problem of the color line—has left few uninfected. Although the darker nations of the world revolt against and condemn the European nations for exporting the bane of color status, some are themselves guilty of the same addiction as a result of having assimilated white racist values. In South Vietnam the darker Vietnamese of the far south is looked down upon by his lighter brethren. In India, while the black Indian of the south considers himself to be the only true Indian, his lighter-skinned brothers of the north consider him undesirable because of his skin. Many "coloreds" in southern Africa consider themselves superior to the black Africans. The story of color among nonwhites in the Americas is all too well known in fiction and fact.

And in all of these places, the lines of power have been coterminous with the lines of color.

Racialism indeed, has blighted the domestic and international relations of most peoples of the world. In its two-hundred years of existence, modern racism has always led to the creation of tensions and instabilities, distrust and bloodshed. Already the most destructive war in the history of mankind has been fought in the name of racial supremacy. Another one could be fought eventually in the name of racial equality.

The foregoing considerations of race in international relations are only the highlights of a much more complex phenomenon. Race has not been nor is it today always a primary or even a significant variable in international affairs. Where it has been operative in the past it has often acted as an accelerator of tension and conflict. Today, it is indisputably one of the most explosive international issues in parts of Africa, west and southeast Asia, and can be ignored only at the risk of international peace. As such it is not only the responsibility of world statesmen and others directly involved in interstate affairs to come to grips with the question of race. It is also the responsibility of the student of international relations to use his analytical skills and competence to understand how race functions in world affairs. *The Study of Race among Nations* is a first attempt to develop useful concepts and tools for the analyst. We can no longer afford the luxury of emotionalism and half-educated guesses on this crucial issue.

The several studies in this volume do not purport to be a definitive statement on how race in international relations can or ought to be studied. They represent rather an effort at retrospectively bringing together some of the concepts and models already in use.

George Shepherd's two contributions evaluate the applicability of present social-science concepts vis à vis race in international relations and offer a research design for the comparative study of white dominance systems. With their emphasis on a systemic approach, these essays direct the student's attention to what is probably the most difficult problem in current race studies—institutionalized racism.

Peter Rose's contribution is largely a review of selected sociological literature on race relations, with suggestions for its application to cross national studies in comparative race relations. James Rosenau's study also suggests how existing concepts and paradigms might lend themselves to "teasing out" the racial variable in interstate relations. Rosenau, however, goes much farther by introducing several hypotheses to be tested. The hypotheses themselves derive from his own work in "linkage" theory, which relates a state's external behavior to internal sets of variables and vice-versa. The hypotheses should be useful devices for gathering the kind of empirical data that lead to greater understanding and more accurate conclusions about the racial input in foreign policy.

Like the other essays, Karl Deutsch's is an application to the study of race of his own work in communication theory as well as the work of others. The importance of Deutsch's essay is the wide range of theoretical and empirical questions it raises for the student of race relations, and the normative implications the answers have for policymakers. Perhaps most important, the essay suggests useful concepts, models, and hypotheses by demonstrating how race intimately interacts with other variables—national and international, political and economic, educational and cultural.

The Study of Race among Nations is more than just a first effort to apply analytical tools to the study of race in world affairs. It is the first of a continuing series to be published by the Center on International Race Relations as "Studies in Race and Nations." These studies will go beyond the theoretical and conceptual, for the editors of the series believe that the scholar has a responsibility to the world he analyzes. Thus, while continuing to refine the tools of empirical inquiry, subsequent studies will be equally concerned with policies and issues and will offer normative theories to be applied to the peaceful resolution of racial conflict in world affairs. To do less would be tantamount to dehumanizing both the scholar, who is human, and his subject matter, which is human behavior. The editors and the staff of the Center on International Race Relations deem it inherently repugnant to disregard the human factor when the subject of scholarly inquiry is essentially man himself and when the findings of that inquiry have a bearing on the human condition. Thus it is hoped that "Studies in Race and Nations" will be a source of greater understanding in the resolution of racial conflict.

Needless to say, the successful completion of this book would not have been possible without the effort of many people. In particular, we want to thank the New World Foundation for providing financial aid for the symposium in February 1969, at which the papers printed here were presented. The Graduate School of International Studies, University of Denver, graciously provided facilities for the symposium, and a direct result was the formation of the Center on International Race Relations. A debt of gratitude is owed the individual contributors and their assistants who, despite the constant demands on their time and competences, made the effort to see their essays to press. Special thanks go to Gail S. Schoettler and Cynthia Kahn, who assisted in the final preparation of the papers for publication. And finally the editors wish to thank John Beck of Heath Lexington Books, D. C. Heath and Company, for recognizing the importance and urgency of publishing and disseminating this and subsequent studies on so vital an issue as race in international relations.

1

The Study of Race in American Foreign Policy and International Relations

George W. Shepherd, Jr.

Despite the emergence of race as a prime domestic problem, very little attention has been given to its role in American foreign policy. This is unfortunate because there is much evidence that race plays a major role, and the failure to understand it leaves American foreign policy at the mercy of one of the most disruptive and demoniac forces in society.

There are many reasons why the assumption persists that race is not significant in American foreign policy. The most prevalent is the ethnocentric belief that the shortcomings of American society at home are not projected abroad in any significant way, since the "foreign-policy process" effectively screens out race consciousness and prejudiced behavior. The fact that the foreign-policy process is not subject to the same popular pressures and prejudices as domestic politics is frequently cited. The increasing appointment of minority-group members in the Foreign Service and other foreign-policy agencies is felt by some to be evidence of the exclusion of racial considerations from the foreign policy process.

All of this can be very misleading, however. The color of a man's skin does not necessarily determine whose interests he serves. And if we accept the judgment of the Kerner Commission that America is a white racist society, what then transforms domestic racial politics into nonracial foreign policy? This question is particularly critical for those who recognize that the old sharp distinctions between the domestic political process and the foreign-policy process are no longer valid, if indeed they ever were. The black revolt in this country has dramatized the role of race in all American political institutions.

For the scholar other obstacles have existed in analyzing race and foreign policy. A legalistic view has been that race as cited under Article II, Section 7, of the United Nations Charter is a matter of "domestic jurisdiction." Yet even many who reject this narrow view have nevertheless confined the political significance of race to domestic politics because of the long-standing general distinction between foreign matters and domestic matters. In addition, many researchers have been dissuaded from further investigation by those who have argued that it is impossible or unnecessary to distinguish race from culture or class in international politics. If this research gap is not, as Gunnar Myrdal claims it is, "a conspiracy of silence," then American scholarship must demonstrate a capacity to deal analytically with the phenomenon.[1]

Several developments have required a change in outlook. Scholars have increasingly freed themselves from ethnocentric biases; foreign-policy analysts have recently pointed out that the distinction between foreign and domestic issues is not a valid one; sociologists have now revised and recast the race concept in terms that are viable for comparative politics and foreign-policy analysis; and most important of all, certain new approaches within political science are more adaptable to the analysis of the role of race in political and international systems.

The first step in considering these developments should be to review the work that has been done and to indicate what the new approaches and priorities might be. Such an examination should not be limited to the approach of one school of thought. It is therefore my purpose to examine the ways in which the role of race in American foreign policy has been approached in the past and several ways it might be more usefully approached in the future.

The Definitional Problem

Gabriel Almond, one of the foremost contributors to new approaches in comparative politics, recently called for an "anthropological perspective" on foreign policy. Almond believes that such a perspective would give United States policy far greater relevance to the primary problem of this age and would enable us to see more clearly that:

The idea of growth in the non-western world—economic, social and political growth—as the central objective of American foreign policy cannot be fully grasped by an elite group which cannot think anthropologically and sociologically. If it is true that the survival of western culture is dependent upon its assimilation in significant measure in the modernizing societies of Asia, Africa and Latin America, our foreign policy must be informed by an anthropological appreciation of cultural differences and by sound theory of social and cultural change.[2]

This advice in itself, coming from one of the leading minds in the development of new approaches, should have stimulated substantial activity in this aspect of American foreign policy. However,

Almond's students, with a few exceptions, have done very little to
pursue this line of thought.[3] Despite an early interest in American
foreign policy, Almond himself has been absorbed by other interests.
The field of developing areas has proven to be more attractive to the
most imaginative advocates of functionalist and systems approaches
to politics. But now that these unknown areas have been chartered in
their major outlines, the task that Almond pointed to still remains:
"to affect the course of cultural change in the non-western areas."[4]
This will not be easy. Americans will have

to act out of cultural character to overcome our parochialism and
ethnocentrism. The central question of American foreign policy in the 1960's is
whether or not the United States still possesses this capacity for growth—not
simply economic growth which will enable us to hold our lead over the Soviet
Union—but cultural and psychological growth which will enable us to provide
moral and political leadership over an expanding free world.[5]

When Almond speaks of an anthropological perspective, he is
including the concept of race within the broad category of political
culture. Yet he does not attempt to define race or analyze its
particular role in American foreign policy, though he does recognize
its importance in American politics.

This raises a definitional problem because most American
foreign-policy scholars have not isolated race from culture; insofar as
it receives any attention, they consider it a subsidiary aspect of the
total spectrum of culture or even political culture.[6] Several social
scientists have questioned the validity of race as a scientifically
measurable social entity.[7] The effect of this uncertainty regarding the
concept of race has led to a tendency to subsume it within a more
tangible and acceptable entity, such as ethnicity or culture. With all
due respect to those who have made valuable contributions in
cross-cultural research, the failure to study race as an independent
variable within culture and across political systems has been a major
neglect, which scholars are only now beginning to rectify.[8]

Race is an important element within culture just as are religion,
political traditions, and family mores. In some cultures it obviously
plays a more important role than in others. But in very few cultures
in the world is there a complete absence of distinction between
groups, either within or external to the culture, on the basis of race.
This racial distinction is facilitated, as Otto Klineberg and others
have pointed out, simply because "Races consist . . . of groups of
men who differ from other groups in their inherited physical

characteristics."[9] Peter Rose gives a similar definition: "A race is a statistical aggregate of persons who share a composite of genetically transmissable physical traits."[10]

An immense amount of mythology and prejudice has encrusted the idea of race in Western history. Because some people resent the hostilities race perceptions create, they attempt to eliminate racism by definition, as an unscientific fiction. This is a mistake. No less a social scientist than Harold Lasswell has pointed out,

True the racist category is an intellectual monstrosity; so for that matter, was the fiction of a proletariat. But the racist symbol has the superficial plausibility of common-sense observation—everybody admits that people differ in certain obvious physical characteristics. In the immediate future there may be little opportunity for massive re-education of the world community, disseminating the best scientific evidence of factors that truly effect human capacities and patterns of conduct. Hence, predispositions exist on a gigantic scale for the mobilization of political perspectives along lines of racist identity.[11]

It is these predispositions and stereotypes in men's minds and in social systems that give race its force in group stratification. Social scientists must deal with those factors that mold human behavior although they may fundamentally disagree with their scientific or teleological validity.[12]

Modern sociology has developed the view of race as a role or pattern variable in society. In this sense racial visibility is a device employed in many societies for making distinctions. As van den Berghe stated, "A salient aspect of multiracial societies is that racial groups are almost invariably hierarchized in terms of prestige, wealth, and power. Hence race can be treated as a special case of invidious status differentiation or a special criterion of stratification."[13] In social and political systems this device has been widely employed for delineating dominant and subordinate groups in society.[14] As a part of cultural pluralism it reinforces other cleavages, such as class or ethnicity. Race has a special role of reinforcing stratification. "Racial consciousness, facilitated by its extreme visibility, creates its own stereotypes of cultural differential."[15] Moreover, van den Berghe demonstrates that it can be isolated as an independent variable for the purposes of analysis. Anderson, von der Mehden, and Young corroborate this finding. As Karl Deutsch suggests, race may well be the visible indicator that triggers more deeply seated cleavage attitudes. Thus a white American may not possess conscious feelings of discrimination toward Indian Americans, but he may have a built-in presumption that Indians are shiftless and lower-class.

Therefore any clearly identifiable Indian who comes to him for employment or credit will be screened in terms of special criteria, if he is not rejected outright.

Thus, while race can be isolated for analytical purposes in terms of racial prejudice because of its close relationship to ethnicity, no complete social or political analysis can be made without considering the interaction between race and other variables. Racial cleavage is a part of the total system. Studies of racism have revealed how frequently those who maintain they have no prejudice nevertheless participate in the decisions of institutions that discriminate, such as banks, schools, and government agencies. This was the important breakthrough of the Kerner Commission Report on Civil Disorder in America. It documented racial cleavage and white racism not as deviant behavior but as an integral part of the political system.

As comparative race studies have shown, there are some social systems in which racial pluralism is a stronger cleavage variable than in others. South Africa and the United States are two of the most obvious examples of high racial cleavage. Most Scandinavian and Western European societies have a very low level of racial cleavage, as is true of Japan and a number of the new states such as Tunisia and the UAR.[16]

Basic Approaches

It is perhaps an unmerited kindness to categorize the previous research in this field within a conceptual framework, but this is possible given the generous and flexible concept of an approach employed by Maurice East.[17] There are four basic approaches, which can be categorized as cross-culture-tension studies, historical and legal studies, national-character studies, and several types of systems analysis. It is a proposition of this essay that all of these approaches have made a certain contribution that now can be utilized within the general category of systems analysis, which provides a new and promising conceptual approach for all work in this field.

Most of the relevant cross-culture studies were done during the period of the Second World War.[18] Social scientists such as Otto Klineberg, E. H. Norman, and R. S. Cattel were motivated by the racial and cultural cleavages that contributed to the racism, ethnocentrism, and aggressions of nations during the interwar period. Much of their work was published by UNESCO, where the concerns of this group of sociologists, anthropologists, and social psychologists have become centered. Otto Klineberg presents a summary of much of this effort in *Tensions Affecting International Understanding: A Survey of Research.*[19]

The merit of cross-culture-tension work has been the extensive documentation of the different meaning that certain concepts have to different cultures. They established that national stereotypes develop early in family and school settings within different cultures, and lead to false conclusions about other peoples and aggressive or negative attitudes toward them. Their extensive analysis of racism, particularly the cultural origins of ideological racism, has contributed to our understanding of Nazism and white-supremacy doctrines.

Although the methods employed make comparisons difficult, the individual studies on national stereotypes are highly valuable to international relations and foreign policy, H. E. Wilson's study, *Latin America in School and College Teaching* (American Council on Education, 1944), showed strong negative stereotypes about Spanish peoples in American education.[20] Through the International Center for the Study of Intergroup Relations in Paris, Klineberg has launched a number of important studies, such as his and M. Zavallani's "A Study of Social Identity in Africa" and Klineberg's own "The Multinational Society."

There are, however, several weaknesses in this cultural-tension approach. First, there is little conceptual agreement on what culture is and, more important, on which elements of culture have special relevance to politics. Unlike modern comparative race studies and comparative politics, which have developed the idea of a political culture with specific components, the tension studies are diverse and unstructured.[21] Race and ethnicity are not treated as functions of the total system, but instead as irrational systems of prejudice, produced as a result of extended conflict and rivalry between national cultures or arising from abnormal psychological influences on groups or individuals. The presumption is that education and insight can eliminate racist practices, whereas modern conflict theorists believe that only a basic restructuring of society can remove the cleavages that make prejudice profitable and powerful.

Therefore the difference is substantial between the national-tension group and the newer approach of the students of comparative race and ethnic studies, represented by Schermerhorn and van den Berghe. The new approach is both systemic and comparative. Race is examined in terms of various forms of plural stratification of society. Richard Schermerhorn suggests in his article "Polarity in the Approach to Comparative Research in Ethnic

Relations" a way of treating subordinate and dominant ethnic groups as independent variables "to set up a four-fold table of possibilities to account for various patterns of integration-conflict."[22] This approach is more adaptable to the various plural patterns of societies in the world. Moreover, it may lead to a theory of race relations more useful to foreign policy and comparative analysis than anything we have had before.

This comparative sociological approach offers a more systematic approach to comparative race studies and therefore is of greater value to international relations and foreign policy. By the development of typologies of plural societies and of the way these societies react to external and internal forces of change and reform, a great deal can be learned about multinational behavior, regional integration, and the interaction of states in general.

The Hyphenate American

Of direct relevance to American foreign policy are the studies of the role of ethnicity in American voting behavior. These became especially important during the 1930s and 1940s when political scientists were seeking the sources of isolationism and cold-war attitudes. Works by Louis Bean, Lawrence Fuchs, and Louis L. Gerson have been of particular value.

Bean's work, which was later popularized in many political-science studies, such as Samuel Lubell's *The Future of American Politics* (1951), showed the direct relationship between significant voting behavior and the ethnic ties to countries of origin. Bean concludes that these ethnic ties were of dramatic importance in the Wilkie-Roosevelt presidential contest of 1940, in which the German-American vote of the Western plains found a favorite son in the appealing but inexperienced Wendell Wilkie.[23]

The most important study of the role of ethnicity is Gerson's *The Hyphenate in Recent American Politics and Diplomacy* (1964), in which he examines the roles of Irish-Americans, Jewish-Americans, German-Americans, and Polish-Americans. These studies support the conclusion of Thomas Bailey that ethnicity is one of the most significant influences on American foreign policy.[24] Our modern Middle East policy continues to reflect this influence.

There are conceptual and substantive weaknesses in this approach, however. These studies give only partial perspectives on interest groups. They fail to place ethnicity within the total political or foreign-policy system. Thus, only a partial glimpse of one important facet is supplied, leading frequently to easy and distorted interpretations, for example, that isolationism is attributable to the continuance of traditional ethnic ties within American society.[25] But even more important from the standpoint of this study is the failure to study the special role of nonwhite racial groups in foreign policy. There is a total absence of any significant empirical studies of the foreign-policy attitudes and voting behavior of blacks, Mexican-Americans, Puerto Ricans, Asians, and Arabs. The comparatively recent emergence of these groups as political forces is only a partial explanation. The reluctance to establish the identity of these groups in terms of foreign ties reflects the general denigration of them in American society. More recently, the political climate has changed and it is now popular to emphasize the significance of nonwhite groups. The danger here is that this could lead to errors in the opposite extreme if a balanced perspective is not maintained.

The Factors Approach

The more traditional approach to the study of American foreign policy and diplomacy has been conducted through factors analysis that considers culture and ideology, but not race, as important factors. Leading exponents of this approach, such as Hans Morgenthau and Charles Lerche, have studied foreign policy in terms of national interest and power. Despite its contributions to the general field of international relations and foreign policy, this "realist" approach has shown little comprehension of the role of race and ethnicity. Where they are considered, most realists ascribe to ethnicity and race a low priority in the power scales.

No major work on international relations or American foreign policy has attempted to isolate race and weigh its significance in relations between nations. Hans Morgenthau discusses the role of national character and is more concerned than most about the relationship between national consensus, unity, and ethnic loyalties.[26] Yet even for him ethnicity is far down the scale of important factor variables, especially as it affects American foreign policy.[27]

Since the emergence of the Third World and the growing recognition of the importance of multiracial cleavages, there has been no revision of this weighting of factors in the power equations of major theorists. The ethnocentric assumption among these theorists is that whereas such cleavages sorely test the national morale and unity of newer nations, the more developed states have integrated their citizens to the point where ethnicity and race have little significance. This myth of national unity was perhaps sustained by pressures of the cold war, reinforced by ethnocentric dispositions.

Still more basic within the factors approach is the bias found in the central concept of the national interest. The realist school sees the national interest in terms of the policies and interests of historically dominant groups. The propositions that societies are often plural and that nations are frequently divided by multinational loyalties and interests run counter to the basic assumptions of this school, which for the most part maintains that assimilation is the reality in American life.[28] The contrary proposition of cultural pluralism, that multinational loyalties exist in plural societies and frequently dissent from the dominant group values, is quite contrary to the popular melting-pot idea.[29] Thus a strong status quo bias exists in the realist approach that does not account for the conflict between dominant and subordinate groups in its effect on foreign policy.

Historical-Legal Approach

Another traditional approach is the international legal view of human rights. American international legal authorities have been concerned with the status of minority groups throughout the world. To a more limited extent this has also involved domestic racial groups. Several American theorists have attempted to draft and adopt international covenants governing the status of minorities.[30] But they have been singularly unsuccessful in persuading the United States government to ratify such covenants.[31] No adequate analysis has yet been made of why the country that has led the world in advocating international codes has been the least successful in ratifying them. But this is not the task of legal authorities as much as it is that of the social analysts of foreign policy. An explanation might well be found in the close relationship between American domestic minority politics and foreign policies.

The limits of this approach are linked to the difficulty of the international legal field in general. A great deal of energy is expended in outlining and justifying international covenants that are either not ratified by most powers or are ignored in practice. There is a need in the field of human rights not only to agree upon the international norms, but also to identify the reasons why the behavior of nations is at such variance with internationally recognized standards. This would entail more extensive consideration of the violation of these existing norms, as has been done to some extent by the United Nations studies of apartheid in South Africa. Great as well as small powers should be subject to this scrutiny, and the findings might well be useful in charting more accurately the role of race in foreign policy. There have been severe protocol limitations on such studies by international agencies, for most nations are prone to consider internal racial difficulties as falling strictly under domestic jurisdiction. Fortunately, international research is not limited by such parochialism and is increasingly determined to probe race issues as they affect international relations.

While more traditional approaches are being considered, it is well to point out the dearth of race studies in the area of diplomatic history. The reason is perhaps linked to the general tendency to subsume race under culture. Thus, ethnic rivalries contributing to the outbreak of World Wars I and II have been studied,[32] and the role of these rivalries in the history of colonialism has also been examined.[33] But, except for a few writers such as Harold Isaacs, very little attention has been given to the role of race as a separate concept in colonization—for example, the British in India or the American colonization of the Pacific Islands. Non-Western ideologists, such as Franz Fanon, have raised the issue.[34] Diplomatic historians could do a great service if they would cut through the shrouds of ethnocentrism that have been thrown over this period of Western expansionism and look objectively at the role of racial ideas at certain points in history.[35] One such period of great importance to American diplomacy was the Versailles Peace Settlement, about which C. Eric Lincoln raises some provocative issues concerning the influence of racial ideas on President Wilson as well as on other major participants.[36]

Systems Approaches

It has already been suggested that the current developments in systems approaches might well provide a key to more significant work in the study of race in international politics in general and in American foreign policy in particular. There are, of course, many difficulties in a systems approach, not the least of which is the vast

variety of views of what a political system is and the ways in which
systems theory can be adapted to international and foreign-policy
subjects. Nevertheless, the intense interest in this approach by many
leading scholars suggests a fruitful area of inquiry.[37]

The advantage of the systems approach to the study of race is that
its role in the social system and in cross-national political systems is
readily verifiable. Because of its sociological antecedents, systems
theory is interested in identifying the function and role of pattern
variables more than their legal or constitutional status. Therefore if,
as I have stressed, the view of race as primarily a cleavage pattern is
employed, race is seen as a variable interacting with other variables
within the political system.

As we have seen, more traditional approaches to the study of race
in international relations and foreign policy tend to subsume race in
culture and thereby to minimize its importance. Such approaches
generally fail to account for the problems raised by pluralism in
multinational systems or in the conflict and cohesion patterns of
subsystems in the world polity. The study of the role of race in
American foreign policy from a systems view can be approached by
an application of methods utilized by theorists of both comparative
politics and international systems.

The comparative-politics approach is especially useful in
understanding the role of race within national political systems. The
idea of a total political system viewed as an input-output model is
useful because the racial variable can be applied at either the input or
the output end.[38] The Almond and Coleman adaptation of this
model to developing nations through a functional structural scheme
is one of the many variations that has been utilized by those
interested in the role of ethnic and racial variables. Van den Berghe's
adaptation of this total systems approach in his *Race and Racism*
shows the significance of different racial systems (competitive and
paternalistic) in the development of political systems.[39] Certain
general propositions about the role of racial variables in
modernization can be demonstrated by comparative studies, as
shown by Guy Hunter in his study of race and industrialization.
Some of the most promising work in this field has been undertaken
by sociologist Richard Schermerhorn, whose models of the dominant
and subordinate relationships of groups are applicable to the
dynamic processes of development.[40]

From all of this work there may well emerge a typology of racially
influenced societies that can be made operational by indicating ways
in which race relations affect stability or precipitate change as
modernization takes place. The influence of external forces on these

patterns is of great importance too. In what ways do racially stratified systems respond to technological innovation? Which structure is most susceptible to external influence and manipulation toward greater egalitarianism? Here the work of van den Berghe and Hunter illustrates what can be done in providing answers to such important questions.

The study of race relations in the United States itself can directly benefit from this comparative approach.[41] For example, if our knowledge of the American ghetto structure is advanced by comparative studies of apartheid in South Africa or of former Belgian colonial policies, then the fields of domestic as well as foreign policy are benefited.

However, the systems approach in comparative politics has certain limitations from the standpoint of race studies. Several writers have noted the bias toward equilibrium in functional-structural theory.[42] Joseph La Polombara and Samuel Huntington have pointed out the excessive zeal of some applications of the functional-structural approach that have led to false conclusions about stability and progress toward modernity.[43] La Polombara especially urges caution in making predictions based on a partial systems analysis.[44] All of this strengthens the insight of Huntington concerning the tendency toward instability and decay as a result of the failures of the political order to mature, along with indices of economic and social growth.

This has opened the way to a revision of systems theory by the cultural pluralists who are aware of the highly relevant role of race. Neopluralists in the field of comparative politics are now criticizing the functional structuralists for their failure to take into account the multinational character of many states. The basic assumption that modernization encourages integration, national consensus, and stability is highly questionable in light of much evidence, as demonstrated in Malaysia, Nigeria, and Peru. In certain new nations it appears that heterogeneity rather than homogeneity is accelerated by the modernization process. Among the most pluralist nations, this disintegration process is most apparent. As Michael Lofchie maintains,

dissensus and disassociation characterize the life of many of the new polities. The violent breakdowns of conciliar institutions (parliaments, legislatures, assemblies, parties, elected local governments) is not explained in terms of patterns of decay (corruption, immobilism, bureaucratisation, Personalism), but in terms of more elemental attributes of the social order: the unmitigated quality of communal cleavages.[45]

Lofchie refers particularly to the effect that deprivation can have upon subordinate groups who, feeling discriminated against, develop hostility and eventually undertake "an assault upon the entire system." It is in this area of psychological alienation because of real or imagined racial discrimination that race may well play a major role in interacting with other ethnic and class cleavages. Research on the relationship between a violent pluralist conflict and the presence of aggravating racial concepts might be very revealing. In Southeast Asia, Africa, and Latin America each of the most serious multinational conflicts of the past five years has had a racial dimension. The more intense and protracted the conflict, the more this dimension grows. For example, foreign intervention appears to aggravate racial and ethnic differences.

Thus the failure of systems analysis to take pluralism into account has led to excessively optimistic conclusions and expectations. The recognition of race as an independent variable in many developing nations may well provide a way of emphasizing the ethnic factors and the communal politics that add a special dimension to many political systems. For the most part, this dimension has not been integrated in the systems models of development and modernization.[46]

Comparative research on pluralism in different nations has only begun. One study that demonstrates the utility of systematic analysis is by Arthur S. Banks and Robert Textor, *A Cross Polity Survey* (1963). It employed for the first time substantial quantification data for 114 polities, using 57 variables, five of which can be adapted to the measurement of pluralism. One of these is race. These data as reworked in 1967 by Marie Haug to give significant classifications of states by pluralist characteristics yielded few surprises (see Table 1.1).[47] The categories were language, race, religion, sectionalism, and interest articulation by nonassociational groups. Yet the groupings are interesting, especially when correlated with other factors such as urbanization, literacy, and "horizontal power distribution."[48] Most of the highly pluralist societies are post-1945 states, and therefore located in the Third World. The high number of African states, with Sudan possessing the highest index of all 114, is perhaps to be expected. With the exception of Ecuador and Peru, there are no Latin American states among the highest three ranks. North Africa and Asia rank second only to sub-Saharan Africa. Among the developed states both the United States and the United Kingdom rank unexpectedly high. The presence of the UAR and Tunisia

Table 1-1

Distribution of 114 World Polities by "Index of Pluralism"

Index of Pluralism Score

0	1	2	3
		Australia	
Argentina		Bulgaria	
Austria		Burundi	
Chile		El Salvador	
Costa Rica		Germany, W.	
Denmark		Honduras	
Greece		Japan	
Iceland		Korea, N.	
Ireland		Korea, S.	Algeria
Luxembourg	Cuba	Mexico	Colombia
Norway	Dominican R.	Mongolia	Israel
Paraguay	France	Netherlands	Jamaica
Poland	Germany, E.	Nicaragua	Libya
Portugal	Finland	Panama	Spain
Sweden	Hungary	Rumania	United Kingdom
Tunisia	Italy	Rwanda	United States
UAR	New Zealand	Saudi Arabia	Vietnam, N.
Uruguay	Venezuela	Turkey	Vietnam, S.
N=17	N=9	N=18	N=10

4	5	6	7	8
		Afghanistan		
		Burma		
		Canada		
		Cameroun		
		Ceylon		
		Congo (Bra.)		
		Dahomey		
		Gabon		
	Belgium	Ghana		
	Bolivia	Guinea		
	Cyprus	India		
Algeria	Czechoslovakia	Indonesia		
Brazil	Guatemala	Iran		
Cambodia	Ivory Coast	Iraq		
Cent. Afr. R.	Liberia	Mali	Chad	
Haiti	Malagasy	Mauritania	Congo (Leo.)	
Jordan	Morocco	Niger	Ecuador	
Lebanon	Nepal	Pakistan	Ethiopia	
Somalia	Philippines	Peru	Laos	
Syria	Senegal	Sierra Leone	Malaysia	
Thailand	Tanganyika	Switzerland	Nigeria	
Trinidad	USSR	Togo	S. Africa	
Yemen	Upper Volta	Yugoslavia	Uganda	Sudan
N=12	N=15	N=23	N=9	N=1

Note: Mainland China is omitted because of no data on two factors in the index pluralism.

among the most homogeneous may be surprising to the nonarea specialist.[49]

Thus Haug's conclusion—"Pluralism is not simply another form of social stratification which can be subsumed under that variable, but constitutes a special condition of diversity which varies widely in degree across societies"[50]—is strong support for the cultural-pluralist critique of current political-systems analysis. Similarly, it can be said of race that it gives a special character to the nature of pluralist cleavages. The study of the role of race in these plural systems on a comparative and cross-national basis has only begun. But the preliminary work of van den Berghe and Haug is a promising start.

The relevance of this to American foreign policy lies first in understanding the effect of racial stratification on the kinds of policies that are produced. Second, a stratification analysis of other national systems can assist in comparative foreign-policy analysis and the assessment of the ability of any one nation to influence the policy of others.

An example of the utility of pluralist concepts is the "colonized people" thesis that Charles Hamilton and Stokely Carmichael develop in *Black Power.* They derive the concept from the ideas of race, culture, and conflict of Franz Fanon, who analyzed colonialism and racism in Africa.[51] These men argue that the position of black Americans is similar to the racially exploited peoples of Africa and that a similar national spirit of resistance is necessary if freedom is to be obtained.[52] St. Clair Drake has also drawn parallels between the colonized position of black ghettos in America and the subordinate role of colonial economies. Moving from theory to action, these social scientists advocate a pan-Negro solidarity system that will be mutually supportive in the United States, the new African states, and the Caribbean countries. Clearly, comparative analysis of the position of minority groups in pluralist societies, between Western and non-Western societies, may have consequences that are important for foreign policy.[53]

The systems approach is also applicable to another dimension of the study of race in American foreign policy: cross-national relations. Foreign policy, after all, is not simply the interaction of one state with other national systems, but includes interaction with the international system itself. This international system, according to systems analysis, is more than the sum of its national parts. It exists on several levels, as Kaiser has shown in his analysis of three basic subsystems: the intergovernmental, which consists of the interaction of states; the transnational society subsystems; and the comprehensive regional subsystems.[54] Like an iceberg the inter-governmental system is most visible—but the ship that ignores the subsurface extensions of the iceberg (the transnational society subsystems) is in danger of running aground. It is this transnational subsystem that is highly suggestive for cross-national racial and ethnic cleavage research. Here, ethnic and racial groups as they affect the political system come first to mind.

Very little work has yet been done in demonstrating the role of racial or indeed ethnic cleavages in the operation of the international system of regional systems. The field of subsystem theory holds particular promise. A considerable amount of work has been done on the development of regional integration. The writings of Karl Deutsch have contributed to systems integration theory.[55] Joseph Nye's work on pan-Africanism has demonstrated the emergence of ethnic and racial cohesion as an important variable.[56] More recent subsystems work on Africa has been done by Larry Bowman, I. William Zartman, and this writer.[57] These studies demonstrate that race consciousness as well as racism are important factors in the emergence of subordinate and nonaligned subsystems in Africa. Bowman demonstrates the subordinate pattern of the southern African subsystem in terms of South Africa and Western Europe, emphasizing economic integration. In contrast, I develop the thesis of conflicting subsystems, in which race is an independent variable, intensifying the ethnic and economic rivalries between the subsystems.

One can imagine the development of comparative subsystem studies in which pluralist characteristics in the global system are examined in terms of the cohesion and conflict patterns both within subsystems and among them.[58] To what extent is race or color an integrating force in the Third World or among nonwhite subsystems? Some study has been done of this by Thomas Hovet in his book on bloc voting at the United Nations, *Africa and the United Nations.* More sophisticated voting analysis can be found in Benjamin Meyers' "African Voting in the General Assembly," in *Journal of Modern African Studies.* Yet even Meyers does not analyze race and pluralist correlations.

The United Nations is only one dimension of the interaction that takes place between states in the international system, and seems increasingly to be a secondary area. The role of race and pluralist variables in the global system as a whole has been examined only by descriptive and speculative literature, such as Richard Wright's *Listen White Man* or Ronald Segal's *The Race War.* Almost no empirical or systemic work has been done on the role of racial identification in the basic and growing differences between the rich and the poor, the West and the non-West.

A subsidiary topic of interest is the way in which great powers develop subordinate systems through the use of racial-ethnic concepts. This was a topic of great concern to Franz Fanon and increasingly occupies the minds of non-Western social scientists. Ali Mazrui's "From Social Darwinism to Current Theories of Modernization" maintains that racist ideas, injected into Social Darwinism, affect contemporary modernization theory. If ideological biases can be transcended, systemic studies of contemporary empire building could show the deliberate or unconscious use of racial concepts by racially stratified societies. The work of historians of colonial history constitutes an immense reserve of material for such projections into the modern period.

That systems theory has direct application to foreign policy has been demonstrated most significantly by James Rosenau. Since he has contributed to this volume (Chapter Three), there is little need for me to elaborate upon his ideas, except to point to some important possible applications. Through the systems approach, Rosenau has shown how the traditional distinctions between foreign policy and domestic politics are invalid and becoming increasingly so all the time. His ideas form a very important link between domestic politics, foreign policy, and the international system. His issue-area concept is a most useful vehicle for analyzing the role of race in American foreign policy.[59] As he himself has pointed out, the issue-area transcends international boundaries: "there is more interaction across national boundaries than most people realize." He illustrates this by reference to the growth of concern for international race relations: "An American who defines himself as a civil libertarian is likely to feel obliged to be as attentive to incidents of racial strife in South Africa as to those in Mississippi."[60] He also points out that civil rights is becoming involved as an issue-area in American foreign policy, as much for practical reasons concerning the allocation of resources as for the moral and intellectual ones described above. Thus the issue-area concept can show how race in its cross-national manifestations is pulled into American politics and foreign policy. Therefore, if a link between civil rights in South Africa and civil rights in America is established in an issue-area, the South African issue becomes a domestic concern in the United States.

Thus Rosenau provides a conceptual framework for analyzing the growing phenomenon of pan-Negro civil rights movements and other color-culture groups in the American foreign-policy process. American blacks seek to project their own aspirations through American policy into such areas as South Africa and in turn are stimulated by this identification to obtain more resources for the rectification of their own grievances as well as those of the South Africans.

Rosenau's proposition on resource allocation and foreign policy is applicable here: "The more an issue encompasses a society's resources and relationships the more it will be drawn into the society's domestic political system and the less it will be processed through the society's foreign policy system."[61] A suggested corollary to the above proposition might be that the more clearly a linkage is established between a foreign-policy issue and a domestic issue, the more that foreign issue becomes subject to the domestic political process. In the race field, as with the ethnic, the linkages appear to be of growing significance in American foreign and domestic policy.

The issue-area concept needs further refinement, especially if it is applied to race and cross-cultural relations. At present its boundaries are not sufficiently defined. What are the component parts of issue-areas? Conceivably one might place all foreign-policy interaction with other states in the situational factors that influence an important issue. Also, what is the relationship between issue-areas? Is there not competition and conflict? But these conceptual problems do not seem insoluble and should prove challenging to the inquiring mind.

Little has been said about methodology. It should be obvious that certain methodologies are appropriate to some problems and not to others. Traditional historical methodologies are most applicable to the problems of diplomatic history, such as the study of the role of race in colonial systems. Quantitative analysis may be applicable to the study of pluralist systems, as Haug has shown, and has proven useful in the study of racial behavior, particularly voting patterns. There is a great need for collection of data, and the use of new methods can be of great assistance, but the greatest need is for new concepts and problem-solving approaches. I feel that conceptual designs should not be dictated by a desire to measure and quantify. Many of the most important subjects in this field cannot be measured effectively because of inadequate data. The danger is that important subjects are by-passed simply because they do not lend themselves to computer measurement. Too often, great effort in accumulating data is wasted on a poorly conceived research design. More extensive empirical information and creative insights into problems are the primary needs. Although the systems approach appears to offer the best prospects at the moment, it is necessary to adapt certain systems theories to the particular subject at hand.

Conclusion: Priorities in
Approach and Subject Matter

It is not my purpose to try to spell out specific research topics, but only to survey approaches and to suggest possible new approaches and subjects in which work should be undertaken.

The most productive approach to the issue of race in foreign policy and international relations appears to lie within the area marked out as comparative and international systems. No significant policy determinations can be made without an adequate grasp of the major conditioning variables both within the American system and within the systems with which the United States must interact, from nations, to national systems, to regional subsystems and the global system itself. This calls for the development of a more adequate systems theory applicable to an understanding of conflict, development, and interaction between multinational states.

We have seen how important the cleavage variables of race and ethnicity are in the formation, growth, and conflicts of societies. And it has been pointed out how most of the predominant approaches in comparative politics and international relations do not give adequate attention to the important role of race and other pluralist variables.

The structural functionalists, as much as they have made a contribution in breaking through the legalistic concepts in comparative politics, have a built-in equilibrium and stability bias that does not adequately account for alienation and conflict arising from the dominant and subordinate relationships of racial-ethnic groups. This has contributed in large measure to the false optimism about integration and progress that has been characteristic of the work of many functional structuralists both in the analysis of new nations and in respect to the American political system itself.

The work of international-relations theorists, with few exceptions, has not given much weight to racial and ethnic variables. The more traditional approaches have given very low priority to race and cultural factors, and the new systems approaches are also prone to the same equilibrium biases of the functional structuralists, intensified perhaps by ethnocentric biases. Thus few of the international systems models outside of the Banks and Textor study have even recognized the importance of racial and ethnic variables. This is less true of the recent interest in international subsystems, but even here there are outstanding examples of the misleading consequences of overlooking the importance of these variables.[62]

In all of the major subsystem studies that have been published, none gives much weight to racial and ethnic variables. This accounts for the unfortunate preoccupation with the subordinate centrifugal character of these systems, indicating a dependency on great powers, to the exclusion of the centripetal forces leading toward self-identity.

A new and more comprehensive approach is suggested by the cultural pluralists and ethnic-conflict theorists, such as Schermerhorn and van den Berghe. The contribution of these sociologists to the emergence of a new field in comparative race relations based upon systems theory has important implications for political scientists who have been drinking deeply from the well of sociology during the past two decades. The appeal of Gabriel Almond for the development of an anthropological perspective in foreign policy reflects this influence. If this advice is taken seriously, particularly in terms of the findings and insights of cultural pluralism, a broader base can be built for comparative politics and international systems theory as well as race studies. The adaptation of this pluralist approach to comparative and international race relations interests suggests four general types of studies:

1. **Comparative race systems theories.** These might concentrate on the adaptation of cultural pluralism to systems theory on a comparative basis. The power-conflict theory of Schermerhorn appears most promising. This is as useful for modern as for underdeveloped societies. The black-power theorists such as Charles Hamilton and St. Clair Drake, who apply the racial-culture conflict theories of Fanon concerning the colonial situation to the subordinate status of nonwhite groups in American society, indicates one practical application of power-conflict theory.

2. **Comparative empirical studies of the modernization process in different pluralist settings.** As the cultural pluralists have demonstrated, the response of modernizing societies varies substantially according to the nature of their pluralist and racial structure. South Africa responds differently from the United States to technological change or resolutions of the United Nations.

This is a vast area for study, since most of the work already done is not of a systematic comparative nature. Those nations in which the racial variables are particularly high might well be given first priority.

Examining the extent to which pluralist stratification in certain societies is affected by and in turn affects socialization, participation, governmental capacity, consensus, the political order, the distribution of benefits, and a dozen other ways of defining the major components of modernization will greatly extend our knowledge of the role of race under varied conditions. The comparison of conditions and policies in developed countries would be as significant as the study of emerging nations.

3. **Race in international subsystems.** The role of race and ethnicity in the formation and growth of international subsystems is open to extensive examination. Previous work in this field has tended to minimize these influences. Ideological and economic factors have been emphasized to the exclusion of race and ethnicity. The centrifugal as well as the centripetal force of cross-national racial systems needs to be considered along with other variables. In Africa the collapse of pan-Africanism and the emergence of new regional integration systems as well as nonaligned subsystems are most significant. And the conflicts between these subsystems, such as the black-white confrontation in South Africa, constitute a priority area.

4. **Racial variables in American foreign policy.** These variables can best be approached from stratification theory. Material from the above three categories would be important background. The extent of participation in foreign policy by nonwhite minority groups in American society offers one highly important area for empirical work. Models of the input of situations and the output of decisions offer a means of getting into the racial issue.

Using the colonial theses of black power theorists, the loyalty links of black Americans with overseas groups and nations can be analyzed. The ways in which this changes with real participation in the system may be of great significance to American politics. A proposition worth investigating is that the Black-Americans' alienation from American foreign policy rises with their participation in the American political system and their acceptance of their African heritage.

The character of intervention in areas of conflict in the world such as southern Africa, the Congo, Southeast Asia, and the Middle East, as influenced by racial-ethnic ties in addition to ideological and economic variables, presents another set of issues that might be examined from the standpoint of Rosenau's issue-area concept. An interesting proposition to consider here is that the intensity of the racial conflict determines the strength of the cross-national issue-area and consequently the scope of international intervention.

Studies might well be launched in the developing field of comparative foreign policies in which highly pluralist societies are compared with relatively homogeneous nations in terms of aggressive or peaceful behavior on the global scene. One general proposition is that aggressive behavior of a nation is closely associated with a high level of pluralism, especially when the political system is conceived as being wider than national boundaries.

These four areas for work are only suggestions. It would be presumptuous to draw up a research priority list at this time, and no one program could possibly undertake all of it. Denver's Center on International Race Relations at the Graduate School of International Studies has elected to focus for the immediate future on only a few aspects of this immense task. Other scholars and centers have already contributed substantially to the general fund of knowledge. By presenting an overview of the various approaches that have been made and suggesting a framework for envisioning the work of the future, I hope to draw attention to neglected areas of research. These can no longer be overlooked if we are to be relevant to the kind of world that has emerged in the past two decades.

At the outset, Gabriel Almond's plea for a new perspective in foreign-policy research was quoted. He raised the question whether America still has the capacity for cultural and psychological growth to eliminate parochialism and ethnocentrism from its foreign policy. There is a greater urgency now about this because, if anything, the United States seems to have moved increasingly from a sober and informed anthropological view toward the security-minded policy that Almond deplored. The Vietnam fiasco is in part a result of this, and there are seasoned observers who feel that the racial-ethnic dimensions of the confrontation building in southern Africa and perhaps in the Middle East and Latin America contain even more serious aggravating agents than those faced before. These new crises have already involved the United States. Therefore we must be concerned not simply with matters of approach and theory about race and systems, but with the wisdom of policy. The task of disposing of these problems is not only one for the moralist or the decision maker. Political science, as Aristotle knew so well, must not be intimidated by its awesome responsibilities from performing the task of developing policy guidelines out of its theoretical propositions and empirical observations.

2 The Development of Race Studies

Peter I. Rose

Throughout human history men have set themselves apart from others, making clear distinctions between those called "we" and those called "they." The ties of kinship, faith, culture, and tradition, and real or imagined racial differences, separately or in combination, have often been responsible for the instigation and perpetuation of conflicts within and between societies and have long been recognized as such.

Chroniclers from the days of Babylonian civilization to the modern era have recorded and discussed—sometimes in great detail—patterns of intergroup relations, varying forms of subjugation of both mass subjects and minorities, and different kinds of pluralism: political, cultural, and social. The subject of "race relations" is a very old one, antedating by many centuries the emergence of anthropology and sociology, the two modern disciplines that have concentrated on the subject.

Any truly comprehensive review of "race studies" would have to go back into antiquity and encompass the works of scholars from every quarter of the globe. Such a survey would help us to see the legacy upon which many current ideologies have been built and would indicate the persistence of certain tendencies, not least the ethnocentric proclivities of observers. Recently, several historians have attempted to collate this material, and their books offer fascinating background for study.

My concern here is more limited. This review concentrates on modern Western and, particularly, American perspectives and the studies that have been conducted by social scientists who (however they saw themselves) are now considered specialists in the field of race relations. A rather arbitrary point of departure has been chosen: the time when anthropological data began to be systematically accumulated and the word "race" began to have specific biological meaning in the vernacular of several European societies.

Development of European Racial Theories

Scientific research on "the races of man" did not begin until the early part of the eighteenth century. Then students of racial differences, whether they viewed Europeans as innately superior to others (as did Bernier, Linnaeus, and Buffon) or leaned toward a somewhat more egalitarian stance regarding the potentialities of all peoples (as did Blumenbach), favored the notion that all human types were subdivisions of a single genus, *homo sapiens.* This theory was to be challenged by men who argued that racial differences were attributable to separate origins and that not all men were the direct descendants of Adam and Eve. The foremost zoologists and naturalists of the first half of the nineteenth century tended to follow suit. Louis Agassiz, Samuel G. Morton, and his disciples, Josiah C. Nott and George Robin Gliddon, were such "polygenesists."

Whether they adhered to a single- or multiorigin doctrine, the number of races these proto-anthropologists described depended largely upon the classificatory system each found most efficacious for his particular purposes.[1] Moreover, whether one spoke of three races or thirty, there was a rather consistent tendency to equate biological characteristics with social attributes. According to one commentator:

The distinction between the old "descriptive" and the new "scientific" anthropology is of course an arbitrary one, for it is obvious that an observer like Buffon was a better scientist than some undistinguished latter-day measurer of skulls. Nevertheless a rough line can be drawn between the bulk of the anthropologists who worked before 1859 and those who came after.[2]

The year 1859 is selected as the crucial watershed, for it was then that Charles Darwin's *Origin of Species* was first published. Darwinian theory gave legitimacy to the polygenesists' views, and many took the superordinate status of "whites" as evidence of the fact that the fittest survive and that the aggressive, not the meek, inherit the earth. While eschewing mere observation and description for the more sophisticated mechanical techniques of measuring racial differences, most anthropologists of the late nineteenth century concurred that their findings revealed the inferiority of non-Caucasians and continued to link biological and social evolution with one another.

Following Paul Broca, the French anthropologist and founder in 1859 of the Anthropological Society of Paris, many agreed that the differences separating human groups are primordial. They argued that, "since racial differences find their expression in opinions and behavior, the brain has something to do with race and the measured shape of the skull is the best way to get at the contents of the brain."[3] Elaborating upon earlier techniques, a variety of cephalic indices were devised to aid in the classification process. In time, other methods of dividing mankind "scientifically" were used. By combining certain skull types, hair textures, nasal forms, skin colors, and the like, general groupings were suggested—not, it seems, unlike those three- or four- or fivefold paradigms proposed for two centuries.

Inevitably, even such arbitrary pigeonholing proved difficult to justify, especially when it came to "placing" such people as the brown-skinned, straight-nosed inhabitants of India or the black-skinned but hairy Australian aborigines. Some opted for a sixfold classification; others for a tenfold one; and so on.[4]

Although not all scientists agreed, many continued to claim that "colored" people were degenerate, simple-minded, untamed, and uncivilized. "Scientific racism" was used to justify the slave system in the United States and to support the exploits of colonialists as they continued to bear the white man's burden in distant lands, especially in Africa.[5]

In time, increasing numbers of anthropologists began to seriously question the position of the "scientific" racists. They moved toward conceding that "racial groups" are most properly defined simply as statistical aggregates of persons who share a composite of genetically transmissable physical traits. For most, the concept was to be clearly distinguished—both semantically and empirically—from such ideas as language, nationality, personality, and culture.[6] This particular change of attitude did not come about overnight, however. In fact, some anthropologists, like many other observers of the passing scene, were confounded by indigent people of southern and central Europe who were moving across the continent and migrating to the United States in ever increasing numbers. Many wondered, especially in this country, whether the motley array of poor immigrants could ever be adapted to the American scene. Not a few contended that they did not have the makings of *real* Americans.

Franz Boas, the most important ethnologist since Edward B. Tylor, emphatically disagreed with the latter view. His perceptive scholarship here and abroad was chiefly responsible for the new departure in the study of races and nationality groups. In *The Mind of Primitive Man* (1911) and subsequent publications, Boas dismissed the hypothesis that race determines ability and performance. He and his students denied that culture was determined by biology and helped to dispel widely held beliefs about racial groups—that they are temperamentally different, that there are racial cultures or such things as racial moralities, that some races are biologically and intellectually superior to others.[7] Research findings tended to invert the assumed relationship, and Boas argued that even physical attributes themselves (such as size and head form) might well be influenced by the social and cultural environment. Thus he wrote:

Heredity may explain a part of the pronounced mental similarities between parents and children; but this explanation cannot be transferred to explain on hereditary grounds the similarity of behavior of entire nations in which the most varied lines occur. These assume their characteristic forms under the pressure of society.[8]

Today, many anthropologists continue to follow the general course set forth by Boas shortly after the turn of the century. As recently as 1961, the Fellows of the American Anthropological Association affirmed the Boas assertion. In their studied opinion they unequivocally stated, "All races possess the abilities needed to participate fully in the democratic way of life and in modern technological civilization."

In one way this forceful statement denies to the discreditors the notion that those categorized as members of a given racial group (such as the far from "pure" American blacks) are innately inferior. In another sense it begs several questions that remain scientifically legitimate. As Theodosius Dobzhansky, co-author of the well-known *Heredity, Race and Society* (1952) and *Mankind Evolving* (1962), has recently written: "Faced with a revival of 'scientific' racism one is tempted to treat the matter with the silent scorn it so richly deserves . . . [Yet] it may perhaps be useful to add a warning against exaggerations which some writers bent on combating racism are unwittingly making."[9] Specifically:

The contention of racists is that cultural achievements of different races are so obviously unlike, their genetic capacities for achievement are just as different. It is, however, a matter of elementary genetics that the capacities of individuals, populations, or races cannot be discovered until they are given an equality of opportunity to demonstrate these capacities.[10]

Putting it in somewhat different terms, Manning Nash makes a similar point. "The scientifically responsible student of race is at a distinct disadvantage in trying to confront the propositions on racial inferiority. He is in the unenviable position of trying to defend the null hypothesis."[11] Nash goes on to suggest that an elementary distinction is needed between the study of race (the pursuit of knowledge about phenomena) and the study of the "ideology of race."

Lately we have begun to see significant strides in the direction of clarifying these elusive distinctions. The discussion of Race in the new edition of the *International Encyclopedia of the Social Sciences* is a good case in point. While stating that "raciological (biological) explanations of socioculture differences and similarities have attracted the support of a large and not infrequently preponderant scientific consensus," Marvin Harris indicates that "the term *race,* or its various ethnosemantic glosses, is applied in vernacular contexts to human populations organized along an astonishing variety of principles."[12]

Nation-states, such as the Irish, Japanese, or German; tribes such as the Scythian, Iroquois, Zulu; language families such as Slavic, Latin, Semitic; minorities such as Jews, gypsies, Puerto Ricans; and phenotypically distinct but genetically hybrid aggregates such as whites, Negroes, yellows, and Coloureds are cognitively equivalent in many ethnosemantic contexts. Social scientists have tried to diminish intergroup conflict by exposing the disparity between biologically acceptable definitions of race and those which are entertained at the popular level. Since none of the folk usages is informed by valid genetic principles, the lack of correspondence between social race and biological race should occasion no surprise. Social races encompass both phenotypically similar and phenotypically dissimilar populations; actual gene frequencies, the ultimate goal of infraspecies systematics, are obviously not desiderata in folk taxonomies. The cognitive substratum by which so many disparate aggregates are united cannot therefore be regarded as racial in the biological sense.... In distinguishing socially defined races, therefore, attention must be directed toward common sociocultural rather than common biological features.[13]

Elaborating further, Harris says:

Social races are composed of subjectively significant groups, unrestricted by age and sex criteria, in which membership is sociocentric (i.e. appears the same to all egos), is established at birth, endures for life, and confers special behavioral obligations or privileges. Social races differ from other stratified groups (such as classes with low rates of out-mobility) in their methods of maintaining membership and group identity. Social races accomplish this by a special ideological device, the idea of descent. Although the members of a social race are replaced during each generation, the group maintains a continuing identity through varied applications of descent rules.[14]

The Dutch sociologist Harry Hoetink also argues that social scientists would do well to search for a concept that is the sociopsychological compliment of the biological term "race." He suggests (and uses) the phrase "somatic norm image" defined as "the complex of physical (somatic) characteristics which are accepted by a group as its norm ideal." In a somewhat similar vein, the British anthropologist Michael Banton argues that norms are indeed critical and that, at bottom, "race is a role sign."[15]

So-called "Negro" Americans represent a social race, influenced by a specific "somatic norm image" that requires the playing of particular roles. In one sense they are persons who are said to possess certain phenotypic traits that cause others to lump them together. The fact is, of course, that such a grouping actually exceeds the limits of apparent physical similarity, for many who are "mostly white" are called Negroes and relegated to a particular position in the status hierarchy of American society. Deemed inferior, they are expected to play particular subordinate (or, at times, specialized) roles. In turn, the categorical ascription to those called "Negroes" of an inferior or differential place has served to unite an amorphous aggregate into what has begun to take on the characteristics of a community. It is evident that there are more than conceptual connections between personal attributes, cultural norms, and the patterns of social relationships.

Rather than dwell on the matter of racial similarities and differences (still of central concern to physical anthropologists) or on the reconstruction and description of the minutiae of life in small, nonliterate folk societies, increasing numbers of social anthropologists are turning their attention to the comparative investigation of intragroup and intergroup conflicts and tensions. With certain social historians (such as Oscar Handlin, John Hope Franklin, Frank Tannenbaum, Stanley Elkins, David Brion Davis), they are beginning to explore the relation of racial and ethnic minorities to the wider social systems in which they are located and the cultural traditions that underlie patterns of race relations. The works of Melville Herskovits, Robert Redfield, and, more recently, Marvin Harris, Charles Wagley, and Gerald D. Berreman are among the best representations of this orientation in the United States.

Recently, comparative anthropologists, historians, and sociologists concerned with race relations have found themselves cooperating in a variety of ways and using very similar frames of reference. Such was rarely the case in the past.

Racial Concepts in America

Unlike anthropology, American sociology was, at least in the beginning, only partly an extension of the European tradition. Of the many reasons for this, two stand out as particularly significant. First, in contrast to their European counterparts, most American sociologists lacked both a historical and a comparative perspective. This is not to say that the Europeans were not ethnocentric; of course they were (and many did reflect the then current prejudices). Still, macrosocial forces were their uppermost concern, and the comparison of various social systems in time and space was a principal modus operandi.

The American sociologists, by contrast, were mainly interested in *endemic* problems. Meliorism played a major role in the work and thought of the early American sociologists. With some exceptions, they were imbued with the spirit of the Social Gospel and possessed by a faith in progressive social change. In America, "applied sociology" became a fact of academic life before Lester Ward gave it a name.

The majority of America's early sociologists (including all but a few of the first twenty-four presidents of the American Sociological Society, founded in 1905) came from clerical families and from rural backgrounds which, according to some commentators, led to an antiurban stance in much of their work and to a special concern with the problems of city living.[16] Whether the allegation is correct or not, there is little doubt that a concern about "social disorganization" played a significant role in shaping the course of sociological inquiry from the turn of the century into the Depression years. At that time, the center of sociological gravity shifted from Chicago to the eastern seaboard, and sociologists turned away, at least for a time, from a problem orientation.

Ironically, the most influential of the early sociologists, insofar as the study of race and race relations is concerned, did not represent the major trend. William Graham Sumner abhorred the reforming bent of his colleagues. At Yale University, where he taught the first sociology courses in America, he inveighed against sociologists engaging in humanitarian activities, raising their voices against the privations of certain segments of the population, or advocating social legislation. On the last point, Sumner once claimed that "stateways cannot change folkways," a statement that is still used by those arguing against the position that morality can be legislated.

Some of his basic writings have had a profound effect, however, upon the understanding of racial and ethnic relations. Particularly influential are his classic distinction between in-groups and out-groups (the former providing its members with a sense of superiority in relation to the latter) and his now-famous definition of ethnocentrism, which, he said, "leads people to exaggerate and intensify everything in their own folkways which is peculiar and which differentiates them from others."[17]

Moreover, in discussing the concept of mores, Sumner made the seminal observation that "modern scholars have made a mistake of attributing to race much which belongs to the ethos."[18] Although he was a Social Darwinist, he was not entrapped by the rhetoric of the racists. In claiming that social behavior and attitudes (including group antipathies) are learned, not inherited, he (as well as such contemporary anthropologists as Franz Boas) signaled a decided shift regarding the relationship between race and culture, which, as will be shown, grew more pronounced in the ensuing decades.[19]

Others contributed to the growing literature on race *relations.* W. I. Thomas, for example, wrote in one of the first essays on "The Psychology of Race Prejudice."[20] He recognized the extent to which ethnocentrism played a role in the perpetuation of in-group solidarity and out-group antipathy and said that "in race prejudice we see the . . . tendency to exalt the self and the group at the expense of outsiders."[21] (Somewhat later, Sigmund Freud was to write that "in the undisguised antipathies and aversions which people feel toward strangers with whom they have to do we may recognize the expression of self-love—of narcissism."[22]

Most sociologists of the period were interested in the social and cultural conflicts they saw around them, most noticeably in the collision of values, interests, and life styles of the native-born and the newcomers from Europe. In this particular sense, they were "comparative." Their work reflected, however, that they were also wrapped up in their own culture-bound prejudices. Thus eugenicists like E. A. Ross warned the Darwinists that the "fittest" were not surviving[23] and went so far as to express fears over the consequences of unlimited immigration, which threatened to pollute the American blood. Franklin Giddings shared these views as did Thomas N. Carver, Jeremiah Jenks, and other prominent social scientists of the day. Indeed, they gave academic legitimacy and, at times, aid and support to the activities of the Immigration Restriction League and similar organizations.

Although he would never go along with the tirades of the eugenicists or support restrictive immigration, even Robert E. Park, who was to become the guiding force behind the empirical study of racial and ethnic relations in this country, believed for a time that "it is evident that there is in race prejudice as distinguished from class and caste prejudice, an *instinctive* factor based on the fear of the unfamiliar and uncomprehended."[24] Park was to modify his position and eventually to say that "race consciousness . . . is to be regarded *like* class or caste consciousness, that enforces social distance."[25] His emphasis (like that of Sumner) was now on the fact that, while group antagonisms do exist, they are a result of social and cultural conflicts and tensions and not innate aversions. As such, they could be modified.

Sociocultural Theories of Intergroup Relations

The apparent shift in Park's thinking characterized or, perhaps, symbolized the changes that were taking place in the sociological treatment of race. There was a shift from a stress on the biological aspects of human differences, heavily influenced by the early physical anthropologists, to a sociocultural frame of reference. Sociologists became particularly interested in the study of the social rather than biological histories of various peoples in order to explain character and modes of behavior. Later on, a third change was to become evident. Sociologists turned attention to the effects of intergroup contact and the nature of relationships between those who differed from one another because of their cultural backgrounds.[26]

These changes did not come about abruptly. There was a good deal of overlapping between those whose work best represents one phase or another. An examination of the textbooks in sociology that were most widely read during the early part of this century bears witness to the confusion that existed regarding the bases of group differences, the meaning of social experiences, and, especially, the use of such basic terms as "race" and "nationality."[27] Donald Young addressed himself to the last issue in particular and sought to deal with the semantic confusion once and for all.

In 1932, in one of the first major texts to deal exclusively with the sociology of intergroup relations in the United States, Young wrote: "There is, unfortunately, no word in the English language which can with philological propriety be applied to all these groups which are distinguished by biological features, alike national traits, or a combination of both."[28] He suggested using the term "minority." Some years later, Louis Wirth spelled out the new concept in detail.

We may define a minority as a group of people who, because of their physical or cultural characteristics, are singled out from the others in the society in which they live for differential and unequal treatment, and who therefore regard themselves as objects of collective discrimination. The existence of a minority in a society implies the existence of a corresponding dominant group enjoying higher social status and greater privileges. Minority status carries with it the exclusion from full participation in the life of the society. Though not necessarily an alien group the minority is treated and regards itself as a people apart.[29]

Stressing both internal characteristics and the relation to the wider social milieu, Wirth continued:

A minority must be distinguishable from the dominant group by physical or cultural marks. In the absence of such identifying characteristics it blends into the rest of the population in the course of time. . . .

Minorities objectively occupy a disadvantageous position in society. As contrasted with the dominant group they are debarred from certain opportunities—economic, social and political. . . .

The members of minority groups are held in lower esteem and may even be objects of contempt, hatred, ridicule and violence. . . .

They are generally socially isolated and frequently spatially segregated. . . .

They suffer from more than the ordinary amount of social and economic insecurity.[30]

Because of these attributes, "Minorities tend to develop a set of attitudes, forms of behavior, and other subjective characteristics which tend further to set them apart."[31]

Quite obviously, the emphasis on dominant group—minority relations finally moved the question of whether groups are superior or inferior to their position in the minds of others and to their treatment by others—together with their own response patterns. It should also be apparent that Wirth was greatly concerned about the deleterious effect of the placement in inferior status position of particular ethnic groups. Still he and others, such as E.K. Francis, stressed the fact that most ethnic groups, including many of those called minorities, frequently shared a positive sense of unity or "we-feeling," an ideology (however vague and unreflective it may be), and an interdependence of fate (whether based upon religious, political, cultural, or racial characteristics). Moreover, ethnic group ties were seen as being maintained as long as individuals felt bound to the community—a community dependent as much upon the idea of communality as on actual proximity; a community one could feel if not touch.[32] The Jews are a classic case in point.[33]

Wirth was among the many sociologists who worked with Robert E. Park at the University of Chicago in the halcyon days of empirical sociology. Beginning with the founding of America's first department of sociology by Albion Small in 1893, led to eminence by Robert Park, Chicago was for many years the center for sociological training in the United States. There, under the tutelage of Park and Ernest W. Burgess, a number of important studies of social structure and community organization were conducted—studies that described, sometimes in intimate detail, the experiences of immigrants, life in the ghettos, the social and economic gap between the gold coast and the slum, and examinations of the "other side" of urban existence.

"As sociological study approached the status of scientific procedure," wrote E.B. Reuter, "its emphasis shifted from the description of social structure to the study of social processes."[34] And, he continued:

The interest in differences was replaced by an interest in uniformities; the interest in traits, whether inherited or acquired, whether biological or cultural, gave way to an interest in relationships. Social traits were seen to form and change in the experience of living together.[35]

This change in emphasis was abundantly clear in the work of the Chicago sociologists. As early as 1926, Park had suggested that "in relations of races there is a cycle of events which tends everywhere to repeat itself."[36] The process involved the coming into contact of different groups, a period of competition followed by a detente (accommodation), and, ultimately, assimilation or amalgamation.

In time others proposed their own "race relations" cycles; more recently, some have rather sharply criticized the use of such rigidly mechanistic models.[37] Yet Park's sequential typology represented a new departure in the theoretical study of intergroup relations and stimulated new research into the similarities of groups undergoing the strain of confrontation and adaptation to new situations. Not least important were the studies on the marginal man first conducted by Everett V. Stonequist and those of social distance by Emory S. Bogardus—both stimulated by the pioneering work of Park.[38] In fact, Stonequist and Borgardus, each in his own way, symbolize what may best be described as a bifurcation of directions in race-relation research. One was essentially sociological, the other psychological. Though there was to be much overlapping, the former followed the trend of emphasizing the behavior of peoples in varied social situations; the latter stressed attitudes and the behavior of individuals.

From the late 1930s on, studies of the nature of prejudice (considered as "a negative social attitude") and of the "prejudiced personality" paralleled those on intergroup relations. Although psychologists concerned themselves in the main with cognitive, affective, and conative dimensions of prejudice and the responses of individuals to certain social situations, and sociologists concentrated on group processes, the two trends were never entirely divorced from one another. Many of the most important studies in the field as well as most postwar texts illustrate this interdependence. Among the former are John Dollard's *Caste and Class in a Southern Town* (1937), Gunnar Myrdal's *An American Dilemma* (1944), Bruno Bettelheim's and Morris Janowitz's *The Dynamics of Prejudice* (1950), Melvin M. Tumin's *Desegregation* (1958), Robin M. Williams' *Strangers Next Door* (1964), Kenneth B. Clark's *Dark Ghetto* (1965), Gary T. Marx's *Protest and Prejudice* (1967), and Elliot Liebow's *Tally's Corner* (1967).[39] Each of the studies mentioned here deals partly or exclusively with the black in comparison to other groups in America as seen from outside and within the dark ghetto or rural sector. Each stresses both the social structure in which intergroup relations occur as well as attitudes and behavioral responses. Taken together they illustrate what Richard Schermerhorn has called the major thought patterns of American specialists: preoccupation with problems of prejudice and discrimination; the depiction of minorities or ethnic groups solely in the role of victims and progress in research primarily concerned with "updating" previous studies.

Courses and Research on Race

The first courses in the United States that were concerned solely with "races and nationalities" were offered at the University of

Chicago in the late 1920s. One of the most significant was an interdisciplinary seminar in which sociologists, economists, historians, and political scientists took part. Robert Park, Louis Wirth, Robert Redfield, and Herbert Blumer were the organizers. Members of other departments reported on multiracial and multiethnic societies in various parts of the world. During this same period, Louis Wirth began teaching "American minorities" and helped to organize the American Council on Race Relations, on which he served as chief officer. Hughes, Wirth, and their colleagues developed the Committee on Research and Training in Race Relations, which was one of the first of its kind anywhere. In summarizing the days when the subject of race relations was first regarded as a distinct field for undergraduates to study (in contrast to being an area only for scholarly research), two themes were evident. One was the place of minorities in this country—"Negroes and the various groups who came later." The other was the broadly conceived comparative study of race relations. "Park," says Hughes, "spoke of it as the study of the expansion of Europe."[40]

In a short time the first theme became action-oriented and focused on attempts to reduce intergroup conflicts, interesting social workers as well as sociologists. Summarizing the trend, Wirth noted the change "from the earlier preoccupation with the study of differential traits and capacities of various racial and cultural components of the human family to the present dominant interest in the processes of interaction between racial and cultural groups and in the development of effective methods for understanding and dealing with the problems of racial and cultural relations."[41] Yet, perhaps understandably, he underplayed the fact that preoccupation with the bases for prejudice and attempts to reduce the malaise of those with minority status portended a narrowing perception of intergroup relations, which for a time led to a somewhat myopic concern with *America's* racial and ethnic problems. Elaborating on the latter point, Everett and Helen Hughes wrote in 1952 (two years after Wirth's commentary was published):

It is an odd thing to say, but a true one, that many of the people who are now studying racial and ethnic relations are doing so from an ethnocentric point of view. This is true sometimes in one, sometimes in both of the following senses: they show little or no interest in the contacts of peoples outside the United States, or at most do not get beyond North America. Moreover, they look at cultural and racial relations almost entirely from the point of view of what have come to be called *minorities;* often, indeed, from the point of view of some particular minority. . . . It is not the special interest in one, but the exclusion of the others from view that makes the point of view ethnocentric.[42]

The comparative approach, by contrast, was far more sophisticated. Attempts were made to examine examples of groups both in harmony and in conflict from various societies and cultures and to develop theories of race relations. It captured the imagination of some sociologists as well as political scientists and anthropologists. Yet it never seemed to have the same appeal as did the problem-oriented, parochial, and seemingly more immediate subject of "American minorities," at least not until the postwar period and the time when the study of culture change and of new nations came into vogue.

The "dominant" and "subordinate" themes are most apparent in postwar synopses of research and texts on race relations and in course outlines. There have been numerous attempts to review research in this field.[43] In addition, many post World War II textbooks and readers have developed the findings of researchers and have provided certain guidelines for students concerned with the general topic.[44]

With rare exceptions, most of the books written or compiled by these social scientists have been concerned with the American scene. A recent nationwide study of the focus of over seven hundred sociology courses in race relations taught in American colleges and universities conclusively indicates a major emphasis on America's problems.[45] Moreover, most of these courses, like many of the textbooks used in them, are highly eclectic overviews rather than theoretical explorations of basic social structural issues. Although they are marked by an aura of scientific certainty and contain many data, these courses (and many textbooks)[46] remain infused with a sense of moral indignation. Discrimination is seen as a stain on the fabric of American society which, as one respondent put it, "must be understood, then eradicated."

Few can fault the passion expressed by most who teach these courses. Few can disagree with their desire to improve the character and quality of life in the United States. Yet as Tamotsu Shibutani and Kian W. Kwan have recently written:

Ironically, one of the major barriers to a better comprehension of these phenomena is the indignation of the investigators. Social scientists are human beings, and their emotional reactions to the injustices they see make difficult the cultivation of a detached standpoint. Men who are angry often look for a responsible agent to blame, and this search for culprits often vitiates research. . . . When difficulties are perceived in moral terms, there is a tendency to explain events by imputing vicious motives to those who are held responsible.

Furthermore, moral indignation often blinds the student to many facts that would otherwise be obvious. All too often deeds regarded as reprehensible are assumed to be fundamentally different from those that are approved, and the moral dichotomy often prevents one from recognizing that both may be manifestations of the same social process. John Dewey once wrote that the greatest single obstacle to the development of the social sciences was the tendency to approach human problems in terms of moral blame and approbation, and in no field is this more true than in the study of inter-ethnic contacts.[47]

Elsewhere I have referred to this as the problem of the "limits of conscience." It has indeed inhibited much meaningful assessment of the nature and course of racial and ethnic relations. Fortunately such American writers as Shibutani, Kwan, Hughes and Tumin and such Europeans as J. S. Furnivall, Harry Hoetink, and Michael Banton (to name but a few) have begun to speak out against the deleterious effects of these "limits." Unfortunately, however, few have heeded their admonitions. Having avoided the pitfalls of early racist doctrine to which some of their predecessors subscribed, and having overcome the tendency to oversimplify complex social relationships by taking the view that "the folkways make everything right," they have not been able to come to terms with the liberal rhetoric that has become so much a part of the sociology of race relations. (Hoetink calls this the "sociologistic vision," especially pronounced in America.) As a result, the same platitudes about "good guys" and "bad guys" circumscribe many approaches to intergroup problems and underlie the majority of courses currently being taught (and texts being written) on the subject of race and race relations. Too many continue to reflect in word and activity the understandable but somewhat misguided ethnocentric stances mentioned by the Hughes over fifteen years ago.

Tomatsu Shibutani and Kian Kwan are among a small number of American sociologists who have attempted to offer an alternative to the ethnocentric positivism that seems to mark the work of so many of their colleagues. Their work is very much in the tradition of Robert E. Park, the Hugheses, Herbert Blumer, and E. Franklin Frazier. Like Park and his colleagues, Shibutani and Kwan feel that race relations should be viewed not as social problems but as social phenomena that exist *wherever* ethnic groups meet.

To this end, they set forth "to formulate generalizations concerning the characteristics of various social processes and the conditions under which they occur, regardless of where they happen."[48] The bulk of their volume, *Ethnic Stratification: A Comparative Approach*

(1965), is devoted to an elaboration of the social processes themselves: "differentiating processes" (how color lines come into existence); "sustaining processes" (including patterns of adjustment and accommodation); "disjunctive processes" (dealing with tension and conflict, political tactics, and the consolidation of power); and "integrative processes" (concerned with such matters as acculturation and assimilation). *Ethnic Stratification* contains a far more comprehensive (and up-to-date) treatment of these subjects than is to be found in any single text now available for classroom use. It also offers an antidote to those who seek an alternative to the many books whose principle raison d'etre seems to be "resolving social conflicts." Nowhere is this more evident than in Shibutani and Kwan's discussion of the loaded term "prejudice."

Though offering no direct substitute, they present an elaborate discussion of "Popular Conceptions of Ethnic Identity"[49] dealing with such relevant issues as categorization, stereotyping, and ethnocentricity. Emphasis is given to the relative positions of groups in the stratification of different societies and to the differential meaning of subordinate status. "As incredible as it may seem to most Americans," they write, "systems of ethnic stratification are upheld for long periods by the willing support and cooperation of the people who are being subjugated."[50] Extensive examples and "natural histories" drawn from the world literature on interethnic contacts lend some (but not conclusive) support to such generalizations.

The volume ends with a tightly knit "theory of ethnic stratification" in which the authors, a social psychologist and a sociologist, assert that:

The population in most communities is heterogeneous, the people being divided along class, religious and ethnic lines. . . .

The relationship between such groups varies; it may be one of coexistence, stratification, or sustained opposition. . . .

Those who occupy the same habitat . . . sooner or later become involved in a common web of life; in most cases they participate in a common economic system. . . .

Ethnic stratification is one aspect of community organization; individuals are placed in a hierarchical order, not in terms of their personal attributes but in terms of their supposed ancestry (Here we note similarities to Harris' notion of "social races"). . . .[51]

Having defined an ethnic group as "people who conceive of themselves as being alike by virtue of common ancestry, real or fictitious, and are so regarded by others,"[52] Shibutani and Kwan go on to say that "where a color line develops the fate of an individual depends upon the manner in which he is classified. The color line is a particular type of social structure."[53] And, since social structures are here viewed as "patterns of concerted action" (a somewhat dubious conceptualization),

ethnic stratification persists as long as people on both sides of the color line approach one another with common expectations of how each is to act in the presence of the other. The color lines consist of a set of conventional norms. Where there is a high degree of consensus, violations of norms arose emotional reactions; deviating acts appear immoral, perhaps even unnatural.

The consensus of which they speak is built up through a "communicative process" in which perspectives are shaped and reaffirmed through a succession of culturally relevant gestural interchanges. (Although they do not refer to him, Shibutani's and Kwan's ideas are very close to those expressed by Edward T. Hall in his book, *The Silent Language,* in which he describes "primary message systems."[55]) Thus acculturation is seen as being determined by the ease with which subordinates can communicate with those who are dominant, both in the political arena and in all phases of social life.

Institutionalized segregation may be used effectively to block communication channels, isolating dominant groups from subordinates and resulting in the development or continuation of separate "cultures." Thus efficient communication is viewed as an "inverse function of social distance."[56] Rather tautologically Shibutani and Kwan then assert that "as members of minority groups become acculturated, they become more like those in the dominant group and attempt to identify with them."[57] Here one might ask whether identification or even heightened aspiration is necessarily the path to domestic tranquility. The evidence in this country is not conclusive. Closing the cultural gap does not necessarily close the social one. Moreover, competition for scarce resources or limited rewards by those who have grown closer to the dominant group in terms of desires and goals (the "revolution of rising expectations") may exacerbate tensions and cause the reinstitution of ethnic or racial barriers ("backlash"). Although Shibutani and Kwan are aware of these possibilities, they tend to handle them in a manner reminiscent of the previously mentioned period of Social Darwinian sociology.

They write that "if values are in short supply, individuals compete for them and *new patterns of concerted action emerge initially through natural selection.*"[58]

As it is developed, the argument becomes Parkian as well as Darwinian: when competition is intensified, it is transformed into rivalry or conflict that becomes fixed and, eventually, institutionalized. They have come full circle. While denying their intention to offer another cyclical theory, Shibutani and Kwan exhibit it time and again. The argument develops as follows: Most societies are hierarchical and many are heterogeneous. In those that are both, ethnicity is a critical variable. Shutting out those who differ intensifies separatism; opening the door increases communication and may alter traditional norms on the part of the subordinate minority in favor of those of the "host" society. A demand follows for a greater share in power, which often results in a backlash that throws the minority back on itself and reasserts the hierarchical, heterogeneous character of the society.

Of course, no society that actually goes through such a process—and American society is, in a sense, going through it today with regard to its black population—is *ever* truly the same again. Theoretically the circle may close (as in the case of any self-fulfilling prophecy), but in real terms there is no "cycle of events that repeats itself everywhere," as Robert Park[59] and, to some extent, Shibutani and Kwan would have us believe. (If one wants to use a simile here, a spiral would come closer than a circle.) My criticism is meant only to point out the dangers of looking for simple models to cover all contingencies, especially by those offering definitive theories of ethnic stratification.

Still, the Shibutani and Kwan volume is a significant addition to the literature and an important text. Not only does it offer a refreshing perspective; it also provides a rich compendium of information obtained from an extensive perusal of the available literature in related fields. I refer here to a source of data that has hardly been tapped by the sociologists: the studies of social anthropologists, economists, and area specialists. As for American sociologists who have done their own field work abroad, one recent commentator has claimed that "by the 1960's . . . they could almost be counted on the fingers of two hands!"[60]

A brief digression is in order here. Since the Second World War a number of economists and political scientists concerned with development began to study nation building and to search for similar

patterns in societies undergoing reorganization. In many ways their
work was far more sophisticated than that of the problem-oriented
"race relationists." They turned to the basic sociological categories
and began to substitute such concepts as "political system" for
"state," "functions" for "powers," "roles" for "offices," and to rely
on the premises of functional analysis.[61]

Their work needs no summarizing. However, despite its breakthrough quality, particularly in working out ways of understanding
the relationship between the anatomy and the physiology of political
life, it has tended to avoid or overlook or underplay the significance
of the race factor as a critical variable in the comparative study of
social change and international relations. As for the few sociologists
and anthropologists who have worked on this race factor, Schermerhorn has suggested that five approaches seem to dominate the field.

The first is the gathering of new data with little attention to
theory, some of the early descriptive work published by the Institute
of Race Relations in London, for example. The second involves the
gathering and theoretical interpretation of new data. Three examples
are Robert E. Park's posthumous *Race and Culture* (1949), Everett
and Helen Hughes's *Where People Meet* (1952), and the recently
published book by Harry Hoetink, *The Two Variants on Caribbean
Race Relations* (1967). The third approach centers on the organizing
of vast quantities of data collected by taxonomic means. Three
well-known volumes characterize this orientation: Alain Locke and
Bernhard J. Stern, *When Peoples Meet* (1942), P.A.F. Walter, *Race
and Culture Relations* (1952), and Brewton Berry, *Race and Ethnic
Relations* (1958).

Shibutani and Kwan's volume is a good example of the fourth
approach: the attempt to pull together vast quantities of collected
data by means of a unified or a specially constructed theory. Hubert
Blalock's *Toward a Theory of Minority Group Relations* (1967)
illustrates the latter. Finally, there is a very limited series of
comparative case studies dealing with particular societies and
utilizing the same theoretical framework for each. One of the first
books using this approach is Charles Wagley and Marvin Harris,
Minorities in the New World (1958). A more recent example is Pierre
van den Berghe's *Race and Racism* (1967).[62]

Van den Berghe's recent book is the more sophisticated of the last
mentioned examples. It reviews the dominant trends in the study of
race relations, many of which have already been touched on in
previous discussion, and then explicates several key concepts,

particularly the ideas of race and racism. Offering an operational definition similar to that suggested by Marvin Harris, van den Berghe writes, "we consistently use the term race . . . to refer to a group that is socially defined but on the basis of physical criteria."[63] To avoid confusion with the layman's usage, he would call groups sharing certain cultural characteristics, such as a language or religion, ethnic groups or ethnicities. The important difference is that, like races, ethnic groups are socially defined; but their definition is based primarily on cultural rather than on physical criteria.[64]

In this view racism is defined as "any set of beliefs that organic, genetically transmitted differences (whether real or imagined) between human groups are intrinsically associated with the presence or the absence of certain socially relevant abilities or characteristics, hence that such differences are a legitimate basis of invidious distinctions between groups socially defined as races."[65] Although such racism is to be found in all eras of human history and in various parts of the world, van den Berghe focuses his attention upon Western racism and racial stratification. The latter is said to result from one or more of the following conditions: military conquest (in which the victor establishes his political and economic domination over an indigenous group, such as the European powers in tropical Africa); gradual frontier expansion (in which one group pushes back, overruns, or exterminates the native population, such as European expansion in North America and Australia); involuntary migration (such as the capture and transportation of African slaves into the United States, Brazil, and the West Indies); and voluntary migration (in which alien groups move into new lands seeking political protection or economic opportunities, such as the old European and recent Puerto Rican, Mexican, and Cuban migrations to the United States mainland).[66]

Western racism is a fairly widespread phenomenon with definite historic and cultural roots. Of special importance is (or was) its congruence with certain prevailing forms of economic exploitation (including slavery in the New World and colonial expansion there and elsewhere), although this is not necessarily a consequence of racism, as the Marxists believe.[67] (Debate still continues over the question of pre-eighteenth-century racism. I would contend that racism, even as defined by van den Berghe, is a much older phenomenon.)

In any case, van den Berghe is correct when he points to the fact that Darwinism gave legitimacy to the ideology of racial superiority, particularly for those who had taken up the white man's burden. He adds an interesting addendum to this conventional wisdom:

The egalitarian and libertarian ideas of the enlightenment spread by the American and French Revolutions . . . paradoxically contributed to [racism's] development. Faced with the blatant contradiction between the treatment of slaves and colonial peoples and the official rhetoric of freedom of equality, Europeans and white North Americans began to dichotomize humanity between men and submen (or the "civilized" and the "savages").[68]

He continues:

The scope of applicability of the egalitarian ideals was restricted to "the people," that is, the whites, and there resulted what I have called "*Herrenvolk* democracies,"—regimes such as those of the United States or South Africa that are democratic for the master race but tyrannical for the subordinate groups.[69]

According to van den Berghe, *Herrenvolk* democracies are apt to be more highly developed economically and more complex socially.[70] In Karl Mannheim's terms, they would be more Democratic than Aristocratic in spite of obvious disparities (disparities often explained in Social Darwinist terms).[71]

Attempting to go beyond the traditional theories that rarely seem able to relate race relations to the total society, van den Berghe offers his own paradigm. To avoid the pitfalls of the past, he seeks to provide a system of classification which meets the criteria of comparative applicability, historical usability, specification of variables, and integration (meaning the integration of the specific syndrome of race relations within the rest of the social structure). Pointing out that one frequently finds similarities in *social structural relations* which transcend cultural differences (such as the plantation systems in North and Latin America), van den Berghe states:

If two societies with widely different cultural traditions can more or less independently develop similar racial situations and institutions, if, conversely, the history of a given country can be marked by profound changes and discontinuities, and, furthermore, if abrupt qualitative changes in race relations can be shown to coincide with structural changes in the society at large, it is reasonable to accept that basic aspects of the social structure exert a considerable degree of determination on the prevailing type of race relations.[72]

He then presents his two "ideal-types": the traditional master-servant pattern of paternalism and the modern competitive one. The

Table 2-1

A Schematic Outline of the Paternalistic and the Competitive Types of Race Relations

Independent Variables

	Paternalistic	*Competitive*
1. Economy	Nonmanufacturing, agricultural, pastoral, handicraft; mercantile capitalism; plantation economy	Typically manufacturing, but not necessarily so; large-scale industrial capitalism
2. Division of labor	Simple ("primitive") or intermediate (as in preindustrial large-scale societies); division of labor along racial lines; wide income gap between racial groups	Complex (manufacturing) according to "rational" universalistic criteria; narrow gap in wages; no longer strictly racial
3. Mobility	Little mobility either vertical or horizontal (slaves, servants, or serfs "attached" in space)	Much mobility both vertical and horizontal (required by industrial economy)
4. Social stratification	Caste system with horizontal color bar; aristocracy versus servile caste with wide gap in living standards (as indexed by income, education, death and birth rates); homogeneous upper caste	Caste system but with tendency for color bar to "tilt" to vertical position; complex stratification into classes within castes; narrower gaps between castes and greater range within castes
5. Numerical ratio	Dominant group a small minority	Dominant group a majority
6. Value	Integrated value system; no ideological conflict	Conflict at least in Western "Christian," "democratic," "liberal" type of society

Dependent Variables

	Paternalistic	*Competitive*
1. Race relations	Accommodation; everyone in "his place" and "knows it"; paternalism; benevolent despotism	Antagonism; suspicion, hatred; competitiveness (real or imaginary)
2. Roles and statuses	Sharply defined roles and statuses based on ascription, particularism, diffuseness, collectivity orientation, affectivity; unequal status unthreatened	Ill-defined and based on achievement, universalism, specificity, self-orientation, affective neutrality; unequal status threatened

3. Etiquette	Elaborate and definite	Simple and indefinite
4. Forms of aggression	Generally from lower caste: slave rebellions; nationalistic, revivalistic, or messianistic movements; not directly racial	Both from upper and lower caste; more frequent and directly racial: riots, lynchings, pogroms; passive resistance, sabotage, organized mass protests
5. Miscegenation	Condoned and frequent between upper-caste males and lower-caste females; institutionalized concubinage	Severely condemned and infrequent
6. Segregation	Little of it; status gap allows close but unequal contact	Much of it; narrowing of status gap makes for increase of spatial gap
7. Psychological syndrome	Internalized subservient status; no personality need for prejudice; no "high F"; pseudotolerance	Need for prejudice; "high F"; linked with sexuality, sadism, frustration; scapegoating
8. Stereotypes of lower caste	Childish, immature, exuberant, uninhibited, lazy, impulsive, fun-loving, good-humored; inferior but lovable	Aggressive, uppity, insolent, oversexed, dirty; inferior, despicable, and dangerous
9. Intensity of prejudice	Fairly constant	Variable and sensitive to provocative situations

Social-Control Variables

	Paternalistic	*Competitive*
1. Form of government	Aristocratic, oligarchic, autocratic; either centralized or "feudal"; colonial	Restricted or pseudodemocratic
2. Legal system	Lower caste has definite legal status; law on side of racial status quo	Lower caste has no definite legal status; resort to extralegal sanctions (e.g., lynchings)

Note: By independent variables I mean here those basic structural factors that determine to a large extent the prevailing type of race relations in a given society. By dependent variables, I mean more specifically aspects or components of the racial situation.

schematic outline in Table 2.1 illustrates the independent, dependent, and social-control variables associated with such polarity.[73]

Van den Berghe also introduces (or reintroduces) the concept of pluralism. His usage differs from the Tocquevillian view of a variety of competing interest groups each with some sort of veto power ("political pluralism") and from the widely used sociological notion of "cultural pluralism."[74] Rather, to him, as to J. S. Furnivall, J. H. Boeke, and M. G. Smith,[75] the defining criteria of a plural society are institutional duplication *and* cleavage between corporate groups. In theory, "social pluralism . . . is present in pure form to the extent that a society is structurally compartmentalized into analogous and duplicatory but culturally alike sets of institutions, and into corporate groups which are differentiated on a basis other than culture." In practice, social pluralism sometimes goes hand in hand with cultural pluralism because racial groups as previously defined often learn to share certain common values and beliefs and form subcultures of their own. Van den Berghe calls this "secondary cultural pluralism," arising from structural pluralism.[76] Again, one thinks of the situation of enslaved black Africans who became Negro Americans and are now developing a new "Afro-American" or "Black American" ethnicity.[77] Still, recognizing the persistence in this country of social separation and cultural assimilation for many American minorities (like the Irish, the Poles, and the Jews), theoretical distinction remains relevant for empirical purposes. This is further evident in *Race and Racism.*

Van den Berghe uses case studies of four segmented or plural societies, Mexico, Brazil, the United States, and the Union of South Africa, each of which is the product of a historically unique set of factors resulting from the colonial expansion of Europe after the late fifteenth century.[78] He examines similarities and differences between them on such dimensions as the respective degree of acculturation, the role of religion, the character of indigenous social organizations, the fate of the local population, the extensiveness of miscegenation, the presence of slaves, demographic and economic features, the major cleavages and dimensions of intergroup conflict, and, finally, the attitudes of those in the dominant positions. The body of his book is concerned with these comparisons but, since this is only tangential to our immediate theoretical interests, I will summarize only his general findings:

the system of race relations developed in the pre-modern phase of the four societies examined showed great similarities despite great differences in the cultures of both dominant and subordinate groups. In all instances a typically paternalistic system united in symbiotic interdependence a servile or quasi-servile labor force ... the stereotypes of subordinate groups were similar ... the dominant group rationalized its position by virtue of cultural and racial superiority....

the paternalistic regimes were all characterized by two social processes ... physical intermixture or miscegenation [and] ... the extensive and relatively rapid assimilation of the subject groups to the culture of the dominant group....

[Differences are apparent in] the contrasting role of Catholicism and Protestantism....

another "generalizable difference" between the four cases concerns the nature of the indigenous cultures which the conquerors encountered....

in all four cases the paternalistic system of race and ethnic relations was undermined by a series of changes in the social infra-structure. In the political sphere aristocratic, colonial, or white settler regimes became transformed into "representative" governments with wider participation in the polity, though in South Africa and until recently in the United States the democratic process was still restricted to the dominant racial caste.[79]

One last summarizing point must be added, the one that links van den Berghe's findings to his overall theory and relates back to the paternalism-competition axis. It is his statement that

even these *Herrenvolk* democracies are clearly different from the colonial government or the planter slave-owning oligarchy which preceded them, if only because they were legitimized in terms of an ideology that could be effectively used to challenge the racial status quo. Thus these *Herrenvolk* democracies contained the ideological seeds of their own destruction, providing the educated elite within the oppressed groups and the progressive minority of the dominant group with a set of values to deny legitimacy to the established order.[80]

I could go on discussing van den Berghe's views and analyses of these particular societies but, instead, let us turn to his comments on the more general matter of social and cultural pluralism.

As noted previously, "race" and "racism" are perceived in different ways by the members of various disciplines.

To the physical anthropologist "race" in the genetic sense is a case of subspeciation in *homo sapiens;* to a social psychologist racism is a special instance of prejudice; for the philosopher racism is a particular body of ideas; the political scientist may regard racism as a special kind of political ideology; to an economist race is one of the "nonrational" factors, influencing, to be sure, economic behavior but falling outside the scope of his discipline; a historian may look at race and racism as by-products of, and rationalizations for, Western slavery and colonial expansion; a cultural anthropologist may regard race and racism as traits in the cultural inventory of a people.[81]

The sociologists, according to van den Berghe, should limit their perceptions to seeing these phenomena as special instances of *structural* or *social* pluralism. Whether one agrees with so narrow a view or not, it is significant to note that van den Berghe, perhaps better than anyone else, indicates that "cultural and social pluralism are not simply two facets of the same reality." He continues, "Since race is a more rigid basis of cleavage than ethnicity, social pluralism can subsist longer and, indeed, even in the nearly total absence of cultural pluralism, whereas the converse is not true."[82] This is why several sociologists have attempted to draw clear distinctions between racial and ethnic groups even in the study of American society.[83]

When one uses the concept of social pluralism, four levels of society must be examined: groups, institutions, individuals, and values. Boundaries are significant in the first instance; duplication in the second. (It is said that "institutional pluralism is the opposite of functional differentiation." Thus a segregated school system is pluralistic, an alternative one is not.) At the individual level, mobility through both structural and cultural space is most relevant. Finally, at the value level, consensus or its absence is crucial (for instance, "freedom does not mean the same to most whites and to most Negroes in the United States").[84]

Value consensus is often considered the critical level and the key to social stability, at least by those who are concerned with the study of whole societies. A problem arises when "whole societies" are not homogeneous but are socially pluralistic. What, then, is the basis of social integration? Some would claim that pluralistic societies are in constant turmoil and are always lacking in integration, although the evidence belies such a claim. Van den Berghe and others suggest that many pluralistic societies are held together by a combination of political coercion and economic interdependence. (He suggests that neither alone is sufficient to maintain stability.[85])

Here, van den Berghe has touched on a critical theoretical debate that has particular relevance for those wishing to apply sociological perspectives to the study of intergroup relations. I refer to the controversy over functionalism versus conflict theory. One should remember that, despite an impressive amount of research in race relations (particularly within the United States), there has been a dearth of theory. Race relations was not particularly important to the founding fathers of sociology; few wrote much on it as a subject per se, and few modern theoreticians have shown much interest in it either.[86]

I have already indicated the biases of most of the American sociologists who have worked in the area of racial and ethnic relations and have stressed the ideological character of their concern, the pragmatic approach to data gathering and the melioristic orientation by which they hope to save society or its victims. One fact, alluded to previously (in a passing reference to a shift in sociological gravity from Chicago to the East), has been the bias of many theorists at least since the mid-1930s. Imbued with a structural-functional orientation that emphasizes stasis and system maintenance through the acceptance of certain values by society's members, it was difficult to cope with race relations, which are contentious almost by definition (at least the definitions most popularly used). Michael Banton pursues this point in a brief review of race-relations theory (or its lack). He suggests that "By its very nature this [structural-functional] approach is not well suited to the study of circumstances in which two societies interact or in which social patterns are maintained by force rather than agreement."[87]

Some alternatives have been offered. One is Ralf Dahrendorf's thesis as presented in *Class and Class Conflict in Industrial Society* (1959), which begins with a very different basic assumption from that of Talcott Parsons and other functionalists. To them, "integration" means largely what A. R. Radcliffe-Brown (and, before him, Emile Durkheim) had contended. Social behavior and the institutions of society are seen in terms of the functioning of the social system (the individual being "adjusted" if he accepts his place, "deviant" if he does not). To Dahrendorf this is only one view. Another is the "coercion thesis," the argument that society is held together by various constraints.

Banton illustrates the dual perspectives of consensus and coercion rather cleverly in the following example:

It may be useful to view the attitudes of miners towards work underground in terms of coercion theory: they work because they have to, not because they want to. At the same time, it may be more profitable to view their leisure behaviour in the welfare centre from the standpoint of the consensus theory, highlighting their common outlook and values concerning matters outside the employment situation.[88]

Though it may seem obvious that, in the case of the study of race relations, there is no alternative but to use the coercion approach, Banton says that "no sociologist has linked up race relations studies to the intellectual tradition behind the coercion theory, permitting the lessons learned in this long controversy to be applied to the racial field."[89] No one, that is, except Pierre van den Berghe and Richard Schermerhorn (two men of whose most recent work Banton seems unaware).

For many years Schermerhorn, the author of *These Our People* (1949) and *Society and Power* (1961), has been concerned with the strains extant in plural societies and the relative position of members. An early proclivity for a "conflict approach" gave way to a less dogmatic view. In a paper entitled "Polarity in the Approach to Comparative Research in Ethnic Relations" published in 1967, Schermerhorn asserted that "the task of intergroup research is to account for modes of integration-conflict (as dependent variables) in the relationships between dominant groups and subordinate ethnic groups in different societies."[90] As for independent variables, he suggests two that are "most promising": (1) the degree of enclosure in the subordinate ethnic group[91] as measured by such indices as endogamy, ecological concentration, institutional duplication, associational clustering and the like; and, (2) the control of scarce values by dominant groups.[92] In addition, the direction of "movement" toward or away from one another by those who hold and those who lack power is "The Contextual Feature" and, as an intervening variable, must also be taken into account.

Altogether, his idea may be graphically presented as in the accompanying diagram.[93] *A, B, C,* and *D* are various patterns of intergroup relations. The first two represent situations where there is agreement regarding the maintenance of stability (though in one case it is through togetherness and in the other through institutionalized separation), and the latter two indicate situations where there is a collision between the desires of the separate parties toward their respective positions and life styles.

Congruent and Incongruent
Orientations Toward Centripetal
and Centrifugal Directional
Movement by Superordinate and
Subordinate Groups

	A	B	
Superordinates	Cp	Cf	Tending toward
Subordinates	Cp	Cf	Integration
	Assimilation	Cultural Pluralism	
	Amalgamation	Federalism	

	C	D	
Superordinates	Cf	Cp	Tending toward
Subordinates	Cp	Cf	Conflict
	Forced segregation	Forced assimilation	
	with resistance	with resistance	

Cp — centripetal
Cf — centrifugal

The important point is Schermerhorn's graphic portrayal of the necessity to consider both systemic and relational matters (the whole-to-part "functionalist" orientation and the part-to-whole "conflict" orientation) at least when considering intergroup relations at a macrosociological level. This concern with the "dual perspective" is one of the principle issues discussed by Schermerhorn in his latest work, still in preparation, "Comparative Ethnic Relations."[94]

A central question of comparative research in ethnic relations is: What are the conditions that foster or prevent the integration of ethnic groups into their environing societies? Here integration is not seen as an end state (as would be the "integration" of blacks in the United States), but as "a process whereby units or elements of a society are brought into an active and coordinated compliance with the ongoing activities and objectives of the dominant group in that society." Again, integration and conflict are viewed as dependent variables subject to a variety of social and historical factors.

To the question—How are societies as wholes maintained by their constituent elements?—those following the Durkheimian tradition would tend to say

societies as wholes can survive as "going concerns" only if fundamental needs are met. These needs, usually called functional imperatives or functional requisites . . . include such items as provisions for physiological functioning and survival, reproduction and replacement, shared goals and perspectives, socialization, communication, organization of roles, control and regulation of deviance, and general regularization of activities in patterned forms . . . if these needs are to be met reliably and predictably, they must be supported by structures, i.e. by uniformities of action that recur when called for by the situation. Here generic principles must become specified into determinant patterns and organizations and institutions.

The point is that whatever character societies assume, they must be, according to functional theory, mutually supportive to maintain the stability of society.

Two other principles of functional analysis are relevant here as well. One is the principle of hierarchy, or what some would call "the functional basis for stratification";[95] the other is the principle of symmetry. The latter is best illustrated by such Parsonian terms as complementarity, boundary-maintenance, mutuality of role expectations, pattern consistency, and the like.

Robin M. Williams, a functional theorist in his own right, sums up the approach in the following statement, also quoted by Schermerhorn:

Even with all its careful disclaimers and qualifications, the [structural-functional] scheme does have the net effect, for many readers, of emphasizing stability, and, by omission, understating the problem of radical discontinuities and rapid, massive, and violent conflicts and changes in social systems with sub-systems.[96]

Schermerhorn asks if it is possible that some functional requirements may actually contradict others. Although the answer is yes, he does not conclude that one should dispense with the concept of system altogether. Rather, it "means that any use of system analysis must be more flexible, relativistic, and circumspect, alert at the same time to inductive and categorical difficulties."[97] One factor that Schermerhorn feels has inhibited greater flexibility is "the excessive dependence on cultural factors to carry the explanatory load." Here he is referring to the tendency of Parsonians to be "ends-oriented," stressing norms and values rather than means, especially scarce means. "If we are to take systems analysis seriously," Schermerhorn claims, "it must encompass the structures of both ends and means."

Continuing along this same line of reasoning, he asserts that those who study social systems must bear in mind the admonition of Georg

Simmel that "contradiction and conflict not only precede unity but are operative in it at every moment of its existence."[98] They must do, in part, what the conflict theorists do—look at the other side and, in Lenski's words, see social systems "as stages on which struggles for power and privilege take place."[99]

As suggested previously, what Schermerhorn calls "power-conflict theory" would seem, on the face of it, far better suited to the study of racial and ethnic relations. In a way it is:

Beginning with the immediate experience of limited social encounters, the power-conflict theory stresses the obvious fact of inequality in most interactions, i.e. that what one has, the other wants, what one wants, the other has. . . . What divides the two contenders is the inherent scarcity of means. The attempt to control these means leads directly to open or concealed conflict in which the exertion of power is needed to attain the goal. Such encounters occur at all levels of society and between all sorts of concrete groupings like nations, political parties, regional associations, ethnic groups, labor vs. management, rural vs. urban sectors and the like.[100]

But this angle of vision is also seen as limiting. A better approach is to view system analysis and power-conflict theory as dialectically related perspectives, at least with regard to ethnic relations. Keeping in mind the typology referred to earlier, in which there is a graphic, if limited, portrayal of this dialectic, Schermerhorn's thesis may be summarized as follows:

1. Comparative study requires a view of ethnic groups in a macrosociological perspective, i.e. in their relation to total societies [a point made forcefully by van den Berghe and discussed above] . . . .

2. In observing these relations one should be aware of the two main theoretical interpretations of total societies given by the system analysts and the power-conflict theorists. (Talcott Parsons and Marion Levy representing the former; Gerhard Lenski and, to a lesser extent, Ralf Dahrendorf representing the latter).

   a. Applying system analysis to comparative ethnic relations actually centers attention on the function the ethnic group performs for the entire system, viewing the ethnic group itself as a sub-system gradually fitted into the wider society by a series of adaptive adjustments regulated by the norms and values of its institutions that eventually become internalized by members of the ethnic groups involved.

b. From the standpoint of power-conflict theory, one can view each ethnic group as being in an embattled position, fighting for its life, its identity, or its prestige, subject to perpetual constraints that threaten its survival, its freedom, or its life chances in a precarious world.

3. Actually, neither perspective can exclude the other without unwarranted dogmatism. As Robin Williams has stated 'all interacting human populations show both coerced and voluntary conformity.'

4. The problem is, at bottom, an empirical one. It is important, therefore, to search out, by inductive inquiry, observation and analysis the meaning of Williams' proposition (as well as A. R. Radcliffe-Brown's statement that 'opposition, i.e. organized and regulated antagonism, is . . . an essential feature of every social system'). No field of inquiry is better fitted to exemplifying the dual relevance of such ostensibly clashing theoretical perspectives than the sphere of ethnic relations.[101]

Evident throughout the remainder of Schermerhorn's study is the shift to a more dialectical view in which there is a constant interplay between the two dominant perspectives. For example, in a chapter on "Some Unexplored Types of Integration," he considers the problems of legitimation, cultural congruence, and goal definitions from the point of view of those holding power and attempting to maintain a particular system and of those who are subordinates (minorities as well as mass subjects). I will dwell only on the last problem.

Here the question is, in part, how do minority-group members see themselves in relation to others and what are they prepared to do about this conception? Louis Wirth had outlined policies adapted by minority-group members. His famous paradigm suggested these alternatives: assimilation, pluralism, secessionism, and militance.[102] I have also addressed attention to this problem and to certain choices offered in order to indicate various responses to discrimination in the United States. My own typology was based upon responses to two theoretical questions: Does the subordinate accept or reject the dominant group's image of his group's inferiority? Regardless of the answer to the first question, is he willing to play (or even desirous of playing) a segregated role? My typology, originally published in 1964, looks like this.[103]

	Dominant Image of Subordinates' "Inferior Status"	
Segregated role?	*Accepted*	*Rejected*
Yes	1. Submission	3. Separatism
No	2. Withdrawal	4. Integration

Although this typology goes somewhat farther than Wirth's, it has, in Schermerhorn's terms, the same inherent problem. It emphasizes only the attitudes and behavior of the subordinates and *assumes* discrimination on the part of the dominant group. Its utility is limited to the specific cultural context for which it was designed, namely the United States.

Schermerhorn points out that such typologies tend to examine only one side of the transaction. It is essential to consider what dominant groups want the subordinates to attain. Here he reintroduces the idea of centripetal and centrifugal tendencies and offers a slightly revised version of the typology presented in his earlier paper and referred to above.[104]

Schermerhorn's treatise goes on as he discusses many other matters tangential to the problem of "the *development* of race studies." Included here are other "typologies of problem relevance," classification schemes that divide societies in "multi-national sectors" or along a continuum according to the dominance of either the polity of the economy (as "Pol-Ec Societies" or "Ec-Pol Societies"), discussions of cross-sectional research on plural societies in which he illustrates attempts at rapprochement between diachronic and synchronic approaches,[105] and more. These later chapters are richly illustrated with data drawn from a wide variety of empirical reports on ethnic relations in various parts of the world.

Ultimately, Schermerhorn offers the following paradigm for comparative study. Like that presented by Pierre van den Berghe, it is divided into three segments:

1. Independent variables:

    a. Repeatable sequences of interacting between subordinate ethnics and dominant groups, such as annexation, migration, colonization, etc.;

    b. The degree of enclosure (institutional separation or segmentation) of the subordinate group or groups from the society-wide network of institutions and associations; and,

    c. The degree of control exercised by dominant groups over access to scarce resources by subordinate groups in a given society.

2. The *intervening or contextual variables* that modify the effects of the independent variables:

    a. Agreement or disagreement between dominant and subordinate groups on collective goals for the latter, i.e. assimilation, pluralism, etc.;

b. Membership of a society under scrutiny in a class or category of societies sharing overall common cultural and structural features, i.e. Near-East societies, Sub-Saharan African societies, etc.; and

c. Membership of a society under scrutiny in a more limited category of societies distinguished by forms of institutional dominance, i.e. polity dominating economy or vice versa.

3. The *dependent variables* to be explained are the interweaving patterns of integration and conflict either in the relations between subordinates and superordinates on the one hand, or between subordinates and the total society on the other.

a. Differential participation rates of subordinates in institutional and associational life (including rates of vertical mobility) as compared with rates for the dominant group;

b. The extent of satisfaction or dissatisfaction of both subordinate and dominant group members with the differential patterns of participation as they see them, together with accompanying ideologies and cultural values; and,

c. Overt or covert behavior patterns of subordinates and dominants indicative of conflict and/or harmonious relations; assessment in terms of continued integration.[106]

This model pulls together many disparate issues to which Schermerhorn (and others previously cited) have addressed themselves. It is offered as a tentative guide for study.

Often during the early days of research in this field, American sociologists (and others) followed the lead of the physical anthropologists. They deduced that if dark-skinned people were backward in technological and "moral" matters while white-skinned people were more advanced and more civilized, there must be some connection between the color of their skin and their ability to perform complicated tasks (including the task of governing themselves). Somewhat later, with the advent of cultural anthropology and, particularly, with the "Boasian challenge," there came a growing concern about the impact of society on its members—and vice-versa. (Actually, as suggested earlier, many sociologists first became involved because of their worries about the effects newcomers were having on American society.)

In time the sociologists became increasingly concerned with the victims of discrimination and the causes of prejudice. Research on minority communities and on the attitudes of members of dominant groups began in earnest. The findings tended to corroborate the view that racism was pervasive and that discrimination was damaging to those marked by oppression.

Some propositional inventories did begin to appear and, though limited to a single society, there was some discussion of "a theory of intergroup relations." Robin M. Williams' SSRC Bulletin, *The Reduction of Intergroup Tensions* (1947) is the best example we have of this approach. Such inventories were useful indicators of endemic problems and were guidelines for action. They are also helpful sources for those who wish to compare American racial attitudes and, to a lesser extent, behavior with that in other societies.

More typical of sociologists who ventured, literally and figuratively, beyond America's borders to make comparative studies of racial and ethnic relations are those who have set forth inductive typologies for measuring their findings. Using the conceptual and methodological tools of their discipline, they have begun to fashion models of intergroup relations offering what Richard Schermerhorn calls scaffolding for subsequent theory. Perhaps the most significant point is that sociologists like Shibutani and Kwan, van den Berghe, and Schermerhorn are beginning to fight against the main currents of a discipline where practitioners often seem better and better equipped to learn more and more about less and less. This is a significant movement away from microanalysis and a return, in many ways, to macrosociology.

Before leaving this matter of "direction" one last caveat must be stated. Macrosociology (at least in the realm of race studies) is becoming fashionable among rather different groups of sociologists. First, there are those who agree with William Bruce Cameron that "not all things that count can be counted and that not all things that can be counted count." Eschewing what is seen as nothing more than quantophrenia, they want to get at the "broader issues," the subjective aspects of human relations, to make their contribution more effective.

Then there are those who advocate a New Sociology (sometimes called "underdog sociology"). They are quite explicit in their answer to the question "Which side are you on?" Such sociologists feel that most of their colleagues (especially the sort just cited) are tools of the "welfare-warfare establishment" and contributors to the continued exploitation of those with whom they wish to align themselves: the poor, the sick, the downtrodden in every part of the globe.

Finally, there are those who are less concerned with debates over quantitative versus qualitative study, over involvement versus detachment. Their goal is expanding the horizons of knowledge. They would tend to agree with Comte's statement: *voir pour prevoir; prevoir pour pouvoir.* Or, putting it somewhat differently: first, science for the sake of knowledge and, then, knowledge for the sake of providing solutions to problems that beset man and his world.

Such sociologists are primarily interested in describing and explaining the reasons for differential patterns of race relations. They are only secondarily concerned with the policy implications of such patterns. This is as it must be if honest appraisal is to mean anything. Their work should be an important complement rather than a substitute for policy studies and for the cross-national researches of political scientists, social psychologists, and anthropologists such as Almond and Verba, Buchanan and Cantril, Stein Rokkan and his colleagues, Beatrice Whiting, Campbell and LeVine.

At bottom, the comparative sociologists are addressing themselves to a basic question about research in race relations: the question of whether one can eventually come up with a grand theory replete with postulates of relevance to all (or most) contingencies. This is a large order, but a goal worth pursuing. We need such theorizing. Of course, this is not all that is needed.

There are many other problems—and challenges—facing sociologists and other social scientists concerned with both theoretical and applied race studies. I would suggest that particular attention be paid to the following:

1. Further examination of the functions and dysfunctions of racial categorization in particular societies and cultural areas, with attention to *all* parties. Such studies, closely akin to some of the best recent work conducted in the United States (e.g., Milton M. Gordon's *Assimilation in American Life,* 1964) or in the Caribbean (e.g., H. Hoetink's *The Two Variants on Caribbean Race Relations,* 1967) would be a boon to comparative research. They would be particularly useful for:

2. Comparing societies along the same critical dimensions (or variables) of power and size, ideology and institutional structure, attitudes toward subordinates, types of participation, "minority reactions," and the like. This would further the development of:

3. Propositional inventories (like Robin M. Williams') but with implications both for social theory and for social policy at a *regional* and *international* level. This would help to bridge concerns with:

4. National and international systems, particularly with regard to assessments of race (and ethnicity) in relation to other critical factors in the growth of new political movements and the matter of pan-national racial identity, or what has been called here, direct and indirect linkages.

These are, of course, but a few of the approaches that might be taken. By listing them I have exceeded the limits of this essay, to discuss "the *development* of race studies" in the United States. They are simply suggestions for where we ought to go. I would argue that the collation of descriptive data should continue and that racial conflicts here and abroad be reported with as much accuracy as possible. But I would also hope that innovative interdisciplinary research would be a critical part of any plans for institutes or centers studying race relations.

3

Race in International Politics: A Dialogue in Five Parts

James N. Rosenau

Prologue

The Author: The more one ponders the task of assessing the role of race in world politics, the more staggering it becomes. Where does one begin? What is the problem? Is the problem an empirical one of measuring the extent to which race operates as an independent variable, or is it a theoretical problem of determining the circumstances under which race may operate as a relevant variable in world politics?

The Author's Moral Conscience: Others have not been staggered by the vastness of the problem.[1] Why should you? The problem is simple: the world is troubled by racial tensions and one thus begins by demonstrating their pervasiveness, showing how the relations between nations are shaped by the existence of racial conflicts within them.

The Author's Analytic Conscience: I wonder. Just because an issue arises within societies does not mean that it necessarily agitates relations between them. Race is intimate and proximate. It is pervaded, the psychologists say, with sexual connotations and other deeply felt personal needs. How, then, can it possibly operate as a variable that shapes the relations of such large aggregates as nation-states? Conceivably a host of other considerations enter in as the issue escalates from the level of interpersonal relations to the local community, and then to the national community and beyond. Indeed, it could be argued that by the time racial tension reaches the level of international conflict, it has been transformed into a contest for economic and political advantage.

Originally published in the Monograph Series in World Affairs, Social Science Foundation and Graduate School of International Studies, University of Denver, 1970. Permission to reprint this article is kindly granted by the Graduate School of International Studies.

Author: In other words, the task is a theoretical one of developing a set of mutually consistent hypotheses that allow for clarification of the various roles that race may play in international politics.

Author's Moral Conscience: Why do you always shy away from confronting a problem directly? There is nothing theoretical about the problem of race. Racial conflict is a daily problem everywhere—a real problem for which solutions are needed today, not later after you have overintellectualized the obvious.

Author: But there are some impressive data that raise serious doubts about the potency of race as a source of human conflicts. One analyst, for example, found that if a person has information about others' beliefs, he is more likely to respond to them in terms of these beliefs rather than in terms of their skin color.[2] If this is so at the level of interpersonal relations, it becomes difficult to imagine how physical characteristics could be dominant at the level of interpersonal relations.

Author's Moral Conscience: How incredible can you be! Recently a chief of state broke down in tears while delivering a public speech at a United Nations conference on the treatment of blacks in Rhodesia.[3] Now surely that is concrete evidence that race operates as a variable in behavior at the international level!

Author: One example does not prove anything. Certainly it does not justify the assumption that race *is* an important variable. Such an assumption may salve one's moral conscience, but it does not make for systematic inquiry. Race is so loaded with value connotations that the analyst has an obligation not to rush headlong into the subject. Someone has to be dispassionate, to pause and develop a theoretical perspective, if the affronts to human dignity that mark life today are ever to be eliminated.

Author's Moral Conscience: You are inclined to be dispassionate because your skin is white. If it were black, you wouldn't be arguing for theoretical perspective. Could it be that your championship of a social-scientific approach to the problem is a form of racism?

Author's Analytic Conscience: I don't see how that follows.

Author's Moral Conscience: By arguing for scientific detachment you in effect defend the postponement of an effort to solve the urgent problems that can reduce chiefs of state to tears. Such an approach even leads you to raise the possibility that the problems are not racial in character! Have you considered the possibility that your approach serves unrecognized racial prejudices while it preserves your self-image as an open-minded liberal?

Author's Analytic Conscience: Yes, I have, and I must reject that possibility, at least for the present. It seems to me that the requirements of scientific analysis are such that no assumption is beyond reconsideration. Social science is color-free. One either accepts its procedures or one does not; and while one's acceptance or rejection may be partly a consequence of one's status in life, prejudice is by no means the most likely basis for a commitment to social science. Quite the opposite is the case, I believe, insofar as my own commitment is concerned. I believe that human problems can best be solved through the application of human intelligence, which means that a problem must be understood before successful attempts can be made to solve it. If we are to make progress in ameliorating racial conflicts, we need to comprehend their dynamics, and for that we need a theoretical perspective. If racial tensions in the local community are transformed into contests for political and economic advantage when they reach the international arena, then clearly it makes little sense to approach these contests as if race were still the dominant variable.

Author's Moral Conscience: But why seek abstract theory for phenomena that are self-evident? It hardly takes any knowledge of public affairs to recognize that race is a central factor on the world scene. Look at the Congo, or Biafra, or the UN's condemnations of apartheid in South Africa. Or consider the British efforts to obtain new policies toward blacks in Rhodesia. Skin color is even an issue in the Communist world, with the Chinese citing it as the basis for excluding the Russians from conferences in which the plight of non-Western peoples are to be considered. And these are but a few of the most obvious issues of world politics that presently turn on questions of race. Many others could be cited—including the international consequences of race relations in the United States—and thus it seems absurd to pose the problem in abstract terms. What is needed is comprehension of how racial factors affect world politics. The fact that these factors are significant can be taken for granted.

Author's Analytic Conscience: Nevertheless, such an assumption makes me uneasy. If one looks at virtually any textbook published in the field of international relations in recent years, one will find virtually no discussion of racial factors. Indeed, of eleven texts published since 1960, the entry "race"—or some equivalent—could be found in only five of their indexes, and in three of these five the index referred the reader to less than three paragraphs of actual text.[4] Surely this suggests that it is presumptuous to treat the importance of racial factors as given!

Author's Moral Conscience: You're straining. You know as well as I that most texts posit a "billiard ball model" of world politics in which international actors are not differentiated in terms of their domestic political structures (much less their ethnic and racial composition). Even less do the text writers cast international relations in terms of the operation of independent and dependent variables, so that is hardly surprising that race does not emerge as a focus of extended attention on their part. Moreover, if you want to pose the issue in terms of its recognition by experts, it should also be noted that no less an authority than Arnold Toynbee has stressed that the future of world politics may be organized along racial lines.[5]

Author's Analytic Conscience: You are right. It would not be hard to find experts on both sides of the question. But that is all the more reason to start from scratch and to delineate clearly the problem we are trying to solve. If equally competent observers differ on the importance of racial factors, dare we take their significance for granted? To do so is to prejudge our conclusions as to whether and how race affects world politics. One's moral conscience may say that it has a crucial effect, but careful inquiry may fail to yield proof for such an assertion. Compelling moral issues often prove to be a composite of lesser processes and values when they are subjected to close theoretical and empirical scrutiny. Just because international actors cite race as a basis for their behavior is no reason to assume that their behavior does in fact spring from racial sources. Why should the Chinese Communists be taken at face value in this regard when everything else they do is picked apart for underlying motives?

Why should the current impulse of American blacks to search their African past for identity necessarily be a key link in the causal chain whereby U.S. foreign policy toward events in Africa is formed? Not all domestic conflicts have international repercussions. Why should it be presumed that racial conflict is of the kind that always spreads beyond national boundaries? Indeed, exactly what do we mean by racial conflict? Is it not possible that experts differ on the importance of racial factors either because they fail to define what they mean by race or because they use different definitions?

Author's Moral Conscience: There you go again, avoiding the problem by casting it in a methodological context. One can always sidestep the need to reach substantive conclusions by dwelling on definitional nuances and noting that different observers use different definitions. To insist on drawing exact boundaries is to paralyze inquiry. There is no lack of definitions of race and racial conflict. On the contrary, it is an overworked subject with an abundant literature filled with precise and neatly italicized definitions.[6] So let us not get bogged down in a sterile discussion of whether a particular attribute or event is or is not essentially racial in character. We know what we mean by race—it pertains to inherited physical characteristics. So why can't we bypass questions of definitional nuance by agreeing on this formulation? Can't we simply agree that to the extent that inherited physical characteristics create issues among individuals and groups, then to that extent there is racial conflict?

Author: It would make things much easier. No definition is completely satisfactory anyway, so perhaps a broad definition such as that is best suited to a wide-ranging assessment of the role of race in world politics.

Author's Analytic Conscience: I'll accept that. But a definition is not a theoretical perspective, and our agreement on this broad definition of race does not relieve us of the responsibility for specifying the main dimensions of our problem. Neither empirical observations nor moral solutions can be obtained outside of a theoretical context. The observer can never grasp reality in its entirety, but must select some of its aspects as important and dismiss others as trivial and, in order to do so, he must have some idea of how its component parts interact with each other. His hypotheses about how these components interact are his theory, whereas it is not the purpose of a definition to account for the interactional dynamics of the defined object. For this a theoretical perspective is needed from which hypotheses can be derived that specify how, why, and under what circumstances physical appearance and its inheritance can enter into the external behavior of nations and thus serve as the basis of international conflict. Unfortunately, such a perspective is not to be found in the literature on international politics and we must start from scratch.

At the risk of further offending an impatient morality, therefore, we must insist that the task is theoretical. We need to develop some tentative hypotheses about the ways in which race can enter inter foreign policy and international politics before we can reach meaningful conclusions about the role it actually plays. Data gathered in the absence of hypotheses can provide conclusions about particular historical situations, but only through the derivation and testing of explicit and interrelated propositions can enduring knowledge about the potency of race variables be developed. As indicated elsewhere, the alternative to theory building is an endless series of case analyses that are neither cumulative nor comparable,[7] and there is no dearth of these analyses insofar as the role of race in international conflicts is concerned. Hundreds upon hundreds could be listed.[8] But they are not cumulative. Those that focus on South Africa offer little guidance for the analysis of the Congo, and those that explore the Congo are of little help in comprehending the situation in Nigeria, much less situations in the future that have yet to emerge. The need to develop testable hypotheses would seem to be inescapable!

Author's Moral Conscience: Your capacity for avoiding the real problems is apparently unlimited. How can you say that the available literature lacks perspectives appropriate to the analysis of race? The field of international politics has a surfeit of models and approaches that can be as easily applied to racial conflict as to any other kind that mars the relations of nations. You yourself have outlined a scheme in which the "racial environment" is one of six international environments to which the institutions and functioning of nation-states may be linked.[9] And you have also suggested that political behavior can be differentiated in terms of four basic issue-areas and that racial conflicts fall naturally into the status area.[10] Why, then, develop still another formulation? Why not apply an existing framework? If your own conceptual schemes are still too crude, then one of the more developed approaches can be used. The trouble with you general-theory types is that your first impulse is always to move up rather than down the ladder of abstraction. Mankind is suffering too much to allow for abstract theorizing on the part of social scientists, especially since there is no shortage of frameworks that can be adapted to the analysis of racial factors in international politics.

Author's Analytic Conscience: Name one—leaving aside my own, which are still so crude that they cannot be regarded as theoretical. At present the linkage and issue-area frameworks are a collection of analytic categories and not a set of testable hypotheses. It is not even clear that they can be rendered theoretical through further refinement. And the same can be said about the other frameworks. Name one that is either theoretical or readily adaptable to the derivation of relevant hypotheses.

Author's Moral Conscience: I can name many. North's "mediated S-R" model,[11] Kaplan's systemic formulation,[12] Snyder's decision-making approach,[13] Deutsch's linkage-group scheme[14]—these are but a few of the available models that lend themselves to the analysis of racial conflict at the international level. In the case of North's model, one need merely treat a racial conflict as an environmental stimulus (S) that is perceived by officials (r) in such a way as first to trigger the expression of their attitudes toward race (s) and then to lead them to engage in behavior directed at the conflict (R). Similarly, each of Kaplan's several "states" of the international system specifies the circumstances under which nations engage in such basic kinds of action as mobilizing for war, forming alliances, and going to war. Hence all the analyst need do is to ascertain which state of the international system prevails at the time a racial conflict occurs and then trace the systemic consequences that it predicts. In like manner racial phenomena are readily incorporated into Snyder's decision-making approach. Indeed, the approach allows for their occurrence within a society or external to it. In either case the analyst can probe how awareness of the phenomena is fed into and then processed by the society's decision-making organization, culminating in action abroad designed to cope with the foreign-policy implications of the phenomena. As for Deutsch's linkage-group scheme, it seems especially suited to the analysis of racial conflicts that transgress national boundaries. Racial groups are prototypical of Deutsch's conception of a linkage group, and the international repercussions of racial conflict can thus be clearly traced through his scheme.

I'm not saying that all the available models are equally applicable to the analysis of racial conflict. Some may well be more appropriate than others and I'll bow to your judgment in this respect. But I do insist that it is irresponsible to start from scratch in the search for theoretical perspective. The necessary conceptual equipment is abundantly available, and all you have to do is select those concepts and models that seem most suitable.

Author's Analytic Conscience: If only the tasks of analysis were that simple. It is true that racial conflicts are not precluded by any of the existing frameworks, but neither are they explicitly conceptualized as part of the frameworks. With one possible exception,[15] none of the analysts even hint at, much less hypothesize about, the potency of race as an independent variable. North's model, for example, certainly does allow the analyst to treat racial factors as stimuli that are mediated by perceptions before resulting in behavioral responses; but it in no way indicates the kinds of perceptions and responses to which such stimuli might give rise. As far as the model is concerned, a racial conflict is no different from a nuclear explosion, a peace overture, a quadrennial olympics, or a tariff conference as an independent variable. Each is a stimulus and each fosters perceptions that mediate the resulting responses, but the model does not differentiate among types of stimuli. And much the same can be said about the Kaplan and Snyder approaches. Neither identifies race as an independent variable. Indeed, neither even specifies a general type of independent variable of which race can be presumed to be one case. To derive from Kaplan how a balance-of-power system processes a conflict in one of its member societies differently from how a loose bipolar system does is not to facilitate very useful conclusions as to the differential impact of, say, racial and economic conflicts on each type of system. Similarly, Snyder's framework does not differentiate how various types of situations affect the processes of foreign-policy decision making, so that a racial conflict is the analytic equivalent of a patriotic motive, a diplomatic offer, or a bureaucratic ploy. As for Deutsch's scheme, it is true that racial minorities can readily be treated as linkage groups, but so can a number of other minorities, and Deutsch does not delineate how racial ones might function differently from other types.

So it is not evasive to conclude that a model appropriate to the analysis of race is not available. The existing frameworks offer a number of concepts that can usefully be employed once it is determined how inherited physical appearance operates as a variable. If it is found to be similar to other sources of behavior, then the existing frameworks can be adapted. If, on the other hand, race is found to have unique characteristics as an independent variable, then the adaptation of the existing models is likely to be difficult, and an attempt to generate a new set of integrated hypotheses may prove to be the wisest course.

Author: I am lost again. You speak of determining the operation of a variable and of generating hypotheses in the same breath. The former is an empirical task and the latter is a theoretical task. Which comes first? What can we accomplish in this essay? Should we take an inventory of empirical findings relevant to the potency of the race variable? Or should we try to conceptualize the points at which the variable can operate in international political processes, whatever its potency? Or should we go beyond either of these to the development of a set of integrated hypotheses that specify the variations in international political processes that are caused by the variable potency of racial factors? You have said so many things fending off my moral conscience that I need clarification. I am still not clear on the nature of the problem to be confronted here.

Author's Analytic Conscience: The problem is threefold. It is empirical. It is conceptual. And it is also theoretical. The three tasks are interdependent, and thus we need to undertake all of them. This is not the occasion to compile an exhaustive inventory of the relevant findings, but plainly we cannot proceed without making at least a preliminary assessment of the potency of inherited physical appearance as a source of individual and group behavior. Likewise, while we do not have time to engage in an elaborate conceptualization, we can hardly proceed to derive hypotheses unless we have at least a broad notion of the main gates through which race can enter the international arena. And, as has already been stressed, we cannot avoid the task of theorizing. This third step must be taken even though time and space permit the derivation of only a crude set of hypotheses that may eventually be proved false. Unless we can derive some hypotheses, further research is not likely to be generated by our empirical survey and our conceptualization. Bad theory is better than no theory, since, as long as they are reasonable and internally consistent, hypotheses at least stimulate subsequent investigation.

In short, let us start with a discussion of the potency of race as an independent variable, proceeding thereafter to a conceptual outline of the ways in which racial factors can be brought into the international arena and, lastly, to the derivation of some hypotheses that link the race factors to various degrees or forms of international behavior. You are the author, so go ahead. I'll keep your moral conscience at bay until you have completed all three tasks.

Empirical Considerations

Author: At least three main conclusions are likely to emerge from any inventory of the welter of available empirical materials that bear on the relevance of race to international politics. One is that a person's physical attributes have personal and social significance, and since major dimensions of a person's physical appearance are linked to race, racial identity acquires emotional and social importance. Hence, despite persuasive scientific evidence that intelligence, skills, and orientations are not race-linked, people continue to be sensitive to what their lineage signifies for their capacities and impulses. As such, race can come to mean all kinds of things for an individual, becoming part of his fondest hopes and his deepest fears. In like manner, racial groups can come to have their own histories and identities that, being rooted in the intimacy of personal experience, can generate and sustain conflict within and among groups. Insofar as public affairs are concerned, therefore, race consists as much, if not more, of subjective as of objective fact. Its role is best understood not in terms of scientific definitions and findings, but in terms of perceptual definitions that are held by different people at different times.

Secondly, it is clear that consciousness of racial identity is a pervasive and worldwide phenomenon. Blacks and whites are not alone in their sensitivity to the psychological dynamics of racial identity. Perhaps their colonial heritages render them especially vulnerable in this regard, but it does not require a long history to heighten racial feelings. The evidence is overwhelming that awareness of inherited physical characteristics can acquire a symbolic meaning and serve as a source of conflict elsewhere than in those areas of the world where black and white are proximate to each other. Black and yellow are also conscious of differences in appearance,[16] as are those with various shades of black, or with various shades of yellow, or, indeed, as are virtually every cluster of people whose visible characteristics vary. More specifically, sensitivity to physical differences can be found to mark the relations between tribes in Africa, between Africans north and south of the Sahara, between Chinese and Malays—to mention but some of the more salient instances of racial tension that are not of a black-white hue. Among Filipinos, to illustrate even more specifically, "there is an almost obsessive preoccupation with color and physical characteristics. It appears in almost every aspect of everyday family life, in dating and mating, in the raising of children, and at every point of contact between people of varying groups and kinds in the population."[17] In short, the decline of white colonialism in most of Africa and Asia has not been accompanied by a corresponding diminution of race as a source of conflict. Africans and Asians have won their political freedom, but insofar as race relations are concerned the newly won independence "has often meant . . . displacement of European white racism by a non-European non-white racism."[18]

Despite its intensity and pervasiveness, however, the potency of race as a variable can be exaggerated. This is the third conclusion to emerge from an inventory of the materials on the relevance of race to public and international affairs. The color of a man's skin and his other physical characteristics may be a visible badge that has deep psychological meaning for him, but his clothes, speech, and style of life are also readily apparent and, equally important, these evidences of class and ethnicity reflect his economic circumstances and social standing, not to mention his education, religion, and politics. Race is just one of the many variables that can underlie individual and group behavior. Although analysts vary on the relative potency they attach to racial variables, there is wide agreement that these variables do not operate alone and that other variables may be just as important, if not more so, as sources of behavior in particular situations. As already noted, for example, racial identity has been found to be less important under certain circumstances than beliefs.[19] Data comparing the strength of race and class identifications suggest similar patterns, as is illustrated by the attitudes and behavior of middle-class American blacks.[20]

Teasing out the effects of race as an independent variable thus presents a formidable empirical problem. Normally the several identities to which a person is responsive are not contradictory but mutually reinforcing. Ethnic groups are usually predominantly of the same race. Ordinarily racial minorities are poor and located predominantly in the lower class. And, in turn, class differences reinforce and are reinforced by religious practices, educational attainments, occupational skills, and a host of other factors, each of which contributes to the behavior the analyst is seeking to explain. Only rarely do two or more of the variables come into conflict in such a way as to make their relative potency self-evident. Some American blacks do get professional training and move into the middle class. Some blacks adhere to the Jewish religion. Some holders of a Ph.D. earn little money and are classified as lower-class. Such exceptions, however, are few in number and, indeed, often require the analyst to resort to experimental techniques of inquiry in order to contrast the potency of various factors.[21]

Nor is the problem any less complex at the international level. Non-white nations also tend to be poor nations. The former tend to be located south, the latter north, of the equator, and this geographic and climatic distinction is accompanied by differences in resources, technology, and social organization. How, then, can the potency of racial factors be assessed? How much of the conflict between, say, African and North Atlantic nations is attributable to race variables and how much of it to other sources? The answer is not self-evident but, given the temper of the times, it is easy to exaggerate the potency of racial factors. The immediate visibility of physical characteristics, and the ideological meaning that has come to be attached to them in recent years, makes it all too tempting to ignore the complexity of international behavior and to assume that, in the words of one analyst, "The gap is primarily a gap between races."[22] Race may be the primary variable in certain situations, but the sources of international behavior are so complex that it seems preferable to proceed on the basis of a different assumption; namely, that race is among the more important variables. Situations vary and so does the potency of the variables that sustain them. Hence, rather than attach primacy to race or presume that its potency is equal to or greater than that of such factors as technology and resources, it would seem both sufficient and advisable to start with the presumption that skin color and other physical characteristics are not irrelevant to international situations and that they may be the key factors in many situations.

Author's Analytic Conscience: Excuse the intrusion, but haven't you, perhaps inadvertently, just engaged in exaggeration? You caution against overstatement, but then conclude that racial factors are neither irrelevant nor even secondary. You have offered no evidence for this conclusion. Is it not conceivable, as I suggested at the outset, that they are irrelevant?

Author: Admittedly, the foregoing offers a summary rather than a documentation of the empirical evidence, but the main point that emerges is that the operation of race is not constant. To conclude that the evidence is sufficient to start with the assumption that physical characteristics are not irrelevant is hardly to assume that they are relevant. We assume only that race varies in its potency, which means that primacy may be a proper description of its influence in certain circumstances and irrelevance an appropriate description in other circumstances. Although many of the empirical investigations on the subject are confined to noncomparable case analyses, it is clear that the role played by racial factors is not the same in every situation. In some, such as the United Nations' involvement in Rhodesian and South African affairs, its role is paramount. In others, such as the United States' involvement in the Nigeria-Biafra conflict, its role is not paramount, but neither is it negligible. In still other situations, such as the United States' policies in Vietnam, its role seems virtually irrelevant in comparison to strategic and political variables.

Stated in more general terms, human behavior seldom springs from a single source, and the social scientist is fortunate indeed when the variance in the situations of interest to him can be accounted for by one or two variables. Usually a number of variables contribute to the total variance, and the task of analysis becomes that of determining which variables account for, say, ten or more percent of the total variance. Most analysts are content if they can perform this task and are willing to accept the presence of unspecified variables that account for the variance that remains after those that account for more than ten percent have been identified and contrasted. Following this line of reasoning, exaggeration of the potency of racial factors can be avoided by posing the conceptual problem to be faced here as that of identifying the processes through which race can operate as an independent variable in such a way as to account for at least an arbitrary ten percent of the variance among international situations. Once these processes have been identified we can turn to the theoretical problem of hypothesizing about the conditions under which the potency of the race variable is likely to increase or decrease.

Conceptual Considerations

Any conceptual framework that can be used to theorize about the role of racial factors in international politics must identify the units of action, the independent variables that underlie their actions, and the dependent variables that represent their actions. That is, the framework must clearly specify three main elements: (1) the persons or groups whose behavior brings consciousness of physical characteristics into the international arena; (2) those sources of their behavior that can infuse it with racial consciousness; and (3) the types of behavior in which they can engage that reflect racial factors. Having enumerated these components, the analyst can move on to the construction of hypotheses that link changes in the sources of behavior to its nature and extent.

In order to develop such a framework, the analyst must limit the scope of his interests. The number and variety of persons and groups who can engage in the relevant behavior are so great, and the sources of their behavior and the forms it can take are so multitudinous, that he cannot possibly undertake to account for all the international processes and repercussions to which race may be related. Perforce he must narrow his attention to those actors and types of behavior that seem central to his concerns. Since the aim here is to develop hypotheses that permit inquiry into the impact of racial factors upon international politics, I shall organize the framework in terms of the external conflict behavior engaged in by those who act on behalf of national societies. This is not to deny that the external cooperative behavior of foreign-policy officials can be pervaded with racial consciousness.[23] Nor is it to ignore the capacity of private persons and groups to engage in external conflict behavior that derives from a preoccupation with physical characteristics. However, international politics is sustained essentially through the interaction of national governments, and its contents are shaped mainly by situations in which the goals and actions of governments conflict. Hence foreign-policy officials are the actors around whom the ensuing framework is organized; its dependent variables are conceived in terms of the conflict behavior in which they can engage; and its independent variables are conceptualized in terms of five kinds of sources from which racial considerations can arise as a basis for conflict behavior. Lest this be regarded as too narrow a framework, let it be added that the activities of private citizens and groups constitute a key variable in one of the five clusters of independent variables (see the discussion of societal variables below).

Author's Analytic Conscience: This is too important to postpone until the discussion of societal variables. Is it not unrealistic to construct a framework in which minority groups and mass publics are not treated as actors? The attitudes of publics in Africa and Asia toward race relations in the United States are an important dimension of current international affairs. And certainly there is considerable international relevance in the demand of the Black Panthers for a UN-sponsored plebiscite that would pave the way for a separate state in the American South. Yet phenomena such as these would not be subsumed by the foregoing framework.

Author: Yes, they would be, as independent variables that contribute to the behavior of foreign-policy officials. The presumption is that if the attitudes of foreign publics toward American race relations are in fact important, then they will operate as societal variables underlying the behavior of foreign officials and as systemic variables shaping the behavior of American officials. Likewise, if in fact the demands of the Black Panthers are as relevant as they appear, then they are bound to constitute conditions to which officials are responsive and, accordingly, to which the analyst is sensitive. Our framework is designed to render the subject manageable, to provide a perspective from which any relevant phenomena can be analyzed. The fact that the behavior of government officials serves to organize the perspective does not mean that nongovernmental actors and processes are excluded from it.

Author's Analytic Conscience: One other question before you go on: by organizing the framework in terms of a foreign-policy rather than an international political focus, have you not precluded the direct analysis of racial conflicts in the international system? Since the external actions of national societies are your prime concern, your model cannot possibly also trace and explain the outcome of their actions. To account for outcomes one must focus on what happens when two or more actors react to each other, that is, the interactions of national societies rather than the actions of their foreign-policy officials must organize the analysis.[24] Moreover, the interactions that sustain world politics have a dynamic of their own that cannot be explained only through the behavior of the actors that constitute the interaction. Racial conflicts, for example, can spiral and be self-sustaining because the parties to them have mutually reinforcing hostile perceptions of each other, and any attempt to explain such conflicts that does not allow for a direct focus upon the spiraling process would appear to be insufficient. It is as if one sought to explain the Detroit riots by examining the behavior of blacks independently of the behavior of the police. Plainly the behavior of all the actors in a situation, be they individuals or nations, must be seen in juxtaposition if the dynamics of their conflict are to be revealed. So it would seem that the basic premises of your model are faulty.

Author: The point is well taken, but I question its relevance at this stage. A focus on interaction phenomena makes eminent sense when the system under consideration is system- rather than subsystem-dominant—that is, when no actor in the system is capable of altering the structure of the system through his own actions.[25] Under these circumstances the analyst need not dwell at length on the behavior of the actors that constitute the system. He knows none of them individually can alter its structure. Thus, he need only know the shared attitudes guiding their participation in the system and can concentrate on the spiraling and other interaction processes to which these shared attitudes give rise. Rioting Detroit is a case in point. It approaches a system-dominant situation in the sense that no individual black or white person can alter its tension-ridden structure. Hence the analyst can proceed quickly to an interaction focus. He knows what the main actors bring to the interaction—a shared distrust of white society and particularly, its policemen on the part of most Detroit blacks and a contrary set of attitudes on the part of most Detroit whites—and consequently he can investigate outcomes (riots) per se.

International systems, on the other hand, are not system-dominant. They are dominated by their national subsystems, any one of which is capable of altering its structures, if only by virtue of its sovereign capacity to alter its manner of relating to the system. Hence, while international systems do have their own dynamics, including those that make conflicts spiral, a great deal more needs to be known about the behavior of their national subsystems before these dynamics can be meaningfully analyzed independently of the actors who sustain them. The comparative study of foreign policy is only in its infancy,[26] so that students of international systems have been compelled to construct models that are so abstract as to be almost inapplicable to concrete issue-areas such as those that encompass racial phenomena. Stated differently, national societies are far more varied in their composition and orientations than are the components of system-dominant systems, with the result that the student of international politics cannot proceed on the basis of an assumption that certain common dimensions underlie the behavior of most of the actors that concern him. The tendency to form alliances when threatened or to fight when attacked may constitute a shared predisposition that allows for the construction of convincing abstract models,[27] but it is hardly the basis for insight into the ways in which racial considerations enter into and sustain international conflicts.

Furthermore, since the actors who sustain international conflicts are significantly more complex than the individuals or groups who contribute to conflicts in local communities, the number of interacting variables at the international level is proportionately greater and, accordingly, the potency of racial factors is presumably more intricately woven into the fabric of conflict than is the case in less comprehensive systems. Teasing out the role of race in Detroit's riots would thus appear to be considerably easier than delineating its operation in international situations. Until more is known about how racial considerations are introduced into the processes of world politics, it seems imprudent to organize our hypotheses around the functioning of international systems. Only a foreign-policy focus seems capable of identifying the processes through which racial variables enter international politics. If the price of such a focus is an inability to account for outcomes, then it seems a small one to pay in exchange for greater knowledge of the conditions that make race one of the values over which conflicts in international systems may be waged. Besides, as will be seen, key aspects of international systems are not excluded from the ensuing model. They constitute one of the five main clusters of independent variables, and I have no intention of minimizing their importance as stimuli to external behavior on the part of national societies.

Author's Analytic Conscience: But if the 120-plus national societies of the international system are varied in their composition and orientations, how can you expect to develop useful theory? Does not a foreign-policy focus lead the analyst toward an endless series of case studies and away from hypotheses that can be used and tested for theory-building purposes?

Author: Let me get on with the analysis. You may be holding my moral conscience at bay, but you keep asking questions that prevent me from outlining the model. The questions may be important but they have been dealt with elsewhere,[28] and by asking them again here you only confirm the charge that theorizing is used to avoid confrontation of the substantive issues. Obviously the 120-plus societies of the world are varied in their composition and orientations, and the danger exists that one will employ a model that leads only to case histories of these differences. But I have no intention of facilitating additions to the existing welter of case studies. The ensuing hypotheses are cast at a middle level of abstraction, one that allows both for the discernment of similarities among national actors and for the identification of those points where the differences among them are crucial. The actors do differ in their structure and behavior, but in one form or another the same variables are operative in all cases and it is comparisons among these variables that my hypotheses seek to make possible. From such comparisons the variations among the 120-plus phenotypical actors can be reduced to a few meaningful genotypical actors. If, for example, the racial composition of a society is treated as a dichotomous independent variable, such that one can compare the external behavior of racially homogeneous and racially heterogeneous actors, then presumably useful hypotheses that are neither too abstract nor too bound to time and place can be developed.

Author's Analytic Conscience: But given the variability among societies, their distribution across a racial-composition scale would be so scattered that dichotomization of the variable would constitute gross distortion of its effects on foreign policy.

The Author: That is a minor question that can be readily resolved when the time comes to process empirical data in terms of the hypotheses. Let's get on with the task of identifying the variables out of which the hypotheses have been fashioned. Let us start with the dependent variables through which race may operate in the international arena and then turn to the independent variables from which its operation may derive.

Since national societies can engage in innumerable forms of foreign conflict behavior, it is neither possible nor necessary to elaborate an exhaustive list of dependent variables. Rather it is sufficient for our purposes to specify six major types of foreign conflict behaviors that constitute a continuum ranging from a minimum to a maximum degree of violence and that can be treated either as separate variables or as a single variable in the ensuing analysis. For the most part I have not been able to derive hypotheses that predict specific forms of conflict behavior and have had to settle for predicting whether the conflict behavior, whatever its form, will be more or less extensive or more or less violent. Listed in order of increasing violence, the six forms of conflict behavior are as follows: verbally supporting or denouncing one side in disputes between two other societies or between two factions within another society (as distinguished from not taking sides and adopting a neutral or accommodating stance); recalling or expelling diplomatic personnel; imposing negative sanctions that restrict or prevent the exchange of goods, people, or ideas; severing diplomatic relations; issuing military threats; and undertaking military actions.[29]

Author's Analytic Conscience: Something seems to be missing here. What is the relevance of race to these various forms of conflict behavior? Societies engage in these forms of behavior for all kinds of reasons besides those derived from considerations of race. How do you plan to differentiate those conflict behaviors that are based on racial factors from those that are not?

Author: The presumption is that concern over inherited physical characteristics can lead to verbal denunciations, the recall of ambassadors, and every other form of conflict behavior. However, in deriving the hypotheses, no attempt has been made to differentiate between race-pervaded and race-free conflict behaviors. It is highly probable that the conflict behavior the analyst observes in order to measure the operation of the dependent variables will have stemmed from a variety of sources. A decision to employ economic sanctions or sever diplomatic relations, for example, is rarely a response to a single stimulus. Racial sensitivities may underlie such a decision, but in all likelihood, so will economic and political calculations as to the consequences and risks of such behavior. Yet this is not a serious problem. Our concern is with racial factors and the likelihood that other factors may also be operative is irrelevant as long as we can be confident that we have identified the presence of racial ones. Thus, if data reveal a significant association between the racial factors that are treated as the independent variables in the hypotheses and the degrees or forms of conflict behavior that are treated as dependent variables, then it seems reasonable to assume that the operation of racial factors has been identified and measured.

It follows that in selecting the independent variables we must differentiate precisely between those that involve racial considerations and those that do not. If we do not clearly delineate the racial factors that can give rise to conflict behavior, then we can never be confident that the observed behavior reflects their presence. The selection of independent variables, however, is not a simple matter. There are so many ways in which race may contribute to foreign conflict behavior that we obviously face a sampling problem. Not only do we need to select independent variables that are likely to account for at least ten percent of the variance in the dependent variables, but we must also select a sample that is representative of the various types of sources from which a concern for race can arise.

In order to achieve representativeness we have fallen back on an earlier analytic scheme that posits five basic clusters of independent variables as sources of foreign policy.[30] In effect, the five clusters encompass variables from five basic types of systems in which the foreign-policy official is located. Listed in order of increasing complexity, these systems are those unique to the individual official; the top policymaking system of which his official role is a part; the larger governmental system from which his position derives; the societal system whose polities he formulates and conducts; and the international system in which his society is located. That is, it is presumed that the behavior of foreign-policy officials is a response to the requirements and demands of five types of systems, each of which contains some variables that reinforce those of the other systems and some that oppose them. The interaction of the individual (I), role (R), governmental (G), societal (SO), and systemic (SY) variables—as we shall respectively label (and abbreviate) each cluster—determines the external behavior of officials at any moment in time, and thus a prime task of the comparative study of foreign policy is to uncover the key variables in each cluster and to delineate the ways in which they contribute to the behavior under investigation. In the more specific assignment of analyzing the dynamics whereby physical characteristics and racial consciousness become a part of international politics, it follows that our task at this point is that of selecting variables in each cluster that can range from a high to a low degree of susceptibility to racial factors. Once these *race-susceptible* variables—as we shall call them—in each cluster have been identified, we can turn to an assessment of their potency by constructing hypotheses that link them to foreign conflict behavior. However, in order to put the operation of racial factors to a stiff test, the hypotheses must not only compare the behavioral consequences of high and low degrees of race-susceptible variables; they must also contrast the behavioral consequences of the high extreme with powerful *nonracial* variables from each cluster; that is, variables whose variance is judged not to be reflective of racial factors at any point. For example, in addition to hypothesizing about the differences between societies that have a high and a low degree of racial tension, my analysis has also been structured to yield a hypothesis that contrasts the foreign conflict behavior of societies that are marked by a high degree of racial tension but that are differentiated in terms of being either developed or underdeveloped economically. In other words, the ensuing discussion singles out both race-susceptible and nonracial variables in each cluster for comparison in the next section. Furthermore, since the variables in each cluster are, given the complexity of the systems involved, too numerous even to be listed, I shall confine the discussion only to those that seem likely to account for significant degrees of variation in foreign-policy behavior. Indeed, in order to avoid the development of an unmanageable framework, the hypotheses derived from this analysis will be confined to only one or two race-susceptible and nonracial variables in each cluster.

Individual Variables

Since racial consciousness is profoundly intimate and personal, it is perhaps appropriate to begin the analysis with the cluster of individual variables. These refer to those aspects of an official that cannot be expected to characterize his predecessor or successor. They are unique to him, arising out of his experience in other nongovernmental systems (such as the family, the church, and the professional association) in which he currently occupies or previously occupied a role. No two persons have the same prior experiences or present affiliations, so that some of the talents, values, training, orientations, loyalties, and personality traits that a person brings to his official policymaking role are bound to be different from those of other occupants of his office. It should be noted, however, that not all of the personal characteristics of an official are necessarily unique to him. Some are so central to the policymaking role he occupies that his predecessors and successors can also be expected to have them. The skin color of foreign secretaries, for example, is not likely to vary from one occupant of the office to the next. Rather it is likely to reflect the color of the dominant group in the society and thus must be viewed as a societal rather than an individual variable.

It is easy to exaggerate the potency of individual variables. There are so many variations in the attitudes, training, skills, and traits of officials that it is tempting to explain the differences in their behavior in terms of these individual characteristics. To a considerable degree, however, such individual characteristics operate within limits set by role, governmental, societal, and systemic variables. The private aspirations and political convictions of an official, for example, must be tempered by the dictates of his superiors, by the requirements of diplomatic protocol, by the constraints of interagency bargaining, by the demands of pressure groups, by the challenges of other nations. Indeed, the requirements derived from role, governmental, societal, and systemic variables have been found to be attitudinal as well as behavioral. Officials not only tend to act in patterned ways, but their responsibilities also conduce to common patterns of thought. Whatever their prior orientations, for instance, defense officials tend to favor increased military preparedness once they enter their offices, whereas those who assume positions in foreign offices become inclined to stress diplomatic rather than military flexibility.[31]

Notwithstanding the political constraints within which an official must operate, presumably the degree to which he is racially conscious may be greater or lesser than that of his predecessors or successors. Not every African chief of state is led to tears in public by his acute torment over the plight of black people. Not every governor of Georgia is as assertive of white superiority as Lester Maddox. Not every German leader is anti-Semitic. Different past experiences and personality needs create differences in the extent to which officials are sensitive to the fact and symbolism of skin color. To be sure, some part of an official's racial consciousness stems from the system in which his governmental position is located. Given the history of Africa and the struggles for national autonomy being waged there, all African chiefs of state are likely to regard physical characteristics as politically relevant phenomena, just as postwar racial tensions in the United States are likely to heighten racial consciousness on the part of American foreign-policy officials. The degree of consciousness, however, is likely to vary within these historical and societal constraints, and thus it would appear to be a race-susceptible individual variable of sufficient importance to justify inclusion in the ensuing analysis. To facilitate assessment of the potency of this *consciousness* variable, the degree to which officials had prior experience in foreign affairs—the *experience* variable—has been selected as the nonracial variable from the individual cluster. Presumably officials with extensive experience of this kind are more appreciative of the limits of foreign policy—and thus more inclined to avoid extreme policies—than are those with no previous experience in foreign affairs. Hence, by constructing hypotheses that predict different behavioral consequences depending on the degree of racial consciousness and the extent of prior foreign-affairs experience of the officials concerned, an estimate of the way in which individual variables may bring race into the international arena can be developed.

An equally important means of estimating the potency of race-susceptible individual variables is through hypotheses that probe what is likely to happen to an official's degree of racial consciousness when it is subjected to the requirements of role, governmental, societal, and systemic variables. Do racially prejudiced representatives at the United Nations allow their private orientations to affect how they perceive—and what they report to their governments about—the deliberations of the world organization? Does a white person mostly free of racial sensitivities espouse and enforce anti-nonwhite immigration policies when he becomes foreign secretary of, say, Australia? Does a black man who was educated in London and who has not been dominated by hatred for whites vote to ignore the rule of law when he becomes foreign secretary of, say, Mali and the question of South African rights in international organizations becomes an issue? Questions such as these suggest how race-susceptible individual variables might interact with other types, and they also suggest the complexity of the problems that I attempt to clarify below as a means of developing hypotheses that assess the relative potency of the independent variables.

Role Variables

Existing policy goals are among the prime variables in the cluster that stems from the requirements of top policymaking roles. Whatever the private attitudes and unique talents of officials, and whatever the systems in which they have had previous experience, the responsibilities they acquire when they enter their offices include commitments to the practices and orientations of their predecessors. The goals of their policymaking roles may be changed if individual, governmental, societal, or systemic variables prove to be more powerful; but until such changes occur, the policy requirements of the roles impinge upon their occupants. More accurately, the requirements are operative to the extent that they neither change nor allow for individual discretion. Some policy goals are couched in such general terms that different role occupants can interpret them in different ways, depending on the strength of their individual convictions or the societal or systemic pressures upon them. For example, chiefs of state in the North Atlantic area are at present required to support efforts to maintain defensive arrangements that inhibit military attacks on Western Europe. Such an attitude and the behavior to which it leads are built into their roles and, barring a return to isolationism in the United States or a substantial moderation of the cold war (barring a shift in basic societal or systemic variables), it is therefore reasonable to expect that all future top officials in the region will adhere to this role requirement. On the other hand, the requirement is not so stringent as to have prevented some of the individual (and societal?) variables from making France alter the nature of its commitment to NATO. DeGaulle did not abandon his European allies or totally reject the necessity of achieving defense arrangements in Europe, but the interaction between his unique qualities and this role requirement resulted in changes in the nature of the French involvement in NATO.

Although the cluster of role variables is not confined to those that involve policy goals,[32] it is within this type that race-susceptible variables are to be found. With the decline of European colonialism and the emergence of many nonwhite nation-states after World War II, every national society has been compelled, irrespective of the nature of its racial composition, to adopt general policies that govern when skin color and other physical characteristics are considered to be relevant to a situation in the international system. In some societies, especially those with a history of racial conflict and oppression, persons entering top policymaking roles are required to accept the pre-existing policy standard that attaches a high degree of racial relevance to most of the major issues that sustain world politics at any moment in time. In other societies, particularly those that have not had a racially troubled past, such a standard does not exist and in these cases other standards lead officials to attach a minimum of racial relevance to most international situations. The presence or absence of such a standard—the *relevance* variable—thus appears to be as appropriate as the race-susceptible role variable for further treatment. In order to assess its potency relative to nonracial role variables, the requirement whereby occupants of top policymaking positions must be concerned about the economic welfare of their societies has also been singled out for additional analysis. Built into most top policymaking roles is the necessity of being sensitive to the need for a continual flow of goods and services—the *trade-and-aid* variable—and as illustrated by recent events in Rhodesia, this nonracial role variable can come into conflict with the requirement that a high degree of racial relevance be attached to the unfolding situation, thus affording an opportunity to assess the relative strength of role requirements that do and do not introduce racial factors into the international arena.

Equally important, of course, is the interaction between the race-susceptible role variables and individual, governmental, societal, and systemic variables. If a racially conscious individual enters a role that does not require the attachment of racial relevance to issues, or if there is a buildup of pressures within the national or international system for the attachment of racial relevance to such a role, are the requirements of the role likely to be altered? More precisely, under what conditions will the degree to which officials are required to attach racial relevance to policy goals vary? Answers to questions such as these are crucial to an understanding of the dynamics of racial conflict in world politics and, as indicated below, there is good reason to hypothesize that the relative strength of role variables is greater than might be supposed.

Governmental Variables

The governmental cluster of independent variables refers to those aspects of the larger political system that determine the nature and extent of the information and demands that reach top policymakers and condition their behavior. The structural features of a government and the party system that sustains it thus comprise the main variables in this cluster. The distinction between a presidential and cabinet form of government, or between a two-party or multiparty system, are examples of structural aspects of government that can shape the behavior of officials. Government variables, being structural in nature, do not contribute directly to the content of foreign policy, but rather affect it by serving as a filter through which the values that underlie individual, role, societal, and systemic variables must pass. For example, the same values introduced into a presidential system and a cabinet system are likely to result in policies that differ somewhat in their scope, decisiveness, and clarity.[33]

In other words, although it is not a distinction that will be stressed here, strictly speaking, governmental variables are intervening and not independent variables. They shape the direction and quality of external behavior, but they do not in themselves consist of values that give content to the behavior. Consequently, the distinction between race-susceptible and nonracial variables does not apply to the governmental cluster. Being intervening variables, they are all nonracial and the task here is thus one of selecting powerful governmental variables that can be used to test the strength of the race-susceptible variables in the other clusters. Two such variables seem especially appropriate in this regard. One, the *executive-form* variable, involves the distinction between presidential and cabinet systems of government. The other, the *authority-structure* variable, involves the degree to which a government is responsive to the demands and tensions of the society. Here the distinction is between open, multiparty authority structures that allow racial groups in the society to assert their needs and closed, single-party structures that do not provide nongovernmental groups with ready access to officials. It is a distinction that facilitates, for example, investigation of whether the substantial difference between the Middle Eastern policies of the Soviet Union and the United States is crucially related to their authority structures. At first glance the potency of this variable would seem to be considerable, since the aspirations of Jewish groups in the United States are heard because of its relatively open structure, whereas the relatively closed structure of the USSR prevents similar aspirations from getting articulated and advanced. An additional advantage of the authority-structure variable is that the degree to which a government is responsive to societal pressures can also affect the extent to which racial groups go outside of established channels and conduct, in effect, their own private foreign policy by seeking support in the international system.

Societal Variables

The fourth cluster of independent variables, those derived from the society on whose behalf top policymakers work, is conceived to encompass both human and nonhuman factors. Any aspect of societies that is related to their functioning and that may vary from one society to another is treated as a societal variable, no matter whether it consists of material resources or human efforts. Thus the daily production of oil, the average rainfall, and the complexity of overland transportation routes are as much a part of the societal cluster as are the degree of social cohesion, the values shared by the population, and the educational structure through which human talent is perfected. Some societal variables combine human and nonhuman dimensions, and one of these, the degree of economic development, has been found to be sufficiently powerful as a source of political behavior[34] to justify singling it out as the nonracial variable with which to compare the race-susceptible societal variable in the ensuing analysis. Internal racial conflicts may contribute to the pace and extent of a society's development, but these are so relatively minor as determinants of its gross national product that the hypotheses contrasting the two types of societal variables will not be significantly contaminated. To simplify the analysis the *developmental* variable will be used dichotomously, a distinction being drawn between societies that are developed and those that are underdeveloped.

An extensive list could be compiled of race-susceptible societal variables from which to select one for further examination. The degree to which societies are racially homogeneous or heterogeneous, the extent to which the leadership of their racial minorities is trained and articulate, and the stratification system whereby the racial minorities have access to wealth and status are but a few of the societal variables that are regarded as race-susceptible and that can introduce racial factors into the international arena. One race-susceptible societal variable, however, seems so powerful in this respect as to warrant its use in the hypotheses developed below: the degree of tension among the racial groups in a society. Since tension gives rise to value conflicts and demands for their resolution, officials and publics are sensitive, either empathically or fearfully, to tensions rather than harmonies among groups. Accordingly, it seems reasonable to presume, without prejudging the relative potency of race-susceptible societal variables, that the greater the degree of racial tension in a society, the more likely it is to attract foreign conflict behavior on the part of officials and groups abroad and the more are its own officials and groups likely to engage in external activities that reflect sensitivity to racial factors. This cannot necessarily be said, however, about the other race-susceptible societal variables. Different degrees of racial heterogeneity may or may not be accompanied by tensions among groups with different physical characteristics; and if tension does not exist, the racial composition of a society is likely to be irrelevant to its foreign conflict behavior. Similarly, if racial minorities and their articulate leaderships accept a stratification system that denies them wealth and status, then racial tensions will not characterize the society and any assessment of the potency of such variables under these conditions would give a misleading picture of the extent to which race-susceptible societal variables can affect world politics. The United States is a good example in this respect. Its racial composition and its stratification system have remained essentially unchanged for decades, but it is only recently that traces of racial sensitivity have been discernible in its external behavior, a tendency that coincides with heightened internal tensions stemming from the intensified demands for wealth and status by American blacks in the 1950s. Thus the *racial-tension* variable would seem to be the most overriding of the many that might be included in the ensuing analysis. Furthermore, it has the advantage of being equally applicable to a society in which the racial minority is dominant (such as South Africa) and one in which it is dominated (such as the United States), thus relieving the analyst of the need to include this important distinction as an additional variable.

Systemic Variables

Like societal variables, those comprising the systemic cluster include both human and nonhuman aspects of the international system. Any human event that occurs in, or nonhuman characteristic that distinguishes, the world external to a society can be viewed as a systemic variable. It is true that many nonhuman dimensions of the international system, such as a society's geographical location and the resources of its nearest neighbors, do not vary and can be treated as constants from the perspective of a particular society. But from the perspective of the researcher committed to comparative analysis, these nonhuman aspects of the international system vary from one society to another and must thus be treated as variables. For example, one geographic variable in the systemic cluster is the number of contiguous societies with which a society shares its border, a number that normally does not change but that is different for different societies.

It will readily be recognized that the systemic cluster encompasses an almost infinite number of variables. Developments within all the other societies external to the environed society, not to mention among them, are alone so numerous as to be virtually incalculable. Thus here I can note only a few of the more general types of variables that are likely to have a high potency and that, conceptualized at a high level of abstraction, operate for all societies. The overall political structure of the global system, consisting of the relationships between the superpowers and the formal and informal arrangements whereby other societies relate to each other and to the superpowers, is the most obvious, and perhaps the most important, systemic variable. The readiness of any society to engage in external conflict behavior is bound to be at least partly conditioned by whether a bipolarity, a balance of power, or some other structure characterizes the global system. If only because the overall structure provides an indication of whether a superpower is likely to contest its conflict behavior, every society must consider the possible systemic consequences before it undertakes the behavior. Accordingly, *global structure* would appear to be a systemic variable of sufficient generality and importance to be included in the analysis. Since it refers to alliances and the norms governing their formation and dissolution, and since such norms derive primarily from considerations of military security and only secondarily—if at all—from a concern for skin color or other physical characteristics, global structure can reasonably be treated as a nonracial systemic variable. Furthermore, in order to simplify matters, I shall treat it as a dichotomous variable, differentiating between a tight bipolar structure in which the superpowers exact a heavy price from other societies for nonadherence to their demands and a loose balance of power structure in which deviance on the part of other societies is tolerated by the more powerful societies.

However, the overall structure of the global system is not so much a direct stimulus to external action on the part of societies as it is a screen through which their reactions to more specific events and trends are filtered. Hence, it would seem desirable to include a second nonracial systemic variable in the hypotheses, one that is sufficiently general to apply to all societies and yet specific enough to constitute direct stimuli to external conflict behavior on their part. Sustained conflicts between and within other societies—the *situational* variable—meet these criteria. Both types of situations constitute concrete development that no society can ignore. Its interests may be at stake in any conflict, if only because one or more of the warring factions may seek its support and threaten possible reprisals if the support is not forthcoming. Every conflict situation abroad is thus a stimulus to some kind of action on the part of every society, and though many may choose to respond through inaction, none can avoid adopting a stance toward each situation. Crucial to a society's stance, however, is whether the external conflict situation occurs within or between other societies. Societies act in terms of the values they perceive to be at stake in a situation, but these values can seem very different if they are at stake in *intersocietal* or *intrasocietal* situations.

Another reason to include the *situational* variable in the analysis is that it provides a way of identifying a race-susceptible systemic variable. Some situations between or within other societies are pervaded with racial tension, whereas such tensions are essentially peripheral to or absent from other situations. This distinction, the *race-dominant* variable, is presumably central to the way in which the international system itself contributes to the role racial factors play in world politics. By comparing how societies respond to race-free and race-pervaded external situations—the two extremes of the race-dominant variable—an assessment can be made of the extent to which race is a source of escalating, or at least self-sustaining, conflict in the international system. This is especially so if the situational and race-dominant variables are combined and comparisons are made between race-free and race-pervaded conflicts that occur within other societies, on the one hand, and between them, on the other. For if race-pervaded intrasocietal situations can be shown to evoke different forms and degrees of conflict behavior on the part of other societies than race-free intrasocietal situations do, it should be possible to develop considerable clarification of the processes whereby racial factors become internationalized.

Although it makes the analysis more cumbersome, combining the situational and race-dominant variables has the advantage of facilitating comparisons between systemic variables and those in the other four clusters. Are officials occupying positions that require them to attach a high degree of racial relevance to issues likely to respond to a class war in a white society abroad in the same way as they react to a race war in a racially heterogeneous society? Are race-pervaded intrasocietal conflicts abroad likely to evoke similar or different behavior on the part of societies in which such tension is non-existent? Do the diplomatic restraints built into foreign-policy roles, particularly those that pertain to the principle of nonintervention in the affairs of other societies, tend to limit the intensity of reactions to race-pervaded intrasocietal situations while not limiting responses to intersocietal situations where the issue of nonintervention is irrelevant? Are underdeveloped societies more or less likely than developed ones to engage in conflict behavior toward intrasocietal situations? Questions such as these suggest some of the possibilities for probing comparison that are opened up by these additional systemic variables included in the analysis.

These variables selected from the systemic cluster have the additional advantage that they can be used as the occasion for the various behaviors that are conceived to constitute the dependent variables. Of course, external conflict behavior does not require a foreign situation to occasion it. In fact, such behavior operates frequently as a creator of situations rather than as a response to them. Yet, if assessments of the relative potency of the various independent variables with respect to the several types of external conflict situations can be developed, it should not be difficult to generalize about their potency as a source of external conflict behavior under all conditions. In effect, by including the situational and race-dominant variables, we have narrowed the theoretical task to that of constructing hypotheses about the forms and degrees of conflict behavior toward four types of international situations that individuals with different backgrounds in different governmental roles are likely to undertake on behalf of different kinds of societies.

Author's Analytic Conscience: That is hardly a narrow task. You have made frequent references to the need to limit the number of variables, but what you have fashioned seems more like an analytic monster than a manageable inquiry. Table 3.1 summarizes all the independent variables that have been singled out for inclusion in the hypotheses. There are eleven in all, drawn from five basic clusters and consisting of four that are race-susceptible and seven that are essentially nonracial in character. You seem to have committed yourself not only to developing hypotheses in which each of the former is contrasted with its counterpart from the same cluster among the latter, but also to comparing across the clusters in such a way that each race-susceptible variable is contrasted with every

Table 3-1

Independent Variables Selected for
Analysis

Variable clusters	Nonracial variables	Race-susceptible variables
Individual	experience	racial consciousness
Role	trade-and-aid	racial relevance
Governmental	executive form authority structure	
Societal	developmental	racial tension
Systemic	global structure situational	race-dominant

possible combination of the other variables. That amounts to no less than 508 hypotheses! And that figure allows for only one dependent variable, but you have suggested the possibility of predicting to six forms of foreign conflict behavior. Surely you are not going to put the reader through the exercise of deriving hypotheses for all these combinations. You have space and time for only a few derivations and, in being forced to cut back, you have played straight into the hands of your moral conscience.

Author's Moral Conscience: You sure have! Science is supposed to be parsimonious, but the foregoing demonstrate the extraordinary complexity of human affairs and thus the impossibility of subjecting them to scientific analysis!

Author: It certainly highlights the complexity of the problem and, admittedly, my efforts to limit the scope of inquiry have been less than successful. However, while I am thus forced to cut back and confine myself to only a few derivations, this does not prove that scientific analysis is bound to fall short of its goal. Parsimony is the ultimate goal of science, not its guiding procedure. One moves toward parsimony as comprehension is acquired, and comprehension requires a recognition of complexity and a readiness to deal with small segments of it at a time. Only after the parts of the problem are understood can the whole be pieced together and parsimonious statements made about its underlying dynamics. The real reason I must cut back is because comprehension, rather than time and space, is limited. A grasp of the role that race can play in world politics is not such that useful multivariate hypotheses can be derived. It would be difficult, for example, to offer convincing reasons for a hypothesis that predicted the differences between the reaction of experienced, nonracially conscious officials of an open, developed society to a race-free situation in another society and the reaction of inexperienced, racially conscious officials of a closed, underdeveloped society to the same conflict—much less to a race-pervaded situation between several other societies. On the other hand, plausible underpinnings for one- and two-variable hypotheses do seem possible. If other things are assumed equal, then it seems possible to develop rationales for hypotheses that predict the behavior resulting from the operation of one or two independent variables. Thus I shall cut back to the task of first deriving univariate hypotheses that assess the operation of the race-susceptible variables in each cluster and then deriving bivariate hypotheses in which each race-susceptible variable is compared with the nonracial variable in both its own cluster and in every other cluster—a total of thirty-two hypotheses.[35] In so doing I shall at least put each of the ways in which racial factors can enter the international arena to a stiff and thorough, though still incomplete, test.

To be sure, other things never are equal, as my ignoring of innumerable multivariate hypotheses demonstrates. To reiterate *ceteris paribus*, however, is not to offer a substitute for parsimony. Rather it is a necessary step toward the construction of parsimonious theory.

Some Hypotheses

Individual Variables

Let us start again at the level of the individuals who occupy high posts in the foreign policy organizations of their governments. Other things being equal, will the degree to which they are conscious of physical characteristics affect the extent of the foreign conflict behavior they undertake or recommend with respect to conflict situations abroad? This is the question to which my initial reasoning must be addressed; and since it requires the derivation of a univariate hypothesis with all other variables held constant, the answer may seem fairly obvious. Action flows from motivation and perception, and if racial consciousness is part of a person's motivational and perceptual equipment, it would seem bound to shape the action he takes or recommends unless it is offset by other motives and perceptions. Such an answer, however, is not sufficient. It leaves untouched the relationship between the degree of racial consciousness and the extent of foreign conflict behavior. To presume that an individual is likely to take or recommend more stringent foreign-policy measures the more racially conscious he is, is not to say that the stringency of the measures will increase in direct proportion to the degree of his racial consciousness. For such a relationship to prevail it must be assumed that racial consciousness is unrelenting in its intensity and global in its scope, thus fostering more stringent behavior as it deepens. Such an assumption hardly seems warranted. By its very nature, racial consciousness is likely to be most intense with respect to close-at-hand situations involving the family, community, and possibly the national society. One may be aware of and care about racial arrangements in more distant parts of the world, but a sense of intimacy about them declines with distance. Presumably this is part of the reason why severances of diplomatic relations, economic blockades, and armed attacks are not daily features of the international scene. The world is full of top officials who are highly conscious of race; yet they do not constantly employ extreme forms of foreign conflict behavior when conflict situations arise abroad. To be sure, other variables attenuate the operation of their racial consciousness, but presumably the restraint situations arise abroad. The restraint stems in part from their lesser concern about race relations in remote parts of the world than about their own country or region. In sum, it does not seem reasonable to derive a hypothesis that posits the dependent variable in scalar rather than dichotomous terms. Rather than referring to more or less conflict behavior, we must confine ourselves to anticipating its presence or absence:

Hypothesis I[1]: Other things being equal, the greater the racial consciousness of an individual who occupies a top policymaking position, the more likely he is to undertake or recommend some form of foreign conflict behavior.

If we now relax the assumption that other things are equal and allow for nonracial motives and perceptions that might offset the potency of this race-susceptible individual variable, the potency of the latter is greatly reduced. In the case of the nonracial individual variable (the extent of an official's prior experience in foreign affairs), it seems reasonable to presume that the more contact the individual has had with the procedures and proprieties whereby governments interact, the more inclined he will be to perceive the narrow limits within which foreign policy can be effective. The capacity of societies to organize their external environments so that their own values are better served is minuscule at best. Even in small communities the task of altering attitudes, mobilizing support, and restructuring institutions is extraordinarily difficult, but the difficulties are greatly magnified when the attitudes, support, and institutions are located in other cultures and separated by national boundaries. Appreciation of these difficulties, however, is not automatic. The inexperienced person might well underestimate the obstacles that must be overcome in the conduct of foreign policy and, imbued with strong convictions about how conflicts abroad should be resolved, act precipitously, perhaps even resorting to forms of behavior consistent with the intensity of his convictions. In other words, not only does it appear that racial consciousness is subordinate to other individual variables, but it would also seem possible to treat the dependent variable as continuous when allowance is made for the influence of an official's previous contact with world politics:

Hypothesis I^2: Other things being equal, the more foreign-affairs experience a racially conscious individual has had before he enters a top policymaking position, the less foreign conflict behavior will he be likely to undertake or recommend.

The potency of race-susceptible individual variables appears to diminish even further when they are contrasted with nonracial variables from the other clusters. As previously implied, this is especially so with respect to role variables. If an official's position requires adherence to policies that give high priority to the maintenance of overseas markets and trade patterns, and he does not have a built-in predisposition toward the attachment of racial relevance to the external environment, then even the most racially conscious official is likely to keep his personal sensitivities in check and stress economic considerations when a foreign conflict situation arises. The probabilities of such behavior doubtless become even greater if there is a prohibition against the attachment of racial relevance, rather than just the absence of such a requirement. Those officials that reverse this order of priority will not long remain in their jobs. To be sure, officials of many countries are presently forfeiting markets in Rhodesia and South Africa because of the apartheid practices of these societies. Such exceptions, however, actually uphold the rule. Priorities are reversed with respect to Rhodesia and South Africa, not because somehow the situations in those societies are such that racially conscious officials are unlikely to contain their private feelings and are willing to risk removal from office, but because the roles of officials who maintain an economic boycott of Rhodesia and South Africa include a requirement that racial relevance be attached to such situations. In other words, with role and individual variables reinforcing each other, other things are not equal in these cases. Where they are, however, race-susceptible individual variables appear likely to be subordinated to nonracial role requirements, a relationship which is perhaps even more clearly discernible in the propriety that marks the interaction of top officials from different societies. Undoubtedly there are many diplomats who are personally prejudiced and conscious of skin color. Yet they receive, call upon, toast, hail, and otherwise honor officials of other races on almost a day-to-day basis. The discrepancy between their public behavior and their private orientation is not mysterious. It can be explained by the courtesies and rituals that comprise the requirements of diplomatic roles. In sum, there are good reasons to be confident that empirical data would uphold the following proposition:

Hypothesis I[3]: Other things being equal, the more a top policymaking role requires a racially conscious individual to minimize the attachment of racial relevance to situations and to maximize the flow of trade and aid, the less likely he is to undertake or recommend foreign conflict behavior.

Taken by itself, the interaction between race-susceptible individual variables and those relating to government structure does not seem worthy of prolonged discussion. Some interaction can reasonably be hypothesized, but it is so much influenced by role, societal, and systemic variables that treating it in bivariate terms is misleading. Nevertheless, if the other variables are held constant, the fact that authority is more concentrated in a cabinet form of government than in a presidential form would seem to have some consequence for the degree to which officials can pursue personal convictions that deviate from the policies of the chief executive. Top executive and legislative posts in a cabinet system derive from the same authority, and the resulting collective responsibility limits the individual discretion of those who occupy the positions. Since the top officials in a presidential system have different responsibilities and bases of power, they are somewhat freer to give expression to their idiosyncratic tendencies. In the United States, for example, Allen Ellender can return from a tour of Africa and publish racist views of that continent without damage to his career as a senator.[36] On the other hand, in England Enoch Powell is quickly dismissed from his post in the shadow cabinet when he gives public expression to similar views.[37] Of course, this difference is most pronounced with respect to two-party cabinet systems. A multiparty system may well include minority parties with deviant views on race, and the political balance may be such as to give some of their leaders seats in the cabinet. In sum, while the foregoing differences should not be exaggerated, and while much depends on the role, societal, and systemic variables that are operative, it does seem plausible to derive the following proposition:

Hypothesis I[4]: Other things being equal, racially conscious individuals who occupy top policymaking roles in cabinet systems of government are less likely to undertake or recommend foreign conflict behavior than their counterparts in presidential systems.

Nor need we dwell long on the interaction between racial consciousness at the individual level and nonracial variables at the societal level, since it does not appear to be a very important interaction in comparison to most of those analyzed in subsequent hypotheses. The factors that operate between the racial consciousness of an official and the economic development of his society are so numerous that the interaction between the two variables would seem to be weak at best. Yet, if all else is held constant, presumably the fact that economic development requires an increasing reliance on achievement—rather than ascription—of status is of sufficient importance to interpose progressively greater restraints on the racial consciousness of officials as their society develops. Although it may not warrant extensive investigation, then, the following proposition can be logically deduced:

Hypothesis I[5]: Other things being equal, a racially conscious individual who occupies a top policymaking position in an underdeveloped society is more likely to undertake or recommend foreign conflict behavior than is a similarly conscious official of a developed society.

If the interaction between individual and societal variables is so weak as to render the derivation of hypotheses hazardous, the connection between individual and systemic variables seems virtually impossible to trace. So many factors can intervene to affect the relationship that it seems doubtful whether individual differences can be specifically linked to differences in either the global structures of the international system or the specific situation to which officials must respond. All else being equal, a racially conscious individual would probably perceive physical characteristics as determinants of behavior regardless of the type of conflict involved, and in all likelihood this lack of differentiation would obtain whether the relationship that prevailed between the superpowers was polarized or not. Hence, for the sake of thoroughness, these hypotheses need to be formulated:

Hypothesis I[6]: Other things being equal, a racially conscious individual in a top policymaking position is likely to undertake or recommend as much foreign conflict behavior toward situations within other societies as toward situations between other societies.

Hypothesis I[7]: Other things being equal, a racially conscious individual occupying a top policymaking position is as likely to undertake or recommend foreign conflict behavior in a tight bipolar system as in a loose bipolar one.

Role Variables

Although individual variables do not emerge as particularly relevant to the introduction of racial factors into the international arena, the opposite conclusion emerges from an assessment of the relative potency of role variables. It will be recalled that the race-susceptible variable selected for analysis is the degree of racial relevance policymakers are required to attach to external developments. Although the high extreme of this relevance continuum is subject to the moderating influence of societal and systemic variables (see hypotheses SO^3 and SY^3 below), its potency does not appear ever to be erased by the operation of other variables and, indeed, in several instances it would seem to be the more powerful variable. The basis for such an estimate becomes apparent in a comparison of the relevance variable and its nonracial counterpart, the trade-and-aid variable. Notwithstanding the strength of the requirement that officials give high priority to economic considerations, there is considerable evidence that they are willing to sacrifice the flow of goods and services when the positions also require them to be sensitive to the skin color or racial policies of potential partners in a trade or aid relationship. Most noteworthy in this respect is the willingness of officials in a number of nations to participate in a boycott of Rhodesia and South Africa; and the unwillingness of Rhodesian and South African officials to recover their markets by altering their apartheid policies is certainly no less indicative of the strength of race-susceptible role variables. Indeed, the recent effort to suspend South Africa from the United Nations Conference on Trade and Development, undertaken and pressed by African and Asian nations despite a stern rebuke in the form of a legal opinion that characterized the proposed suspension as unconstitutional and threatening to the entire structure of the United Nations, offers a good measure of the extensity as well as the intensity of this variable. Repeatedly quoted as believing that "whether it is legal or not, we will do what we think is right," forty-nine members voted for the suspension in the UN's Economic Committee, while twenty-two voted against it and twenty-three abstained.[38] In other words, the relevance variable can even be so powerful as to overwhelm the requirement of all other roles, including those that sustain systemic structures and legal procedures.

To be sure, it was concluded above that a racially conscious official would keep his personal sensitivities in check in the face of requirements arising out of the economic and diplomatic requirements of his role (hypothesis I^3). To posit now the trade-and-aid variable as subordinate is not contradictory. Here I am assessing the potency of a role variable, whereas earlier I sought to trace the operation of racial consciousness as an individual variable, unreinforced by the presence of the requirement that racial relevance be attached to situations.

In view of the extremes within which the relevance variable would appear to operate, a direct correlation between it and the behavior of officials can reasonably be predicted—both when it is the only variable being examined and when account is taken of its interaction with nonracial role variables. In short, the following hypotheses can be derived with considerable confidence:

Hypothesis R^1: Other things being equal, the more the top policymaking positions of a society require their occupants to attach racial relevance to external situations, the more foreign conflict behavior are they likely to undertake or recommend.

Hypothesis R^2: Other things being equal, the more the top policymaking positions of a society require their occupants to attach racial relevance to external situations, the less will they be inclined to take account of economic considerations and thus the greater will be the foreign conflict behavior they undertake or recommend.

But is the existence of a role requirement that racial relevance be attached to situations sufficient to offset the effects of such individual characteristics as lack of racial consciousness or foreign-affairs experience? Although perhaps more psychologically than politically interesting, this is the essential question to which the comparison of the relevance and individual variables is addressed. All the evidence suggests that individual variations are likely to prove less potent than role variables. If the policymaking system in which a position and its occupant is located is to persist, any mismatch between the role and the individual cannot be so great as to permit the latter to alter the former. If the individual is not capable of altering his attitudes and behavior to conform to the minimum requirements of the role, then either he will not be recruited to the role or he will not long remain in it. This process of role socialization would seem to operate for roles which do and which do not involve positing one race as superior to another as part of the relevance requirement. Black officials of Malawi, for example, seem just as unlikely to advocate a racial reconciliation on their continent as are white officials of South Africa. Similarly, just as socialization into the presidency shifted Lyndon Johnson's behavior from speeches espousing the values of the American South to one that echoed "We shall overcome," so may the role requirements of the Rhodesian prime ministership have compelled Ian Smith to cling to positions in negotiating with the British over race relations that, allegedly, were less moderate and more anti-black than he was personally inclined to favor.[39] It will be noted, moreover, that at least the first of these examples does not involve a novice in politics and that it depicts role socialization occurring despite long experience in policymaking. If it is assumed that these examples are typical of the interaction of role and individual variables during periods when the role requirements are reasonably stable, an assumption that seems warranted by the logic of how policymaking systems persist as well as by available data,[40] then the derivation of this proposition follows:

Hypothesis R^3: Other things being equal, the more the top policymaking roles of a society require their occupants to attach racial relevance to external situations, the less inclined they will be to base their actions on predilections derived from their own personal and political experience and the greater will be the foreign conflict behavior they undertake or recommend.

Much the same line of reasoning results from a comparison of the role and government variables. Given the existence of the role requirement that racial relevance be attached to external situations, it seems unlikely that the strength or direction of the requirement will be greatly affected by structural aspects of the governmental process. The executive-form variable may, as indicated above, account for whether an official is able to act on the basis of his own racial consciousness, but the requirements of his role are presumably operative irrespective of whether he is responsive to cabinet or presidential authority. To be sure, governmental structure may be crucial to whether officials are required to attach racial relevance to external situations (see hypotheses G^2, G^3, and G^4 below). Yet, once such requirements become part of top policymaking roles, it would seem that their continued existence is independent of governmental form. Thus it seems reasonable to derive the following:

Hypothesis R^4: Other things being equal, top policymaking officials in a cabinet system of government and in a presidential system, both of whose roles require attachment of racial relevance to external situations, are likely to undertake or recommend similar amounts of foreign conflict behavior.

Since the role requirements of top policymaking positions will reflect the basic aspirations of the societies in which they are located, some moderation of the strength of race-susceptible role variables can be anticipated when their interaction with societal variables is analyzed. In a society that is free of racial tension, or is experiencing a lessening of such tensions, demands that its officials be sensitive to the physical characteristics of the parties to situations abroad will either be nonexistent or increasingly muted. Under these circumstances other variables will operate more effectively and will lessen the extent to which policymakers must attach racial relevance to external events. Racially conscious officials may still be able to follow their personal predilections, but these will not be supported by the requirements of their roles and may even be offset by contrary requirements, for example, by societal demands that officials curb their personal predilections and treat external situations as nonracial in character.[41] To be sure, one can readily think of exceptions. The attachment of racial relevance to external situations is very much a requirement of top policymaking roles in black African societies, for example, even though most of these societies, racially homogeneous, are mostly free of racial tensions. Such exceptions, however, do not hold other variables constant. Black African officials are required to attach a high degree of racial relevance to developments abroad because another societal variable, recent history and the colonial memories of which it is comprised, operates to sustain the requirement even in the absence of internal tensions over physical characteristics. Indeed, whenever this historical variable is operative, the above analysis must be modified. But multivariate analysis that would pick up exceptions of this kind lies beyond the scope of this essay. Here I am interested in the central tendencies that can be uncovered through bivariate inquiry, and thus the following hypothesis can reasonably be derived:

Hypothesis R^5: Other things being equal, the less a society is marked by racial tensions, the less inclined its officials will be to attach racial relevance to external situations and thus the less likely they will be to undertake or recommend foreign conflict behavior.

Similarly, the potency of the relevance variable seems likely to be diminished when it interacts with the nonracial societal variable. Despite the degree of racial tension in a society, as it undergoes economic development the responsibilities of its officials will widen and so will their sensitivities to issues other than those that are racial in character. Hence, the more of such development there has been, the greater will be the division of labor in the society and thus the greater the number of cross-cutting relationships that moderate the demands that racial relevance be attached to external situations. Stated differently, the variety of societal demands to which officials are exposed is likely to be much greater in developed societies than in underdeveloped societies. Hence the potency of the relevance variable seems likely to decline as the developmental process unfolds, a conclusion that leads to the following derivation:

Hypothesis R^5: Other things being equal, as a society passes through successive stages of economic development, the requirement that its top policymaking officials attach racial relevance to external situations is likely to weaken, making them less likely to undertake or recommend foreign conflict behavior.

Reflection about the interaction of race-susceptible role variables and nonracial systemic variables leads to hypotheses that both reaffirm the strength of the former and show them to be subject to some moderation of the latter. Their strength is revealed by an analysis of what happens to the relevance requirement when race-free situations develop abroad. Are officials whose roles require them to attach a high degree of relevance to external situations likely to do so even with respect to conflicts within or between other societies in which the contesting parties are of the same race and thus in conflict over nonracial matters? The answer here is not as obvious as it may seem. Although it might seem that the relevance requirement is applicable only to external situations where racial factors are operative, such a conclusion assumes that role requirements are rational, or at least that they are not so irrational as to require their occupants to read relevance into situations that are manifestly nonracial in content. Yet roles are the products of human expectations and are thus as susceptible to distortion as the perceptions of those who create them. In many societies the relevance requirement does not extend to nonracial situations, but under certain circumstances the relevance variable can become so potent that officials are required to attribute racial significance to virtually any situation, including those in which all the participants have the same physical characteristics. These special circumstances include a sense of racial identification with or antagonism to one or more of the parties to the conflict that is of sufficient strength to produce seemingly unwarranted attributions of racial relevance. The reactions of nonwhite countries to the Suez and Hungarian crises of 1956 are a case in point. The two situations had a great deal in common. They occurred at the same time. They both involved intervention by a great power in the domestic affairs of a lesser power. And both interventions were undertaken for political reasons (the ouster of a hostile regime) rather than racial ones. Notwithstanding the similarity of the situations, however, many nonwhite nations were quick to condemn the aggressor in the Suez incident while remaining silent with respect to the Hungarian affair. Although the reasons for this are doubtless complex and numerous, the relevance variable seems to have played an important role. One observer elucidated the operation of the relevance variable in this way, referring to a November 1956 editorial in a Ceylonese newspaper:

The author of the editorial questioned why it was that Ceylon and other so-called Afro-Asian members of the United Nations responded to the Suez incident within a matter of hours, condemning the United Kingdom, France and Israel for their "aggression" against a weaker state, while even a few weeks after the Hungarian incident, these same Afro-Asian United Nations members still "needed more time to get all the facts" before taking a stand. He answered his own question by pointing out that all of the African and Asian countries had experienced colonialism at the hands of a white colonial power and, thus, anything that even vaguely smacked of white colonialism was met with a very visceral and immediate reaction. On the other hand, he argued, while it was conceptually possible to have white colonialism perpetrated upon a weaker white country, it was simply outside the Afro-Asian range of perceptual reality. Somehow, it was simply not colonialism if it was white against white.

Verbal condemnation of the United States role in the Vietnam war offers perhaps another example of this line. Despite the lack of clear evidence that racial feelings about the nonwhite population of Vietnam are in any way a source of the American role, officials of a number of nonwhite societies have cited differences in skin color as part of their reason for denouncing American actions.

Although it can thus be seen that race-susceptible role variables can be sufficiently potent to override some systemic differences, an analysis of their strength in relation to intrasocietal as compared to intersocietal external conflicts reveals that other systemic variables do affect the extent to which racial relevance is attached to situations. Stated succinctly, the practices of diplomacy and the norms of international law circumscribe involvement in intrasocietal situations, whereas there are few, if any, restraints on conflict behavior toward extrasocietal situations. The principles of sovereignty have long prohibited involvement in the domestic life of other societies, and only as recently as December 21, 1965, the General Assembly of the United Nations reaffirmed, by a nearly unanimous vote, these principles through a resolution on intervention which declared that no state had a right to intervene in the "internal or external" affairs of another state by *any* form of interference or coercive measure.[43] Given this norm, and the reality that to violate it by intervening in the domestic affairs of another society is to legitimate or even invite interference in one's own affairs, officials are less likely to allow the relevance variable full potency when the external stimulus is intrasocietal rather than intersocietal. Indeed, the power of sovereignty is such that this difference seems likely to hold even in the case of intrasocietal situations that are unmistakably of a race-pervaded kind. To be sure, the Rhodesian and South African situations are exceptions, and even international law seems to be undergoing change that allows for treating them as such flagrant offenses to "basic principles of justice" as to warrant violation of the sovereignty principle.[44] However, while the exceptions demonstrate again that the potency of the relevance variable is such that it can never be eliminated, the central tendency is one of dominance by the systemic variable.

The potency of the requirement that officials attach racial relevance to developments abroad would also appear to be responsive to variations in the global structure of the international system. No matter whether an external situation unfolds within or between other societies, the predisposition to attach racial relevance to it is likely to be curbed to the extent that the resulting conflict behavior seems capable of evoking a counter-response on the part of one or more great powers. Enhancing and preserving national security is a basic responsibility of top policymakers in all societies, and the effects of this responsibility are thus likely to interact with those of the global structure variable. That is, though no structure of the international system may ever entirely negate a built-in predisposition to respond to a situation in terms of its perceived racial relevance, those structures that facilitate interventionary behavior on the part of the great powers seem likely to limit the predisposition and reduce the amount of conflict behavior officials of lesser powers might otherwise undertake or recommend. As Kaplan has persuasively argued, the tendency for great powers to intervene in the affairs of other societies is maximized when the global structure is tightly organized in terms of two major blocs.[45] Such a structure is based on a commitment of the great powers to the status quo, and thus it heightens the incentives to resort to drastic measures whenever other societies engage in foreign conflict behavior that might loosen the existing ties within and between the blocs. Accordingly, the sensitivity of officials of lesser powers to the relevance requirements of their roles will depend on the degree of emphasis which the prevailing global structure places on the prerequisites of national security.

In sum, the above analysis yields three propositions relevant to the interaction of role and systemic variables:

Hypothesis R^7: Other things being equal, and irrespective of whether racial factors are operative in external situations, the more a top policymaking position requires its occupant to attach racial relevance to external situations, the more likely he is to do so and to undertake or recommend foreign conflict behavior toward them.

Hypothesis R^8: Other things being equal, top policymaking positions are more likely to require their occupants to attach racial relevance to external situations involving conflicts between other societies than to those involving conflicts within other societies. As a result, the undertakings or recommendations of officials with respect to intersocietal situations are likely to be confined to verbal participation, whereas more severe forms of foreign conflict behavior are likely to be directed at intrasocietal situations.

Hypothesis R^9: Other things being equal, the more tightly structured a bipolar international system is, the less likely are the occupants of top policymaking positions to attach racial relevance to external situations and to undertake or recommend foreign conflict behavior toward them.

Governmental Variables

An assessment of the potency of governmental variables need not be very elaborate. It will be recalled that, being structural rather than substantive in nature, these are essentially intervening variables and that the distinction between race-susceptible and nonracial variables cannot be applied to them. In effect, their only utility is that of testing the strength of the race-susceptible variables from the other clusters. This is not to say, however, that governmental variables are necessarily weak. On the contrary, there is considerable evidence that the distinction between open and closed authority structures, while not in itself founded on racial considerations, is crucial to the racial policies that a society pursues at home and abroad. The differences between Russian and American policies toward Israel and the Middle East have already been cited as an example of the importance of the authority-structure variable, and this illustration could be supplemented with innumerable others. For the degree of openness determines the extent to which information about, debates over, and demands with respect to racial matters are introduced into the deliberations of officials. And, of course, the more they are exposed to the information, debates, and demands of the society, the more likely are the personal values and role requirements of the officials to be adjusted to societal needs and wants. To be sure, officials in closed societies cannot entirely ignore the racial aspirations and tensions of their publics, but their authority is such as to permit them to minimize or even suppress organization and agitation for new racial policies. If the authority structure should open up, however, domestic groups will begin to organize, and foreign groups will begin to feed information into their counterparts within the society, with the result that demands involving race will get expressed if the society has aspirations or tensions in which physical characteristics are central factors. It is not a coincidence, for example, that when illness forced the replacement of Salazar as Portuguese chief executive in 1968, opening up what had been a highly dictatorial regime, there followed protest demonstrations against Portugal's racist policies in Angola, Mozambique, and Portuguese Guinea.[46] Indeed, the future course of Portuguese foreign policy offers a good test of the potency of the authority-structure variable: it is reasonable to anticipate a moderation of Portugal's policies in Portuguese Africa if the post-Salazar regime that eventually emerges is more open than its predecessor.

In short, it would seem that societal and systemic variables on the one hand and individual and role variables on the other are related to the authority-structure variable in opposite ways. Whereas societal and systemic variables are strengthened as a government becomes more open and weakened as it becomes more closed, individual and role variables are, respectively, weakened and strengthened by such trends. Four hypotheses thus suggest themselves:

Hypothesis G^1: Other things being equal, the more open a governmental system is, the less likely will its officials be to undertake or recommend foreign conflict behavior that reflects their personal values.

Hypothesis G^2: Other things being equal, the more open a governmental system is, the less likely will the occupants of its top policymaking roles be to undertake or recommend forms of foreign conflict behavior that are consistent with historical precedents.

Hypothesis G^3: Other things being equal, the more open a governmental system is, the more likely will the occupants of its top policymaking roles be to undertake or recommend foreign conflict behavior that is consistent with existing societal pressures about racial values.

Hypothesis G^4: Other things being equal, the more open a governmental system is, the less likely will the occupants of its top policymaking roles be to ignore race-pervaded external situations and, accordingly, the more likely they will be to undertake or recommend foreign conflict behavior.

Societal Variables

As has been indicated in connection with hypotheses R^5, R^6, and G^3, societal variables tend to be highly potent. Their strength can be discerned in virtually all of the interactions thus far examined, and the ensuing analysis of the interactions involving the race-susceptible societal variable reveals their strength even more clearly. Indeed, the racial-tension variable yields some of the most interesting and controversial hypotheses.

Perhaps no hypothesis is more controversial than the one that assesses the potency of the societal-tension variable by comparing its two extremes with each other. Should we anticipate that the foreign conflict behavior of a society with no racial tensions will be essentially the same as or different from that of a society continuously racked by such tensions? My hypothesized answer to this question is controversial because it runs counter to some impressive empirical evidence. Several analysts, using sophisticated quantitative techniques, have converged around the finding that the external conflict behavior of societies is not correlated with their internal conflict behavior.[47] These studies compare more than eighty national societies in terms of thirteen forms of foreign conflict behavior and nine domestic forms, but the central tendency resulting from all these comparisons is the absence of any relationship between the two types of conflict. Yet the reasoning here leads us in a contrary direction. As racial tensions mount in a society, all of its members, citizens as well as officials, seem likely to be affected. Assuming such tensions stem from efforts by one or more racial minorities to acquire more status in and greater benefits from the society, and from resistance on the part of the groups currently deriving status and wealth from the society, once the tensions begin to increase they seem bound to spiral and eventually to encompass the entire society. Unwilling fully to meet the demands of the minorities, the dominant groups either offer them concessions or resort to repressive measures to maintain their control; as a consequence, the minorities are led to assert their demands ever more stridently and perhaps even to enlarge them, thus encouraging still greater resistance on the part of the dominant groups. This familiar pattern is self-sustaining and self-intensifying. Unless the dominant groups make basic concessions that reverse the trend, no aspect of life in the society remains untouched by it. Accordingly, no matter whether spiraling tension results in widespread violence, it is only a matter of time before its effects spread beyond the society's borders. The minorities turn to comparable groups abroad for support, and the latter in turn press their governments and international organizations for remedial action. Once the tension becomes internationalized, of course, the officials responsible for the conduct of the society's foreign policy get caught up in the spiral and are compelled either to address their external behavior to a defense of the society's racial balance or to ensure that their external behavior reflects responsiveness to the internal tensions.

It could be argued that most of foreign policy is a luxury enjoyed only by tension-free societies because those pervaded with racial problems must turn inward as their tensions mount. To the extent that this is so, there would be no necessary relationship, as Rummel and others have found, between internal and external conflict behavior. Such an argument has much to commend it. If tension rises, resources not previously devoted to the domestic scene must be allocated to the task of alleviating or otherwise coping with them. The recent history of the United States illustrates this, and a comparison of the domestic budgets of a number of countries racked by racial tension would undoubtedly show increases and decreases corresponding to periods of heightened and lessened tension. Yet greater preoccupation with internal problems need not be at the expense of external activities. On the contrary, I would contend that precisely because of the racial tensions, those responsible for foreign policy must be ever more active. They must deal with the consequences of the minorities' appeals for support abroad. The growing criticism in the foreign press must be answered.[48] The good intentions, or at least the sovereign rights, of the society must be asserted. Its prevailing practices must be explained. Its attempts to ameliorate tension must be proclaimed. And, equally important, notwithstanding the society's greater preoccupation with its domestic situation, the processes of world politics continue to unfold and yield foreign situations to which it must respond. Indeed, where once the society may have been able to take a neutral or an accommodating stance toward external situations, the dynamics of its mounting racial tensions seem likely to require it publicly to favor one or another of the contending parties. That is, as groups within the society become more sensitive to status, privilege, and justice, they will apply their refined criteria to external situations, if only as a means of giving greater force to the arguments they advance on the domestic scene. So it is, for example, that racial minorities around the world have been increasingly inclined to take stands on the race situation in the United States, just as American black leaders have become increasingly concerned about American policy toward various conflict situations in Africa and Asia. Indeed, it was the black leaders who, perhaps more than any other group, compared the skin colors of the combatants in Vietnam.

For a variety of reasons, therefore, it seems plausible to anticipate that the foreign conflict behavior of societies will increase as their racial tensions mount. However, since the changing domestic scene is likely to require the allocation of new resources, it seems doubtful that the more costly forms of foreign conflict behavior will be employed. It is likely that they will be eschewed in favor of the less economically expensive techniques of adopting verbal stances toward or recalling diplomatic personnel from the external situations. In sum, this reasoning leads to the following proposition:

Hypothesis SO[1]: The more intense the racial tension in a society, the more likely its officials are to undertake or recommend the recall of diplomatic personnel from some parties to external conflicts and verbally to express support of other parties.

Author's Analytic Conscience: But what about Rummel and his colleagues? Are you simply going to ignore their findings? Are you going to put your impressionistic reasoning ahead of quantitative empirical data? Do you not have an obligation to offer some data of your own to justify your expectation that, as tension mounts in a society, foreign-policy officials will engage in external behavior that reflects it?

Author: This is not the place to analyze Rummel's work. I respect it and delight in the fact that at long last quantitative inquiries have resulted in convergent findings in the study of international politics. However, I do not see my reasoning as a rejection of these findings. We are concerned here with a particular form of tension, whereas Rummel's research includes many forms. For reasons bearing on the intimacy of racial feelings, I would argue that the spiral precipitated by racial tensions is likely to be more intense and with more ramifications than those precipitated by other kinds of conflicts and that, accordingly, it is also more specific than the relationships reflected in Rummel's data. In addition, Rummel himself offers some reasons for believing that certain revisions in his assumptions and procedures would yield findings showing a stronger relationship between internal and external conflict behavior.[49]

As for data to support my own reasoning, I have been able to collect only a few and they are extremely rudimentary, certainly far from what is needed for a thorough test of hypothesis SO[1]. The data come from a comparison of the frequencies with which references with racial content (references to skin color or other physical characteristics) occur in three weekly or biweekly publications distributed in the United States by three governments, that of Pakistan, West Germany, and South Africa.[50] Cast in the format of a newsletter, these publications are essentially public-relations documents, designed to present the American reader with an up-to-date and favorable picture of life in the country distributing the newsletter. If a basic premise underlying hypothesis SO[1] is valid—that racial tensions cannot be confined within a society's boundaries and that its foreign-policy officials are bound to be sensitive to its international implications—it ought to follow that these three countries, being so different in their racial compositions and histories of racial tension, should reveal strikingly different patterns. More specifically, assuming that racial tensions in South Africa are much more intense than in the other countries and that they are least intense in Pakistan (which is racially homogeneous, whereas West Germany has the problem of anti-Semitism), it can be expected that the South African publication would yield the most references to race and the Pakistani one least, the West German publication falling in between. Such an expectation is fully confirmed. As can be seen in Table 3.2, except for one year the figures for South Africa are more than thirty times larger than those for Pakistan, and in all cases the figure for West Germany falls between the other two.

To be sure, these data are skimpy and they do not necessarily reflect the kind of behavior referred to in hypothesis SO[1]. Yet,

Table 3-2

The Racial Content of Weekly News-
letters Distributed in the United States
by Three Governments (entries are the
average number of lines per issue in
which references are made to physical
characteristics)

	1963	1964	1965	1966	1967	1968	All years
Pakistan	.4	3.0	1.2	.8	.2	.4	.9
South Africa	27.8	31.4	33.8	32.6	38.8	36.3	33.6
West Germany	27.0	—	—	16.5	6.3	7.9	7.9

although they certainly are not proof of anything, they are relevant to my reasoning and they do not negate it. Thus while Rummel's data cannot be ignored and are the kind that need to be gathered for hypothesis-testing purposes, it seems legitimate to retain hypothesis SO[1], although it is derived mainly from theoretical rather than empirical sources. Indeed, the foregoing analysis suggests that the potency of the tension variable is sufficient to justify similar propositions with respect to its interaction with nonracial individual, role, and societal variables. Although in hypothesis R[6] considerable potency was attached to the nonracial societal variables on the grounds that the processes of differentiation inherent in economic development were likely to diminish the role requirement that officials attach racial relevance to external situations, such an estimate was based on the assumption that other variables remained constant and did not account for the presence of mounting racial tensions. Once tensions begin to mount, however, it seems unlikely that the extent to which a society has passed through the various stages of economic development would have any consequence for the spiraling processes that accompany racial crises. Similarly, in view of the reasoning developed above, it is hard to imagine how officials who are not racially conscious, or who have had extensive foreign-affairs experience, or whose roles require them to attach greater importance to the economic content of external situations than to their racial relevance, can long remain unaffected by increasing racial tensions within their societies. Their experience may lead them to avoid resorting to the recall of diplomatic personnel, but it seems unlikely that they will be able to maintain a posture of neutrality toward external situations. Some long-time American officials, for example, may feel privately that the situations in Biafra and elsewhere in Africa are peripheral problems relative to the main thrust of world politics, but that is not the basis of their public stance toward such issues, since race became such a tension-ridden aspect of American life in the 1960s. In short, my analysis leads to three additonal propositions that run counter to Rummel's findings:

Hypothesis SO^2: Other things being equal, the more a society is marked by racial tension, the more likely are its officials, irrespective of the extent of their experience in foreign affairs or their degree of racial consciousness, to undertake or recommend the expression of verbal support for parties to external conflicts.

Hypothesis SO^3: Other things being equal, the more a society is marked by racial tension, the more likely are its officials, irrespective of role requirements that minimize the racial relevance of external situations and maximize the importance of trade and aid, to attach racial relevance to external situations and to undertake or recommend the recall of diplomatic personnel from some parties to them and the expression of verbal support for others.

Hypothesis SO^4: Other things being equal, the more a society is marked by racial tension, and irrespective of its degree of economic development, the more likely are its officials to undertake or recommend the recall of diplomatic personnel from some parties to external conflicts and the expression of verbal support for other parties.

But the potency of race-susceptible societal variables is not unlimited. As has already been indicated in the derivation of hypothesis G^3, some moderation of their strength can be anticipated in their interaction with at least one governmental variable, the authority-structure variable. It seems clear that the spiraling processes that accompany mounting racial tensions are likely to unfold more rapidly and fully in open societies than in closed ones. The governments of the latter are not only much more capable of suppressing civil disorder than are those of the former, but their very structure also makes them more inclined to use repressive measures against minorities. The spiraling process may never be entirely subject to governmental control, but its pace and continuity are likely to be responsive to the degree to which officialdom is accessible and amenable to demands for new status on the part of racial minorities. Accordingly, the following propositon can be derived:

Hypothesis SO^5: Other things being equal, the officials of an open society marked by a high degree of racial tension are more likely than those of a closed society with a similar degree of tension to undertake or recommend the recall of diplomatic personnel from some parties to external situations and the expression of verbal support for other parties.

The relationship between racial tensions and the executive-form variable, on the other hand, is less clear. Both a presidential and cabinet system with more than one political party are open authority structures. Thus they will both be sensitive to rising tension and receptive to its inherent demands. Whether the differences in the degree to which responsibility is concentrated in their respective executives will make a presidential system more sensitive and receptive than a cabinet system seems doubtful. The one case in which this difference might be sufficient to account for a large difference in external behavior is a cabinet system in a fragmented society with many political parties. In such a multiparty system, as compared to a two- or three-party cabinet system, racial minorities might have sufficient organizational strength to place their party representatives among the top policymaking officials. Under these conditions, of course, there would be an especially strong inclination for officials to attach racial relevance to conflict situations abroad and to take a stance toward them. Most cabinet systems, however, are not multiracial in composition, so that a general proposition that predicts an interaction between the executive-form variable and the race-susceptible societal variable seems unwarranted. By a process of elimination, therefore, the following has been derived:

Hypothesis SO^6: Other things being equal, the more an open society is marked by racial tension, the more likely are its top policymaking officials, irrespective of whether they hold office in presidential or cabinet forms of government, to undertake or recommend the recall of diplomatic personnel from some parties to external situations and the expression of verbal support for other parties.

An analysis of the interaction between the race-susceptible societal variable and the nonracial systemic variables also suggests that the potency of the former is not unlimited. This is particularly so in the case of the global-structure variable. At least one key aspect of the spiraling process that accompanies racial tension, the tendencies for minorities to seek support abroad, seems likely to be affected by the degree of looseness in the polarity of the global system. The looser the system, the more success the minorities are likely to have in their search for support. Virtually by definition, there is more flexibility in a loosely structured system for new arrangements to develop in the relationships among its members. Hence the evolution of both moral and substantive ties between the minorities and external groups or governments would be tolerated, if not accepted, by the great powers in a loosely structured system. The interaction of the two variables is such that it might even be argued that the external support-seeking efforts of racial minorities contributes to the loosening of the system once it has begun to move away from an extremely tight form of bipolarity. Or at least it would not be difficult to find historical connections between the loosening of the global system and the rising racial consciousness of black groups in Africa during the 1950s. In a tightly structured system, on the other hand, the improbability of obtaining external support would lessen the pressures that the minorities put on officials and, accordingly, their readiness to engage in external conflict behavior. In the light of this reasoning, the following proposition about the interaction between the global-structure and racial-tension variables can be derived:

Hypothesis SO[7]: Other things being equal, the officials of a society marked by racial tensions are more likely to undertake or recommend foreign conflict behavior in a loose bipolar system than in a tightly structured one.

Reflection on the interaction of the situation and tension variables makes it difficult to maintain the assumption that other things are equal. If all the restraints of diplomacy are ignored, an unlikely circumstance (see hypothesis R[8]), a racially tense society could be expected to press officials to take a greater interest in intrasocietal situations abroad than in intersocietal ones. The various parties to the spiraling tension are more likely to perceive counterparts similarly embattled within other societies and to regard intersocietal situations as incomparable, if not as largely irrelevant. The problems of NATO, for example, do not arouse the American black, whereas the problems of South Africa do. Furthermore, from the perspective of minorities seeking support abroad, the unfolding circumstances within other societies will seem to be a much more important determinant of the support they can procure. Support comes mainly from other countries, not from their interactions. To be sure, international organizations can provide support, but their decisions in regard to intervention are highly political and the result of how their members vote, which depends largely on the unfolding circumstances within other societies. For a variety of reasons, therefore, racially tense societies will tend to press their officials to be especially active with respect to intrasocietal situations. This tendency, however, is unlikely to prevail, given the strength of the previously noted pressures not to violate the principle of national sovereignty. Nevertheless, for the sake of completeness, the following can be logically derived:

Hypothesis SO^8: Other things being equal, the officials of societies marked by racial tension are more likely to undertake or recommend foreign conflict behavior toward intrasocietal than toward intersocietal situations.

Systemic Variables

Do race-pervaded external situations evoke more foreign conflict behavior than race-free ones? Is the strength of the nonracial variables from the several clusters moderated in the former type? These are the essential questions to be probed in an analysis of the race-susceptible systemic variable, and the ensuing hypotheses suggest that considerable potency accrues to the combination of racial and systemic factors. This is perhaps less apparent in a consideration of the univariate hypothesis addressed to the first question than it is in the remainder of the analysis. For while it seems clear that race-pervaded situations are likely to arouse the concern of more nations than are race-free ones, it seems equally clear that the former are likely to evoke more violent forms of conflict behavior. Racial factors can lead to the use of military threats and action (see hypothesis n^1 below), but it does not take much reflection to realize that most wars are fought over territory, legitimacy, and a host of considerations that have little to do with physical characteristics. Indeed, reasons for anticipating that racial factors frequently will lead to verbal rather than military forms of conflict behavior have already been noted (see the derivation of hypothesis SO^1). Hence, it seems unrealistic to posit race-pervaded situations as evoking more intense conflict behavior than race-free ones. On the other hand, a contrary conclusion suggests itself if stress is placed on the extensity of conflict behavior. For a variety of reasons, race-pervaded situations seem likely to evoke verbal stances on the part of many more societies than race-free situations. Partly because a sense of justice and basic human rights are so central to racial issues, but perhaps more because race-pervaded situations abroad can serve as a mirror to race relations at home, external developments that are pervaded with racial relevance are not likely to seem so remote as those sustained by other types of values. Except for superpowers and nations in the same region, for example, most societies have no reason to get involved in a nationality war in Cyprus, a territorial dispute over Kashmir, or a coup d'état in Brazil. Why offend the Turks or the Greeks, or the Indians or the Pakistani, or some Brazilians by taking a stand on these situations when their repercussions are likely to be local rather than global in scope? The question is rhetorical, and thus most societies choose to remain silent with respect to most situations outside their regions. Racially explosive situations abroad, however, will not seem so distant or so narrow in scope. The demonstration effect is not geographically bound, and thus a South African can seem very proximate, or at least not so distant as to justify silence. Accordingly, it seems reasonable to derive the following prediction:

Hypothesis SY[1]: Other things being equal, the top policymakers of a society are more likely to undertake or recommend a verbal stance toward race-pervaded external situations than toward race-free ones.

Comparisons between the race-systemic variable and those from the individual and role clusters are not difficult to make. There would seem to be little question, essentially for the same reasons as those set forth above, that the former is capable of erasing the differences among the latter. It is difficult to imagine that officials who are personally not conscious of physical characteristics, or whose long experience in international affairs makes them keenly aware of the limits of foreign policy, could ignore external situations that are pervaded by racial connotations. On the contrary, once such situations come into being, even the least racially conscious and most experienced official seems likely to become sensitive to them and to the external behavior they may necessitate. External situations do not transform personalities, but they can transform personal orientations. Those that turn on the status ascribed to skin color are so laden with uncertainty and so infused with values as to be among those that are capable of transforming individual predispositions.

Given their potential for precipitating chainlike reactions elsewhere in the world, much the same can be said about the impact of race-pervaded situations on top policymaking roles. Even the requirement that officials not attach racial relevance to external situations would seem subject to modification when overtones of racial conflict become manifest in developments abroad. Role variables may be powerful enough to lead to the attachment of relevance to nonracial situations (see hypothesis R^7), but they do not appear so powerful as to prevent the attachment of relevance to racial ones. This asymmetry can be explained in terms of the role requirement that impels officials to maximize their information about the factors at work in the international system, whatever significance they may then be required to attach to these factors. The rationality inherent in this role requirement may not lead immediately to the transformation of the low extreme of the relevance variable, since race-pervaded situations can be slow to emerge; but the more manifest their racial content becomes, the less will officials be able to treat them as nonracial or to consider only their implications for trade and aid programs. The postwar American experience is illustrative in relation to both the individual and the role variables. Starting in the late 1950s, as racial situations on the African continent became progressively explosive, the priorities whereby American officials were preoccupied with the defense of Europe and unconcerned about race relations abroad were gradually changed, if not reversed. And, eventually, so was the value that policy be conducted irrespective of race, creed, and color. Today black ambassadors are assigned to African posts partly because race is relevant to the situations they will have to face, an assessment that an earlier generation of policymakers were required to avoid. In short, there is reason to have confidence in the validity of the following derivations:

Hypothesis SY^2: Other things being equal, top policymaking officials, irrespective of their personal and professional experience, are more likely to undertake or recommend a verbal stance toward race-pervaded situations than toward race-free ones.

Hypothesis SY^3: Other things being equal, top policymaking officials, irrespective of any other requirements built into their positions, are more likely to undertake or recommend verbal stances toward race-pervaded than toward race-free situations.

Nor does the potency of the race-susceptible systemic variable seem likely to be offset by the nonracial governmental and societal variables. Whether a governmental system is opened or closed, or whether it is structured along presidential or cabinet lines, the implications of race-pervaded situations will doubtless be appreciated by those responsible for the conduct of foreign policy. The fact that closed systems can maintain control over the internal repercussions of external racial conflicts is not a reason for the officials of such systems to minimize their existence. On the contrary, these controls may seem especially vulnerable to the demonstration effects that foreign racial conflicts can precipitate, making the policymakers of such societies just as sensitive to race-pervaded situations as those who preside over open societies. Similarly, these sensitivities seem unlikely to be differentially affected by the degree to which the policymakers' society is economically developed. Development may introduce cross-cutting relationships that highlight an ever-wider range of issues and reduce the relative potency of the relevance variable (see hypothesis R^6), but this is not to say that sensitivity will be reduced to situations abroad that are unmistakably race-pervaded. Only when the racial content of situations is unclear does the potency of the development variable seem likely to prevail. For a number of previously cited reasons, therefore, the following propositions can also be derived:

Hypothesis SY^4: Other things being equal, top policymaking officials, irrespective of the authority structure and executive form of their government, are more likely to undertake or recommend a verbal stance toward race-pervaded than toward race-free situations.

Hypothesis SY^5: Other things being equal, top policymaking officials, irrespective of the extent to which their society is economically developed, are more likely to undertake or recommend a verbal stance toward race-pervaded than race-free situations.

Like all the variables considered here, however, the race-susceptible systemic variable is not so powerful as not to be modified by any other. An analysis of its interaction with nonracial systemic variables leads to the identification of ways in which its potency can be expected to vary. For reasons that have already been outlined, variations in the global structure and situational variables seem likely to offset the extent to which race-pervaded situations are the focus of foreign conflict behavior. That is, it is difficult to conceive of reasons why the potency of such situations should be impervious to the increased likelihood of great power intervention when the structure of the international system moves toward lesser tightness or to the greater restraint of diplomacy which the norms of diplomatic practice impose when the locale of racial conflict moves from an intersocietal to an intrasocietal setting. To be sure, the norms may be undergoing transformation in the Rhodesian and South African situations, but these are exceptional cases that are unlikely to set a precedent insofar as most intrasocietal situations are concerned. Even in these cases, moreover, the operation of diplomatic norms is evident. It is hard to imagine that the foreign conflict behavior directed toward them would be confined to verbal stances and economic sanctions if their scope was intersocietal. Accordingly, the following propositions suggest themselves:

Hypothesis SY^6: Other things being equal, the looser the structure of the international system, the more likely are top policymaking officials to undertake or recommend a verbal stance toward race-pervaded situations.

Hypothesis SY^7: Other things being equal, top policymakers are likely to undertake or recommend less foreign conflict behavior toward race-pervaded situations within other societies than toward comparable situations among other societies.

Epilogue

Author's Analytic Conscience: I have two questions.

Author's Moral Conscience: I have one.

Author: Keep them brief.

Author's Analytic Conscience: Your use of the dependent variable is puzzling. At the outset you indicated that the hypotheses would predict six forms of foreign conflict behavior, but in fact they are confined either to anticipating unspecified types of behavior or to predicting that the least violent forms will be employed. At no point do your derivations include the use of violent techniques of statecraft. Why, then, did you conceptualize the dependent variables to include the threat or use of military action?

Author: The expectation that the analysis would yield hypotheses that embraced the full range of dependent variables proved to be unwarranted. In retrospect it is clear that resort to the more violent forms of conflict behavior is never due to one or two factors and that it was unrealistic to expect that univariate or bivariate hypotheses could be derived to embrace all the dependent variables. If the prohibition against multivariate analysis is relaxed, however, it becomes possible to specify one set of conditions that is likely to result in some form of military operations, namely, when the high extremes of all the race-susceptible variables are operating simultaneously. Under these circumstances it seems doubtful whether any of the usual restraints on foreign conflict behavior will be sufficient to curb the impulse to go to war, a conclusion that is now being tested by events in Rhodesia and South Africa. Thus, by altering our procedures with respect to the independent variables, the other dependent variables can reasonably be included in the following derivation:

Hypothesis n^1: Other things being equal, if racially conscious persons hold the top policymaking positions of a society, if these positions require them to attach a high degree of racial relevance to external situations, and if racial tensions in the society are extensive when a race-pervaded situation abroad becomes critical, then the officials of the society are likely to undertake or recommend military action with respect to the situation.

Author's Analytic Conscience: My other question concerns the task of putting any or all of your hypotheses to an empirical test. I wonder if some of your variables can be satisfactorily operationalized. How does one get at the consciousness of individuals, delineate the requirements of roles, or measure the degree to which external situations are race-pervaded? These complex phenomena do not readily lend themselves to observation.

Author: They certainly do not, but I have always felt that the most serious obstacles to research are theoretical and that, if meaningful hypotheses can be derived, all else will gradually fall into place.

Operational definitions can always be developed, if necessary through the use of panels of judges who are asked to classify particular phenomena in terms of the researcher's categories. Useful theory, on the other hand, is much more difficult to generate. As indicated earlier, most inquiries into world politics are nontheoretical and, even worse, few of them aspire to the construction of middle- or high-level theory. Perhaps one reason for this situation is that the empirical complexities always seem too great to justify formulation of generalized propositions. Here we have sought to avoid this constraint by emphasizing the derivation of hypotheses and leaving the task of testing them for later. Doubtless some hypotheses will prove to be ill-founded and unwieldy, if not untestable. But, to repeat, bad theory is preferable to no theory. Of course, good theory is preferable to bad theory, but the extent of our success in this respect cannot be judged until the empirical task is undertaken.

Author's Moral Conscience: One final question. You indicated at the outset some doubt about the importance of the role of racial factors in world politics. Yet your hypotheses and their underlying reasoning attribute considerable potency to race-susceptible variables. It is as if the more you thought about them, the more you recognized how crucial they could be. How do you reconcile your initial doubts and your conclusions?

Author: I told you that moral ends are not forsaken, and may even be served by scientific inquiry.

4 Research Problems on Race in Intranational and International Relations

Karl Deutsch

Social Communication

I will begin this discussion by proposing one series of research problems that is based on a definition of race in a context of social communication. Race will be defined in terms of its effect on the social-communication process in which it is a built-in, rapid, inexpensive, and reliable signaling device. It would permit the identification of a group of persons on the basis of some physical characteristic, very quickly, very cheaply, very reliably, and without elaborate procedures for verification. By this device different observers would usually use the same means to classify people as either members or nonmembers of this group.

If people could be injected with a chemical that would turn them bright green, we would have the equivalent of such a signaling device. The elaborate tattoos of the Maoris would have a similar effect. People wearing these tattoos all over their bodies and faces could immediately and quickly determine whether or not someone else had a tattoo. Efforts to confuse or imitate these marks would be difficult, expensive, and usually unsuccessful. The first major characteristic of the built-in labeling device is its cheapness and reliability.

The second characteristic is its inescapability: in most cases, a person so labeled bears that label from birth to death. These are statements of probability. For example, race has the probability that ninety or ninety-five percent of the people with a particular label will be recognizable throughout life. There is a small group of people who, to the geneticists, may belong to this race but who are not immediately recognizable as members of it. I remember a native Czech in Prague with blue eyes, a short nose, full lips, Negroid features, and blond but tightly curled hair. When photographed in black and white, he looked colored. Furthermore, he had the athletic build, slim hips, and wide shoulders of many black athletes. I have a picture of this boy in his student days practicing archery which would deceive a racist. This is clearly an example of one of the wonderful genetic cocktails that history has produced all over the world in the course of centuries. In the United States it is estimated that between two and two and a half million people of partial Negro ancestry have passed or are passing for white. I am talking in these instances of race as the probabilistic definition; for most, however, it is inescapable from birth to death.

The third trait is the inheritability of physical characteristics, again with a ninety or ninety-five percent probability.

Race involves, therefore, the probability of conspicuous, easy recognition with a high likelihood of inheritance. Let us assume that one could duplicate such a reliable process of cheap and inheritable labeling artificially, with no correlation to any other genetic attributes of people. If you had such a communication label, what would be its effect in a society? Very clearly, it would depend on the statistical distribution of this particular signaling device.

Suppose that we could divide the population into greens and blues. These signaling devices would have no immediate effect in a society if they were statistically distributed by random numbers so that greens and blues were found with equal frequency, with equal chance of being rich and poor, educated and uneducated, propertied and unpropertied, industrially acculturated (people with obsessive, puritanical compulsions about punctuality, precision, and such) and preindustrially acculturated. But as soon as these physical labels became attached to a probability distribution that made some difference in terms of education, property, training, preindustrial or postindustrial behavior patterns, subculture, or anything else, the racial labeling would function as an accelerator of perceptions, a simplifier of perceptions, and a gross distorter of perceptions.

I think it is quite important to speak about the gross distortion of perceptions. A great deal of social learning occurs through making global judgments based on probability. If you have your fender scraped three times by drivers wearing checkered shirts and smoking cigars, you are very likely to give the fourth driver smoking a cigar a wide berth on the road. You will not stop even to think that a sample of three is not very large or representative. On the other hand, if such an accident happened only once you would probably not draw this kind of conclusion.

I would infer that the human mind works as a probability device to a large extent. We learn in terms of probability categories. We use categories that have high precise correlations, are cheap to compute, and are easy to recognize. Very often one event or experience can be aggregated into a whole series of different statistical groupings. If my fenders were scraped I could aggregate the fender scrapers into compulsive neurotics or near-paranoids. I could classify them as cigar smokers, as men who wear Makinaw shirts, as working men, as hippies, as Sunday drivers, or as amicable drunks. Since, in fact, I do not know whether they are drunk or what their educational level is (they may, for all I know, be poets on their way to a writers' conference), I am very likely to end up with the category that is cheapest to compute. A man who is treated roughly or impolitely by a person who has a very conspicuous skin color probably will associate the unpleasant experience with this easily recognizable skin-color group rather than with some other group. Thus, race biases the statistical aggregation of our memories and the formation of inferences.

I have said that race is based on easily recognizable physical characteristics. You ask how easy is easy. You would probably say that whatever ninety or ninety-five percent of the local population can recognize within five seconds is easily recognizable. Race therefore presupposes not only some obvious characteristic in the recognized, but also a trait in the recognizer.

A Polish population in a rural area where most people have round faces, high cheekbones, and short noses is quite likely to impute to a different race a delicate-featured, long-faced, dark-haired boy. In his novel *The Painted Bird* the Polish author, Jerzy Kosinski, writes of the nightmare of a child like this who is displaced into the Polish countryside during World War II and is assumed to be either a gypsy or a Jewish child. According to the novel he is neither, but the recognition patterns of the local rural population function that way. I am told that Kosinski's personal nightmares have something to do with the unrelieved horror of his book. I am also told that in the Polish countryside during World War II many things occurred that give a cast of reality to some of the events described in his book.

Depending on what a group has been trained to recognize, genetically doubtful features could still be considered racial attributes. If the inheritance of these features occurs with any probability and if the recognition habits of the population are stable, a race will be created in the eyes of the population. The genetic differences between a deep black American and an American the color of old ivory are considerably greater than the differences between the light American black and any American of Mediterranean ancestry. The imputation of genetic relationships depends, however, on the mores, the recognition scales, and the habits of the local citizenry rather than on the scientifically determined differences.

A marginal characteristic of race, even in the absence of the physical label, is the probability of close family or personal associations. On the fringes of almost every race are people like Walter White, who will not give up their friends, family, or childhood associates and who therefore are recognized as belonging to a racial group not by physical attributes but by association.[1] To some extent, this is race by choice.

It follows, for instance, that membership in the Jewish community is treated as a racial affiliation in areas where the Jewish population is conspicuously different from the rest of the people. Such distinctions may arise even among people of similar ancestry. For example, a trained Israeli observer may recognize Yemeni Jews as distinct from European Jews. If the recognition were easy and instantaneous and if specifically Yemeni traits were inherited with high probability, the differences between Yemenite and European Jews could lead to racial divisions in Israel. Under these circumstances, such divisions could occur even though a geneticist might say there were no racial differences between Yemeni and European Jews.

In other words, I am proposing to define race as a communication syndrome. This might lead to a series of studies. As a simple social experiment, suppose we took a school under reasonably controlled conditions where youngsters lived together and where, as happens in many schools, the population is somewhat stratified. To make it very simple, let us say that the stratification included a top elite, a middling group, and a number of youngsters at the short end of the stick. This could be a scholastic or an athletic classification, or one based on social scales with the popular versus the unpopular. The elite would involve the football team, the class president, and the chaps who win the scholarships. We could divide this group into halves, separating the different strata unequally. One group would wear blue shirts for the next three months, and the other group would wear green shirts. The same color scheme would apply to all other apparel so that they would really remain conspicuously labeled for most hours of every day.

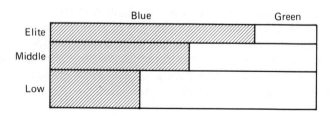

After three months we would probably witness a kind of *Herrenvolk* behavior in perception on the part of the blues whose membership consists of three quarters of the elite, half of the middle group, and less than one quarter of the bottom group. An underdog psychology and perception would develop among the other group. Psychologists could find out by interviews and observation that each group would perceive the other group as it was labeled. This would be particularly true if they had not known each other before and thus did not know how artificial the distinction was between blues and greens. You would find probably that the self-perception of the groups would be distorted after three to six months. This is the hypothesis to be tested. After a while the people in the different groups would start believing this elaborate swindle themselves.

In this experiment we have deliberately taken away history and ethnicity and, through using random numbers, we have taken away individuality. We have combined a clear-cut stratification situation with a clear-cut device for unequal cross-strata labeling. The important thing is to use unequal cross-strata labeling that is diagonal to the stratification line because it is consistent and transitive. The result would be then a development of something like racism: an in-group, out-group perception pattern.

A second hypothesis follows from this: the political effect of visible race distinctions, of the visual identifiability of groups, will be higher as the stratification of society is greater. This social stratification, plus distinctions, is the matrix, the source of strength, of race conflict.

These propositions may be amplified by noting that the social and political importance of visible and inheritable physical characteristics will increase in a society roughly in proportion to seven factors. First is the degree of inequality in the stratification of rewards. The second factor is the degree of insecurity. You could have very unequal rewards but assign these unequal rewards in a very predictable and reliable way to certain people and their children. This would be a closed-class system. The class distinction would be very sharp, but everyone would know that he belonged in a particular class and that he would be likely to stay there. In an open-class system the classes remain highly unequal, but people and their children can change their class position through either effort or accident. Those who are up are not quite secure in staying up, and those who are down have some chance of moving up.

I suggest that in an open-class society the effects of race would be more severe than in a closed-class society. In this sense, the American combination of a persistent high inequality of rewards and a considerable degree of openness may be a more powerful engine for manufacturing race conflict than the more closed British or continental European class systems. You should read de Tocqueville again with a more jaundiced eye and without the eagerness of the apologist for the excellence of our national condition. You may find that the de Tocquevillian democracy can become a stick of dynamite when combined with the racial conditions of economic inequality and physically recognizable characteristics diagonally distributed across the different strata. I think it is possible to predict that the racial conflicts are in danger of becoming worse as the mobility of the disadvantaged groups increases, and as the likelihood of this mobility increases. Later I will discuss some ways this situation could be relieved, but first let us continue the diagnosis.

The third factor indicates that conflicts become more serious in proportion to the density of settlement. This is an important point for metropolitan areas.

The fourth component is that conflict will increase in proportion to the volume of communication flow and the volume of transactions. Again, this goes up as modernization occurs.

The increase in conflicts with the equalization of aspirations is the fifth factor. That is, to the extent that the disadvantaged learn to aspire to the same things as the advantaged, race conflicts will get worse. Therefore, the communications media will increase the danger by using the most powerful tool of subversive education ever invented—mass advertising.

The sixth point is the probability that race conflicts will increase with the impersonality of the society. This can be measured by seeing what proportion of an individual's personal contacts are with unknown people. In the preindustrial society, most people deal with others whom they have known for a long time and whom they will see again. In the mass industrial society, people in both their working and their social lives will again and again meet individuals they have never seen before and are not likely to see again. You can measure the proportion of the two types of contacts, and from this you can get an index of the impersonality of transactions. Valid indicators could be constructed to measure the importance of personal to impersonal transactions.

Finally, factor seven is competitiveness. This is the degree to which the rewards to people depend not on their ability to perform according to some scale vís-à-vís space or time, but on their ability to perform better than the next fellow. For instance, you could arrange at a school to give prizes to an athlete who can run a hundred yards in thirteen seconds. This would be very different from giving a prize to the fastest runner. In the latter case, the runner's situation becomes more insecure if he has fleet-footed colleagues. The same goes for students. If you give a certain prize or reward to all students who have passed a particular measurable level of competence you have a less competitive situation than if you gave a relative standing in class. A law school student knows that if he has bright fellow students he will rank lower in his class than if he is lucky and has dumb bunnies sitting next to him.

Since most of our schools are based on competitive ratings, standings in class, grading on curves, and so on, we are grossly increasing the insecurity of precisely those minority-group students whom we recruit into our top colleges. We are destroying with one hand what we are trying to build with the other by putting these students into competitive situations that create insecurity.

The seven factors I have named—stratified rewards, insecurity, density of settlement, high volume of transactions, equalization of aspiration, impersonality, and competitiveness—are characteristic of ordinary modernization and industrialization as it has occurred and is occurring in many countries of the world. With the economic, political, and social evolution in most of the world's developing countries, one can conclude that this situation will get worse, not better. This is particularly true of the thirty-odd countries in the last three columns of Marie Haug's classification, quoted in George Shepherd's essay in this volume.[2] A glance at these countries unfolds a world map of future troublespots.

This entire line of study will combine the techniques of communication research with the theory of probabilistic reinforcement learning. This is essentially Pavlovian learning. While Pavlov's dogs can be taught to give a physical reaction to a bell or a buzzer, simply because it happens to be associated with food, a conditioned reflex can be increased by making the association probabilistic rather than completely certain. You could subject populations to Pavlovian conditioning by combining visual signals about race with some other perception of competition, insecurity, threat, fear, social distance, or whatever was salient to them. In this sense, the social-communication process becomes a mechanism for manufacturing Pavlovian conditioning in the population on a large scale. This is essentially social-reinforcement learning.

Economic Theories and Discrimination

A second line of research would examine more closely the reward half of this conditioning process. For Pavlovian learning, you need an easily discriminated signal in association with an undoubted reward. The reward only has to be probable, not certain. What research can we do about the rewards associated with race? A number of points come to mind. I will take my examples from the United States, about which we know a little and ought to know more. I would venture to suggest, however, that we would find similar problems already existing in other countries. These would be more extreme in some cases, as in South Africa; in others, they would be milder but growing, as in certain parts of Brazil. The first point would be the economic rewards associated with the economics of noncompeting groups. The economic theory was worked out by E. J. Cairnes in the 1920s and 1930s and is given in a textbook by Gottfried von Haberler. Von Haberler, however, did not draw the inferences for the race situation which I think come clearly from Cairnes's theory.

Cairnes deals with the following problem. Let us assume that we have two kinds of labor in the labor market and that people performing these two kinds of labor cannot move from one group into the other. When one group, called Labor Group A, gets a higher wage, the workers in Group B cannot move over into Group A to take advantage of the higher wage. In this case, one of two things can happen, as the two accompanying diagrams illustrate. In the diagrams, the horizontal axis is the volume or number of jobs offered and the vertical axis is the wage offered. According to the economist Tansig, the situation is pictured as in the first diagram.

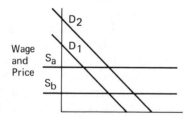

We are assuming that the labor supply is completely free of the two strata. If the demand for labor increased, the demand curve would move from D_1 to D_2. More children would be reared by the members of each labor group to enter their fathers' trade. The result would be, therefore, that wages would not change at all; they would stay stratified.

Cairnes assumes a different situation: a labor group whose supply is vertical. No matter what the changes in wages or what the demand in the market, there will not be any increase in the membership of Groups A and B. Again, at different times a demand might arise from the curve reproduced by D_1 to D_2. In the Cairnes situation, with the

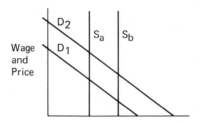

vertical supply lines, more people cannot get into the group. Thus if the labor supply remains the same, the wages will simply go up sharply when the demand for labor increases or go down when the demand declines. The game can be played in reverse using discrimination. Deny an easily identifiable minority group the jobs on the level of D_2 while pushing down the demand for services to the level of D_1. You will get just as much work out of the labor force as before and you will get it more quickly.

Cairnes was using this kind of theory for international trade to show that, given these supplies and conditions, it was quite possible for poorer countries to be exploited by richer countries. Von Haberler and Tansig pointed out that this did not happen very frequently in international trade. More often other countries would come into the market or countries would shift the nature of their exports or start different crops. On the whole, therefore, the Tansig model rather than the Cairnes model would hold. This is where Von Haberler left the argument in 1937.

If you look at these curves again, you will see that they affect to a nightmarish degree the situation inside a country where racial labeling of different groups of wage earners are concerned. Assume that among the twenty-two million blacks in the United States there are approximately ten million wage earners. The supply of black labor is an almost vertical curve, so that, no matter how badly black workers are paid, their numbers will not change. A few women may stay home on welfare and have more babies if their wages are very poor or if their jobs are very unattractive. On the whole, then, being more realistic, the curve would not be completely vertical, but would be very steep. Racial discrimination from the possible wage to what the blacks are really offered will lead to a drastic reduction in the average wage level. The wages of the labor group that does not compete with the bulk of the labor force become an invisible subsidy for the rest of the society.

In a newspaper plant, a white man may be a highly skilled mechanic working at some complicated machine such as a typesetter, and a black man may sweep the floor. If the whole newspaper has a limited wage fund, then the cheaper the wages of the man who sweeps the floor, the more money there is for the typesetter's union to get higher wages for its members. It is therefore the floorsweeper who subsidizes the typesetter's wages. If the typesetters' union is skilled in the ways of this world, they may even.take two black men into their ranks in order to prove to everyone that they do not practice racial discrimination. It is obvious, however, that the children of meritorious elderly typesetters have priority claims to be received into the union. The result will then be that the ninety-eight percent white group of typesetters will be subsidized by a ninety-eight percent black group of floorsweepers, and the typesetters will, in fact, have a share of the floorsweepers' wages.

What is true of the black subsidy of the newspaper wage fund would be true of the subsidy paid by black janitors to white teachers in the New York school system. The New York taxpayers are only willing to pay a fixed sum of money for the school system. Thus racial discrimination that forces blacks to sweep the school buildings at a cheaper rate than white men would charge makes it possible for the teachers to get a little more money or better seniority or other fringe benefits. In all these cases, the labor group that is subject to discrimination, if it cannot escape from its status, can be forced to subsidize the favored group. Under these monopoly conditions it is possible for one labor group to have a share in exploiting the other. The classical Marxist notion of virtuous workers and wicked exploiters has to be replaced by a more existential situation in which the role of worker and the role of exploiter may become unhappily intermingled.

I would suggest that this is the kind of study that too few economists have undertaken. We have large numbers of radical sociologists in the world today. We have bearded and unbearded radical political scientists and psychologists, but I have not yet run across many radical economists. I would like to know where the economics departments of Howard University and Fisk University have been recently. I would suggest that the economic theories of monopoly, monopolistic competition, discriminating monopoly, and the Cairnes model of noncompeting groups all give us intellectual tools to find out why there is a significant amount of potential economic reward in racial discrimination.

Let me make a bridge from the reward to the behavior. In an article on ethnocentrism, Carolyn Ware points out that many groups follow a behavior pattern that has become ritualized and accepted as a folkway, but not understood analytically, simply because it has come to be associated with the statistical probability of reward.[3] This is a prosperity policy. People may never know what trichina worms are, but in an area where trichinosis is frequent, people who do not eat pork may somehow discover that they are better off than their neighbors who do eat pork. In this way the religious taboo—Muslim, Jewish, or otherwise—against eating pork might become established.

Such a prosperity policy often has a very positive effect, but unfortunately it also applies to the folkways of racial exploitation. If it turns out that a group discriminates in racial matters, without having to analyze the complicated economics, the group can simply ritualize its practice. If the discriminatory practice happens to be associated with prosperity, a very stable cultural pattern could develop because the ritual is being restored and strengthened by a reinforcement learning process.

I have discussed the noncompeting groups first. One important way to reduce the average wage of the disadvantaged group is by withholding employment opportunities from them. This can be done in two ways. They can be denied employment on a probability basis. For example, black people of all age groups could be laid off from work by random numbers for a certain percentage of the time. If white unemployment in the United States is about three percent and black unemployment is about six percent, we could simply lay off all black people six percent of the time by random numbers and it would effectively reduce wages, according to Cairnes' theory. We can do something else. We can concentrate this layoff in a particular age group and keep twenty-five percent of this age group unemployed. At the same time, we could employ older black people much more frequently.

This is what occurs in fact. For about fifteen years I have read statements by sociologists and psychologists expressing great alarm about the unemployability of young black people in the age group between sixteen and twenty-five. The people who alarmed the sociologists fifteen years ago because they were unemployable at age twenty—they were dropouts, they could not hold jobs, they did not show up at work, they were drug takers, they were petty criminals, they were all this, that, and the other—seem to evaporate by the time they are thirty-five. I do not read statements about their unemployability now. I would therefore urge some age-cohort research on picking people who were born in 1935 and who therefore belonged to the problem group of young people in 1950. I would ask *Newsweek* the famous question, "Where are they now?" I suspect, as a hypothesis, that consciously or unconsciously (and I am pretty sure unconsciously, in that kind of fit of absent-mindedness in which empires are acquired) we are using the unemployment of the young as one of the most cruel and wasteful processes of forced socialization of black men to the work process. By the time a young black man has been out of work almost all of the time, has been a drifter, a casual worker, moneyless and miserable from his sixteenth to twenty-fifth or thirtieth year, he has a great deal of the resistance and the hope knocked out of him. He is very likely to pick up that broom and show up on that job from age thirty to age sixty-five. It is in one sense a wonderfully cheap method for taming and subjugating the male labor of the group (for black women it is cheaper—they are more willing to work steadily and they have fewer complaints). With black men this terribly cruel process replaces the old slave gang. It is fantastically wasteful because we are throwing away the intelligence, the initiative, the energy, and the sparkle of millions of people. We are impoverishing not only the black minority but the whole United States by doing it.

I must point out that cruel and wasteful as this is, from a certain short-range point of view it is highly functional. Consider New York City with its people who wash windows, sweep floors, wash dishes, make beds in hotels, and do all the other service functions required by the great corporate headquarters and batteries of white-collar workers along the Avenues. The city planner from the University of California, Richard Meyer, estimates that if New York had to be run at white industrial wage levels, the cost of keeping the business and communications headquarters of the nation in the New York area would go up by a factor of twenty percent. You could estimate roughly that twenty percent of the turnover of the white-collar industries of New York is the hidden subsidy paid by a million black and Puerto Rican laborers to the predominantly white white-collar workers in the corporations. The division of this subsidy between the corporations and their white employees depends on the labor market and on the bargaining skill of unions and management. According to this theory, the subsidy is hidden. I would not widely publicize this immediately, but I would put it before scholars in order to stimulate thinking about the kind of research that should be done to get the details and data.

Another hidden subsidy comes in the cost of land. According to the economic theories of John Robinson, the buyers of any commodity can be divided into two submarkets that are cheaply and reliably labeled, so that no customer can move from one market into the other. If a seller has a monopoly or a group of sellers makes gentlemen's agreements not to undercut one another, the sellers can charge an optimum price in each market. Robinson's diagram is shown below. Assume the existence of a Demand Group A, a

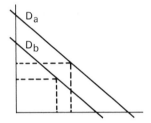

Demand Group B, and a monopoly. You could charge Group B one price and Group A another price and get more money for your total commodity than if you had to charge a uniform price to both groups. By keeping the two groups permanently and reliably separated, you can milk each submarket separately for the maximum it will bear. Robinson developed this paradigm of imperfect competition to show why and how it behooved the country to pay women less than men for equal work.

The preceding discussion of discrimination against black people applies as well to women, who are also a conspicuously labeled subgroup. Being a woman is not inheritable, however, with the reliability to which being black is inheritable, so women can at least escape discrimination across the generations. Also, women can marry members of the favored group and thus recapture some of the results of the exploitation. The black group does not have intergenerational change and does not have much intermarriage. John Robinson's paradigm applies with much greater force to the economics of race discrimination than it does to the economics of sex discrimination.

The classic example of this pattern is the real estate market. If you can clearly segregate real estate buyers who are black from real estate buyers who are white, you exploit the blacks *and* the whites. In the Cairnes labor situation the white worker benefits to some extent from the exploitation of the black. In the real estate market the white suffers side by side with the black.[4]

Recently I obtained figures on the size of this exploitation. In the city of Baltimore a journalist analyzed thirty-six real estate sales in a white lower-middle-class neighborhood into which blacks had moved. The white lower-middle-class people sold their buildings in a panic. The buildings each had an average assessed valuation of $9,000, and they were sold to real estate corporations for an average of $6,000. Within a short time these buildings were resold to black purchasers at an average price of $12,000. The whites lost, on the average, one third of their savings in these houses, taking a cut from $9,000 to $6,000. The blacks were then charged twice as much as the real estate developers had paid. The journalist's work was carefully verified. He even looked into the real estate groups and discovered that they were dummy corporations. When he dug behind the dummy he found some plausible but dubious Jewish entrepreneur, usually with a characteristically Jewish name. The Jewish entrepreneur turned out to be a front man, and behind him were the most respectable banks in Baltimore with the most respectable old-stock families on the boards of directors. The work was done in August of 1968. The newspaper in Baltimore has not yet printed the article, but has commissioned about four rewritings of it.

This is the kind of economics that should be investigated. Such economic processes might work this way in Johannesburg and they might work this way in Rio de Janeiro. They might work all over the world.

So far I have discussed monopoly, monopolistic competition, and Cairnes's noncompeting groups. Let me take another economic theory that is applicable to race relations. This is John Maynard Keynes's multiplier effect. It is known that if you pay a man a wage he will spend it somewhere. If a country exports products, the money it receives will be spent not only by the farmers who raised the coffee or cocoa or cotton, but also by the people who sell goods to the farmers. Ordinarily in international trade, the multiplier effect is about two. For every dollar a country earns in international trade, the economy of that country gets two dollars in real benefits.

A good deal of my argument has been based on the proposition that in a country with racial discrimination, some of the economic relations among race groups take on the characteristics of international trade, just as some of the political relations among these groups assume several of the qualities of international relations, including its dangers. Let us say that fifty-five percent of the school children in New York City are black. If fifty-five percent of the teachers' positions in the New York school system were also held by black people, approximately eight to nine thousand school teachers in New York would be black. If we assume that the average salary of a teacher in the New York school system is about $8,000, the black community would receive $64 million a year just from the income of its teachers. Besides benefiting the teachers and their families, a good deal of this money would be spent in black stores and neighborhoods, stimulating a multiplier effect that might double the amount of the salaries. The economy of the million blacks in New York might eventually end up with more than $100 million. Not all the teachers' income would go to blacks, but if the black community were tightly knit, blacks would probably get about $120 million of the $128 million.

The number of black teachers in the New York school system is below three percent. The subculture technique of requiring written examinations that minimize the things at which black teachers are good and maximize those at which other teachers are good is likely to keep the percentage about the same.

The black usually pays his rent to a white landlord and does most of his shopping with a white shopkeeper (probably forty percent of Harlem's stores are Jewish-owned), while only one fifth or one third of black business goes to black-owned stores. As a result, the multiplier effects of black earnings are siphoned out of the black community. It is very important to understand the economic-reward probabilities involved in the integration-segregation argument. Offering the black people of the United States complete integration under the present distribution of land ownership, store ownership, intermarriage possibilities, availability of medical and professional services, and all the rest means that most of the multiplier effect from increased black earnings would disappear again.

If on the other hand community control and black power increased, despite the similarities of this situation to segregation, the multiplier amount of money would stay in the black community to a much larger extent. The same argument that led to the victory of protectionism over free trade in many countries during the last fifty years is now applicable to intergroup relations within this country. The possibility arises that blacks could gain more through building their own self-contained multiplier economy than they would lose through missing some of the jobs that integration would open up to them. In the long run this is not ideal and this is not the last word on the question. Nevertheless, we cannot discuss black interests, white interests, and our common interests realistically and intelligently unless we know the real economics behind it and not the superficial freetrade textbook economics that has been out of date for fifty years.

Thus the segregation discussed above may benefit the minority if it creates higher multiplier effects in the black community. Let me add to this that there are also discriminatory effects on confidence and risk, on the availability of credit, and on the probability of capital formation. All these are superimposed on the multiplier effects. In some senses, therefore, the economic nationalism and protectionism that exist in international trade have implications for the problems of racial minorities inside national markets. We need essentially an adaptation of the theories of international economics to the theories of interracial economics within both developing countries and highly developed countries.

We must balance the rate of gains versus the rate of costs from the economic processes I have just outlined. These are all research tasks. In the field of interracial economics we need a far more thorough development of economic analysis and economic modeling than we have ever had before. We have to gather and to test in empirical research the data concerning the magnitudes of these gains and costs. Wherever we do not have aggregative data we should take sample surveys. There are techniques for taking well-chosen representative samples which could apply to market research for race discrimination and its consequences as well as to market research for shaving cream. If necessary to discover what the effects are, we will have to send mixed black and white teams of interviewers to everybody in order to be sure that they are getting frank and effective answers on both sides of the dividing line.

The theory suggests that gains from racial discrimination are different for different groups. We ought to do some intensive research on those groups benefiting most from this discrimination. These will be the real estate brokers and the credit interests and, therefore, the banks where real estate and credit operations come together. In the short run, the banks get richer, but over a longer period the banks often saw off the limbs on which they are sitting by making the big metropolitan areas almost uninhabitable and depressing real estate values. Short-range interests and long-range interests may be quite different, but this should be worked out in considerable detail.

Ethnicity and Culture

Let me now leave economics and turn to an approach based on looking at race in the context of ethnicity and culture. We are really dealing with economics, competition, stratification, ethnicity, and culture, to which race is only added as an accelerating and reinforcing signaling device. Race has been defined as a probability. The biological characteristics of race tend to change over a time span of at least six hundred to a thousand years and at most three thousand to five thousand years. I do not think there is evidence of any race older than that. Ethnicity involves traceable descent, concentration of childhood experiences, family associations, peer-group associations, and probability of intermarriage. Where these have a coefficient or correlation of .8 or more, you would have a closely knit ethnic group. We could make a quantitative definition of ethnicity by finding the actual probabilities and determining how strongly they cluster. Essentially culture is a distribution of similar or interlocking memories relating to facts, images, preferences, and basic orientations, as derived in part from childhood learning. One can show how the probability of ethnicity will lead to a probability of culture. The two go together but are somewhat distinguishable.

This distinction is quite important because the distorting and simplifying device of a dark coloring lumps into one category very different individuals. On one hand is a man like Ralph Bunche whose culture is the success-oriented, precision-oriented, performance-oriented, obsessive, puritanical, northwest European, North American culture of the modern industrial age, complete with its risk of stomach ulcers and with all its strengths and weaknesses. Labeled in the same category is the man who subscribes to the kind of culture that leads to what Eldridge Cleaver says about the beauties of rock 'n roll. Now Ralph Bunche is not easily pictured as dancing rock 'n roll to the satisfaction of Eldridge Cleaver. Nevertheless the racial label fantastically oversimplifies and hides not only individual differences among human beings but also the deep cultural differences.

Every people in the world moving from a preindustrial to an industrial system goes through the experience in which some people still have the role of spontaneity, warmth, irascibility, willingness to fight and willingness to take strong stimuli, while others have taken on the pattern of tight-lipped repression, ceaseless work, and willingly accepted frustration in the hope of distant goals. In Germany it is the Bavarians who are cast in this spontaneous role and the North Germans who have taken on the characteristics of the highly industrialized people. Among the Czechoslovakians, the Czechs are placed in the industrial posture and the Slovaks are seen as the people who are better singers, better dancers, and, reputedly, better lovers. You will find this stereotyping between the highly industrialized and the preindustrial culture pattern in country after country. Even white American Southerners have some of this stereotype compared with the Connecticut Yankees. In Israel the oriental Jews get stereotyped as opposed to the Jews from Europe or the so-called Anglo-Saxons in Israel, namely the Jews coming from America and Britain.

Culture is a distribution of interlocking habits of communication incorporation, including language, and a coordination of expectations and role structures which each group wishes to keep distinctive. Ethnicity in terms of family relations and childhood patterns seems to change in two to three generations at the fastest or in fifteen hundred to two thousand years at the slowest. Immigrants usually change language within two generations, but settled populations change languages over a period of five hundred to seven hundred years. Culture, preindustrial to industrial, changes most rapidly, passing from parents to children within ten to twenty years. Think of the industrial revolution or of the great political and social revolutions. Fundamental and fantastic cultural changes, as distinct from language changes, can occur in about fifty to one hundred years. One must keep distinct the race label, which changes very, very slowly; the ethnicity label (family associations and intermarriage probabilities), which changes faster; and the cultural label, which can also change fast.

Culture implies coordinated patterns of aspirations and motivation, coordinated patterns of capabilities, and coordinated practices and institutions for the acquisition and reinforcement of all these characteristics. Special contiguity and high frequency of interaction are usually associated with culture, but they are not essential to it. Separated by thousands of miles, Jewish communities in Eastern Europe and in Baghdad manage to maintain a surprising amount of cultural community. The whole notion of ethnic solidarity is based

on the assumption that West African blacks and American blacks share some cultural traits as well as a visible pigment. Whether or not this is true is a research question. Harold Isaacs notes that American blacks going to West Africa discover that they have become much more American than African and that their main culture has become American at the same time.[5]

Nationality is primarily based upon culture. Ethnicity and race may contribute to it, but they are not essential. During the course of time a single people may emerge across barriers of ethnicity, as has happened in Ireland and England. If race becomes weakened through intermarriage so that the physical signs are no longer spectacular, a common people arises across race barriers. Germanic Vikings were conspicuous. A tall redhead from Scandinavia stood out among small, dark Irishmen, and certainly among small, dark Italians. After the migration of nations, Lombards became over a period of time an inseparable mixture of Germanic and Mediterranean populations. We find racially mixed populations in Hawaii, Hungary, Finland (in Hungary and Finland there is an Asian-European mixture), Russia, Sicily (where Arabs mixed with Italians and Greeks), Egypt, India, Mexico (an Indian-European mixture), Brazil, and many others. Alternatively, whole peoples can be built across different languages, as in Switzerland.

Trends toward a disintegration of populations occur along cultural cleavages, often as a result of the pressure of social mobilization and heightened competition for vertical social mobility. These trends are strongest along lines of language. Social mobility makes language more salient as, for example, when more people become white-collar workers and become more dependent on language for their careers. These are also cleavages for the disintegration of peoples and of nations, particularly when either of these partly overlaps with class. Disintegration rarely occurs along lines of mere ethnicity or of weak or unreliably transmitted racial characteristics. Even here, however, a combination of culture cleavages with class and social stratification can split up or disintegrate a nation. In this sense, Ireland was split away from the developing integration of Britain, and the same phenomenon may occur in Scotland.

We are now living in a period where in some parts of the world disintegration is more frequent than integration. In another part of the globe, six Ibo tribes of Nigeria became one Ibo people over the last forty years, and the survivors of the civil war probably will remain Ibos now that they are even more unified by their sufferings.

For most of the world, however, we now have a reversal of earlier integrative trends, and this may be happening in the United States at the moment. A conscious and deliberate policy may be required to reverse what seems to be a disintegrative trend in this country.

Let me briefly discuss sociological and psychological effects. We can look at jobs, for example. If the population of schoolchildren in all urban districts changes rapidly while teacher populations remain the same because of tenure, we will get an alien occupation of metropolitan schoolrooms that has never existed before. As a result, we will find a culture conflict superimposed on the racial and economic conflicts which will ruin the effectiveness of the educational system in all central cities. This is an irresistible clash: the changes in the ethnic and racial composition of the schoolchildren in the core cities hit an immovable object, the justified insistence of teachers on job security.

We are running into the shop problem, too. As the minorities develop shopkeepers of their own, they will run into the shopkeepers of the other racial groups. This happens in Harlem right now. It will be expressed in municipal votes and patronage. Newark, New Jersey, has a majority of black residents but a minority of black voters. The voting districts of Baltimore preclude any chance of adequate representation of the black voters of Baltimore, even where they are enfranchised. Washington, D.C., has changed the other way, but Washington is not fully self-governing. We will see this problem becoming quite acute in metropolitan politics everywhere.

Something similar will happen within the next thirty years in that model country of racial peace, Brazil, when more and more dark-skinned poor people of the north move into the growing cities of Rio de Janeiro, Sao Paulo, and Brasilia. Conflicts will deepen as the Brazilian educational system slowly improves and the children begin to compete more effectively for white-collar jobs, government positions, and business opportunities. Brazil is now where the United States was forty or fifty years ago, and it may be moving toward the condition in which we find ourselves.

We face the problem of standards again. We tolerated flagrant corruption in New York under Boss Tweed and in Boston under James Michael Curley. This was right, too, because it permitted the immigrant Irish and others to learn how to run a city. After the Curleys came the Kennedys. We have to accept Adam Clayton Powell with equal good grace. We are not enthusiastic about it, but I do not think that we can afford to have different standards of morality for Senator Dodd and for Congressman Powell.

We may have to separate the areas in which revenues are raised. To prevent a flight of taxpayers from the districts where revenues are spent, each area must be centralized in order to tailor its spending effectively to the needs of the people it is supposed to serve. We must decentralize the service functions of the government in order to shorten the feedback from the government to the people it is serving, and we must increase and centralize the revenue-raising functions in order to make them more explicit. This means that the old and traditional Anglo-American tradition of making the tax-raising and tax-spending units identical is becoming untenable. Research problems could be developed along these lines.

The same applies to our admission system in education. Admission to the better schools in the country is highly competitive, but after students have been admitted, they still must compete to a much greater degree than either in Britain or on the European continent. Norman Podhoretz describes in his revealing book, *Making It,* the blessed feeling of relief when he discovered that at Cambridge he was not going to be graded for a solid year.[6] He had to talk to a tutor, but his tutor gave him no grades. If this is good enough for Cambridge University, why should it not be good enough for a black student on our college campuses? I would suggest teaching black students by the Cambridge and Oxford system, where the grading comes not day after day and week after week, but after two or three years. Examining is done by outside examiners after a period of time long enough to show the results of the student's education.

The steady and ceaseless feedback of competitive grading may have or have had advantages, but today it is superfluous. I think the students who go to Harvard today know one thing. They know how to compete. If they did not, they would not be there. There is not the slightest point in making them prove over and over again what they have proved already. Incidentally, students in Germany do not pass many exams; instead, they have years in which they just have to grow up. The process of growing up intellectually and emotionally should not be a competitive process.

Our present performance tests, both for teachers and students, are fantastically biased. If a student has learned French, this shows that he has high intellectual standards. This is equally true for New York teachers, even though French is rarely spoken in Bedford-Stuyvesant. If he has learned Navajo, this also shows a high standard and he gets some academic credit. If he knows the slang spoken in the black districts of Baltimore, he gets no credit. I submit that it takes at least as much verbal skill to understand black slang as it takes to learn elementary or high school French, but the one is a credit subject and the other is not. Many times I have seen poems written by young black students that show high sensitivity and first-rate verbal skills, but not the kind of verbal skills to which the Princeton educational testing service can attach a number.

I surmise that we have a hopelessly warped method of culturally biased testing and, as a student of international and comparative politics, I find that this is not an American peculiarity. All over the world examination systems for government, public service, and business are devised around traditional testing techniques that fit a class of literati. These tests favor certain groups of people and grossly disfavor others. The favored groups naturally defend these tests grimly as a protective tariff around the market for their talents. They use this technique because it looks legitimate and impersonal. Such a practice splits countries and leads to hatreds. The technique of written examinations stressing literary talents in India favored the Hindu clerk and disfavored the Muslims for decades. The result was that these tests produced in the short run a highly literate and cheap Indian civil service, and in the long run a murderous hatred between Muslims and Hindus. This led to the split of India and Pakistan and contributed to the massacres of 1947 that cost one million lives.

You get something similar in Nigeria where the written examinations in the British civil service favored the Ibo tribesmen. I suggest that these examination systems first favored the Ibo and produced as a result the Muslim, Hausa, and Fulani hatred of the Ibo. The next step was the massacre of the Ibo, winners of the examination system, which contributed to the Nigerian civil war.

I think that this use of examination and recruiting methods that looked neutral but that were in fact ethnically discriminatory certainly made situations worse. We should do more work on finding out how the full range of human abilities can be effectively used.

On the other side, just as a privileged minority overreacts in defending these tests (such as New York's Jewish schoolteachers) so the underprivileged minority overreacts in rejecting all of the competitiveness, compulsiveness, precision, and accuracy. I have heard students, both white and black, tell me that precision, accuracy, and hard work are white middle-class prejudices. In that case, I say that if my child has an inflamed appendix, I would much rather have it removed by a white middle-class doctor who knows where the appendix is than by a very poetic, spontaneous, hip individual who remembers it only vaguely and did not do so well in medical school. A cat that lives on catching mice must have a long attention span in front of mouseholes. Whether we call it a white middle-class cat or a black tom cat is irrelevant. There is a degree of performance characteristics which is inherent in watching mice, and there is a degree of performance characteristics inherent in watching or managing machines.

Today at least half or more of the American people, probably nearly three quarters, could not eat and survive without a machine technology. That is true for blacks and whites equally. Black farmers of West Africa are now learning to use strains of wheat—call them white middle-class strains of wheat—which have been raised with the help of white middle-class chemical fertilizer. Every successful nationalism has a phase where, after the rejection of alien values, there comes a demand from within to internalize the values of performance and efficiency in the name of self-respect. This has happened in Japan; it is happening now in India and China, and I think it is going to happen in the black community. The Black Muslims are a striking example of this process.

It ought to be possible to do this on a broader front than just in association with one particular denomination. In the meantime, must we have the biased examination systems? We ought to give a black student from the ghetto area veterans' points and combat points for having grown up in such a situation, just as we give our soldiers special consideration for their service and hardship. I think it takes character and resourcefulness for blacks to get where they are now.

It also may be that we have to change the way we teach the top groups. If we are to train the future leaders of the United States at Harvard, we have to have black students at Harvard, regardless of their test scores, because a student who has not worked with black students, the way they are, not the way they are supposed to be, is not qualified to lead the United States. They would be an essential educational resource, even if they themselves learned nothing. If we had to say that they do not study anything, that instead we are studying them, it would still be important. But in actual fact they are studying something; they are learning something. The more we make this less competitive and more spontaneous and creative, the better the educational process will work.

This means that we have to remember the task of education which is, first of all, to develop identity, self-respect, and motivation. If we destroy motivation, everything else is lost. If we keep motivation, everything else can be added. To paraphrase Nkrumah, "Seek ye the kingdom of motivation and all things will be added to the educational process."

Second, we need to teach communication skills and the accessibility of a much wider range of sources. We would need renovation schools. There is a distinction between a renovative school and a school that teaches its children mainly cognitive additions to the culture of performance, achievement, and self-control which already has been presented to them in their homes. When my children go to school, the schools essentially add something or continue what is already happening in the home. Our children have lots of books at home; the schools teach them to read a few more books. This is quite different from a school that has to teach an industrial culture to children coming from a preindustrial home—for example, the homes of recent migrants. To think that these are the same tasks is a self-deception, and to count educational budgets as equal per capita expense of all students is both a deception of the students and self-deception on the part of the community.

We should do analyses of what schools really have to do and should distinguish information schools from renovation schools. Information schools add information to children who already live in families and in cultural settings which are on the whole adequate and appropriate to much of the industrial culture in which we live. On the other hand, schools for children who are deprived, whether white or black, have a renovative task. They have to provide an industrial element of culture that the family never had or even make up for deprivations from which the family has suffered.

I would assume that renovation schools, serving one fifth of our people (perhaps as many as one quarter of the schoolchildren in this country, since the poor have more children), ought to be based on the assumption that they will require at least twice as much money per capita as information schools. Basically, the latter can run quite successfully as they have in the past on class sizes of twenty-five to thirty students, where the teacher maintains discipline, silence, and long attention spans. Renovation schools cannot possibly have classes with more than fifteen students, and they should have classes of between ten and twelve pupils.

This requires federal financing; it cannot be done by the central cities. The renewal of this country is at stake here. If it is undertaken, however, it will turn out that such conflicts as those seen recently with the New York teachers will disappear. If Oceanhill-Brownsville shifted to a twelve-student class size, the district would need every one of the union teachers, and would make the best of every current teacher and of every new teacher it could possibly recruit, whether white or black or any other shade. The class size and the manpower budgets might make a decisive difference. This might then involve using the existing buildings because you can hire teachers fast, as Oceanhill-Brownsville demonstrated, but you cannot build schools quickly. School buildings would have to be run in shifts and would have to double their maintenance budgets. They would have to develop a staff paid for by the community to make sure that these schools are as well equipped as any of the good suburban schools. If necessary, one ought to get together the Office of Economic Opportunity, the local civic groups, and the local plumbers' union to see what can be done to introduce some civilization and decency into the old buildings. Perhaps they will have to invade some of the old schools with armies of renovators, but I think this can be done. At the moment we have an environment that telegraphs to the child every day, "No one cares for you." If a teacher says once in a while, "We do care for you," it is almost inaudible over the environmental voice that shouts the opposite.

This has some implications for foreign policy. First, the demonstration effects of the American success or failure in handling its own race relations will be worldwide and will be quite decisive for what is now still politely called the "free world." The same will be true for the demonstration effects of what happens in Britain (whether Enoch Powell will prevail or something better), in France, the Soviet Union, Japan, and China. All of these countries are less racially homogeneous than they look.

There will be crucial alignment choices for all the major countries in the world; for example, whether they will support black Africa in its confrontation with Rhodesia and the Union of South Africa. On the whole, we may find that many of the Western countries are unwilling to put serious pressure on South Africa or Rhodesia, but also are unwilling to make sacrifices in their defense. One should realize that this unwillingness cuts both ways, and analytic studies of foreign policy should be done to determine what these two kinds of unwillingness imply. There are similar problems of alignment between Arabs and Israelis, and it will be very important to prevent a possible racialization of the conflict.

There are risks of an arms race between racial groups since the white minority populations, both within countries and in charge of small countries in nonwhite regions, insist on making up for their lack of numbers by higher concentrations of fire power. This is true of Rhodesia and South Africa as compared to the manpower of black Africa and of Israel as compared to the manpower of the Arabs. We will find continually that arms control and disarmament negotiations have this hidden dimension, that the smaller numbers of the privileged white group is to be made up for by the superiority of armaments. Sometimes this is openly averred, but much more often it is in the back of the minds of the negotiators.

In the long run this has an effect on the proliferation of weapons systems. We have to try to de-escalate the regional conflicts, the Rhodesia-Southern Africa discord, the Israeli-Arab confrontation, through multination guarantees, arms reductions, United Nations presence, and in particular resettlement and economic construction plans. If one cannot throw out South Africa, one might possibly get her to pay reparations to black Africa for development purposes. Such a plan might tide the situation over for ten or twenty years and give a new generation of South Africans a chance to become more reasonable. Israel and the United Nations might finance a plan that would give every Arab country two acres for every acre of irrigated Arab land lost in Palestine. I do not know whether this would work, but we have to think of the foreign policy of conflict management in the short run as opposed to conflict resolution in the long run.

The main task of foreign policy is to keep people alive. A potentially suicidal international conflict must be managed just as a patient with a heart condition must be regulated. We have risks of nuclear genocide through the proliferation of nuclear weapons. If the South Africans, Rhodesians, Malawians, and Zambians all get nuclear weapons in the next twenty or thirty years and if the Syrians, Egyptians and Israelis get them, we might suddenly find that these countries have been literally blown off the map. There will be very few survivors to argue the merits of each side in the conflict.

In doing something about this very real point, we may get into the politics of international population transfer. Someday the United Nations may transfer white Rhodesians to a country where they will be welcomed, perhaps to New Zealand, and give them farms or other opportunities which will prevent them from becoming declassé. The problem would be preserving the prestige and economic and social status of ruling ethnic minorities after moving them from their homelands where their old powerful position is untenable. People fear a loss of social status more than they fear death. People prefer murder and suicide to a downward fall in their social mobility and this, I think, is relevant to the problem of compensating the transferred *Herrenvolk*.

Let me finish with some implications of these research problems for world politics. What will happen when, near the end of the century, the world's nonwhite peoples achieve nuclear parity or, in President Nixon's more appropriate term, "nuclear sufficiency"? Almost certainly by the year 2,000 the nonwhite population of the world will have enough weapons to be able to kill all the whites in the world at least once. We may be able to kill them three times, but that is useless. This is something that is coming and we ought to know that it is coming. It will come in a world which will have six billion people, insufficient food, and which may contain some people who prefer to die with a bang instead of a whimper. These problems are now in the pipeline; they are not pipedreams. We ought to begin preparing for them.

A second problem for basic research in world politics is the national ownership of land and capital throughout the world, which is analogous to private property within the nation. This is a problem that Marxists have neglected and hidden from themselves as eagerly as have non-Marxists. There is a concept in Roman law which includes the right of the individual to neglect or to destroy his property. This is the right of exclusion and denial against others, which is largely obsolete in most Western countries and which has been replaced by a stewardship concept. In Britain it is called the residual property right of the crown. In America we speak of property as being imbued in certain cases with a public interest. We speak of a law of eminent domain that entitles the community to expropriate certain items of property from a property holder if it is in the common interest to do so, but it also obliges the community to compensate the owner.

One could argue that the establishment of the state of Israel in 1947 was an absent-minded act of eminent domain performed by the international community with the concurrent votes of the United States, Britain, the Soviet Union, and most of the United Nations. The United Nations, however, did not compensate the former owners, the Arabs of Palestine. I believe that, if there is a law of eminent domain in international politics, the obligation to compensate property owners should be included in it. This has not been worked out yet.

Among the so-called socialist countries, the Russian people are currently property owners over the emptiness of Siberia vis-à-vis the

Chinese and closely resemble the collective, nationalistic property owners of the Western world.

Property in the Roman-law style was not the last word in the national development of countries. I cannot imagine that national property will be the last word in international relations, but very little thought has been given to these problems—which apply to the possession of capital as well as land.

This leads us to the third point. Within the nation we accept those men as our countrymen by whom we are willing to be outvoted. The question arises concerning the sense in which we consider black Americans as participants in local government. A crucial test of true political integration is the willingness of a group to be outvoted. To what extent and on what issues will we consent to be outvoted in the world community? This is a question that not only we but also the Soviet Union must answer, and most countries, particularly large ones, are not very enthusiastic about relinquishing any voting power.

The willingness to be outvoted is related to the agreement to pay taxes. Indeed it is possible for a community to consent to pay taxes before it consents to be outvoted. Harvard pays taxes voluntarily to the city of Cambridge but does not accept the tax jurisdiction of the Cambridge City Council. We may need to study ways in which we could gradually transform what is now international charity, development programs or bribes for joining alliances, into the concept of an international income tax. We seem to be thinking already of the rate for such a tax, and American diplomacy is setting as a yardstick about one percent of the gross national product. We ought to think seriously on the international level of what Oliver Wendell Holmes said, "I like paying taxes, that is the way I buy civilization." When will the Congress of the United States be willing to pay an international income tax as the cheapest way of buying survival at a time when national armaments are clearly becoming incapable of guaranteeing survival?

Finally, there is a fourth field for research in international politics. So far as we know, approximately one child with an IQ over 140, the so-called genius level, is born among every thousand babies. Although our intelligence tests are culture-bound, almost all we know is that this statistic varies within a factor of two. Scottish-Americans have twenty-five percent more highly gifted children than the national average while Jewish-Americans have about twice as many. These figures may reflect a kind of cultural development. On the whole, however, the ratio of one extremely bright child per thousand births is true throughout the world. Two thirds of the world's geniuses are nonwhite. Among the twenty-two million blacks in America, potentially twenty-two thousand are geniuses as far as geneticists can tell.

We identify less than one quarter of the highly gifted people in most countries. Among whites in the United States we may identify and train as many as one third of the gifted. Remember, one half of the highly gifted are women, and that is an additional problem of discrimination. But among American blacks we probably ignore around nine tenths of the highly gifted. The cure for cancer that could save the lives of elderly Southern senators twenty years from now could easily be found by some young black scientist in the United States or elsewhere.

The nonwhite people of the world discovered iron, the number zero, gunpowder, papermaking, and many other things that we now consider characteristic of Western culture. We ought to include in international relations a cooperative effort to identify talented individuals and to train them early. We should subsidize and finance them so that they can follow their inclinations into medicine and science, medical research, scientific work, finding new sources of food and of art and beauty, and doing more social-science research in order to discover additional ways in which people of different races can live together peacefully.

I think these will be some of the tasks which a race program in international relations could study quite profitably and which in time might lead to legislation at both the level of individual nations and at the international level of the United Nations.

5

Comparative Policy in White Dominance Systems: A Framework for Analysis

George W. Shepherd, Jr.

The newly established Center on International Race Relations at the Graduate School of International Studies, University of Denver, has begun work in three major problem areas, one of which, white dominance systems, deals with comparative problems involving United States and African race relations. This essay outlines a research design for studying white dominance systems that can be applied to the United States, South Africa, and areas with other similar racial systems.

Racism is a recognized way of life in South Africa, but in the United States it has been presumed that racism is abhorred by the majority of Americans. The liberal view of man presumes that to resolve racial discrimination in a generation it is only necessary to go on educating our citizens in the equalitarian principles of democracy, to pass antidiscriminatory laws, and to enforce them through public commissions. The American belief in the power of unlimited technology and production reinforced this optimistic view. Because the future was believed to hold abundance for all, no major redistribution was necessary, and the natural laws of growth would provide jobs and positions for all racial and ethnic groups. This American dream of abundance and dignity for everyone was so appealing in itself that few stopped to examine the reality carefully.

This basic assumption of liberal social science that education and economic progress would rapidly transform a racially stratified society into an essentially non-racist society has been clearly challenged by developments in South Africa and the United States. Since 1954, non-violent participation movements have turned to violence and this trend appears to be rising in both white dominance societies.

Obviously the public policy in both systems differs. The critical question is: Has this public policy brought any changes in the racial-segregation patterns of these countries? In order to answer this question with greater insight than the usual ideological and nationalistic biases, we need to develop a research design that will both explain racial stratification patterns and present explicit measures of the effectiveness of public policy. A useful research design for this particular comparison may also have much broader utility, especially in the study of other white dominance systems.

One of the keys to greater insight lies in the comparative method of analysis utilizing the systems concept, which has been called "a genuinely important step in the direction of science."[1] The study of politics has been stimulated greatly by the systems concept in recent years.[2] Yet surprisingly, the study of race relations has been neither systematic nor comparative until very recently.

One practical development in policy-oriented research has been undertaken by the United Nations Institute for Training and Research (UNITAR) in "A Study of the Effectiveness of Policies and Measures against Racial Discrimination."[3] The UNITAR study is a comparative analysis of the effectiveness of public policy in several different national societies that have a "multi-racial population, a significant degree of tension and some accumulated experience in concerted action against discrimination."[4] The supposition of the UNITAR study and similar undertakings is that a systematic comparison will produce useful findings concerning the origins, manifestations and effects of racism as a universal pehnomenon, and thereby a better guideline for public policy in any particular situation can be developed.

The Western White Dominance System

The character of the race relations pattern of each group of nations is influenced by several variables peculiar to each stratification system. Culture, technology, economic and ideological characteristics, in addition to the color factor, are variables that distinguish major groupings. In a white dominance system race is a major determinant of stratification but not an exclusive one. It re-enforces economic differences and intensifies ethnic rivalries by giving a visible dimension to hierarchy. Thus a white dominance system is one in which self-perceiving white groups control the reward system and discriminate against subordinate non-white groups either in attitude or through institutional structures.

Western culture has a particularly highly developed form of color perception arising in part from the religious traditions of Christianity that have equated whiteness with purity and righteousness and blackness with sin and degradation.[5] Other cultures have similar distinctions, as that between Arab and African,[6] the Hindu caste system,[7] or the lightness of skin especially treasured in such Asian countries as Vietnam. But none of these other cultures has as fully developed and continuing a tradition of merit in terms of color distinction, particularly between black and white, as in the white dominance systems.

This white dominance concept took on ideological form in terms of the white civilizing mission of the great imperialist age of the eighteenth and nineteenth centuries. In addition, Social Darwinist precepts contributed to ideological doctrine in the Western world. The chosen people cult has by no means been limited to the Western white world, but its refined ideological expression, especially in the racist doctrines of the German Nazis, Southern Baptists in the United States, and Apartheid supporters in South Africa, has few parallels in the nonwhite world, with the possible exception of Japanese militant expansionism that flowered briefly during World War II.

A most important point of distinction is the technological and economic factor in the Western white dominance systems. Western nations have clearly developed greater technical skill and economic power than most non-Western nations. In racial stratification systems this has had the contradictory effect of strengthening both the subordinate groups and the dominant groups. In this day and age, however, technological power, with its refined communication and destructive capabilities, has probably benefited the dominant groups more than the subordinate groups. Examples of this are the pervasive suppressive power of the South African police and the control power of the National Guard in urban riots in the United States. Others argue that technical and economic progress tend to make inroads into racial stratification by creating more prosperous and professionally powerful classes. The issue turns on the willingness of white dominance groups to accept rapid social change. Technical power increases their capacity to resist as much, if not more, than the capacity of subordinate groups to demand change.

The white dominance systems are the most racially conflict-prone of all because they have produced a strong sense of social deprivation. The contradictory influence of equalitarian ideals has created self-awareness in subordinate groups and given them some expectation of higher status and better opportunities in life. Moreover, these ideals have been developed by Western culture and, to some extent, espoused in the ideology and public policy of the dominant whites. Developments have not borne out the liberal presumption that racial stratification would disappear simply because these ideals have been accepted to some extent by dominant elites and because economic progress creates demands for an educated and specialized working class. Other patterns in which police power becomes the key factor in social control are emerging. This need not be the only alternative; but it may well become just that, if more perceptive analysis of stratification patterns and especially of the white dominance system is not forthcoming.

The Research Design

National white dominance systems can be studied in terms of the origins of stratification patterns and the attempts through public policy either to discriminate in favor of the dominant groups or to eliminate discrimination. This is basically what the UNITAR research design has proposed, although this study made no attempt to establish priorities for study or to differentiate between white dominance systems and others. (There have been two studies under the UNITAR project to date: one of Great Britain and the other of Peru.) Because of the need to develop in-depth studies of each national system before embarking on extensive comparative analysis, it is desirable also to limit analysis to a few white dominance systems at the outset rather than to try to include them all. Across-the-board comparative analysis can be made, of course, where data are reliable: for example, on the extent of integration in public schools, or the proportionate amount of violence involving racial and ethnic minorities. This is meaningless in terms of the basic objective, however, unless the total picture of stratification patterns is also known. Therefore, the UNITAR selection of national units as major actors, in the light of research needs in comparative analysis, provides a valid format for study. Each country is analyzed in terms of its stratification pattern and the public policy employed to modify or reinforce that pattern.

Although the UNITAR research design presents a number of useful categories for analysis, it lacks a theoretical basis and leaves open the important issue of how to measure the effectiveness of policy. The most useful theoretical model for this purpose has been supplied by Richard Schermerhorn, who suggests that we analyze ethnic racial systems in terms of a basic superordinate and subordinate stratification pattern, utilizing two primary independent variables:

The first is the degree of enclosure in the subordinated ethnic group measured by such factors as endogamy, ecological concentration, institutional duplication, associational clustering, rigidity and clarity of group definition, segmentary relations of members with outsiders, etc. The second independent variable of importance is the control of scarce values by the dominant group shown by such indicators as the comparative number of members in superordinate and subordinate groups in upper echelons of political, economic, educational, or prestige hierarchies in the society.[7]

In addition, an intervening variable—the contextual character of society which denotes social trends—must be taken into account in order to comprehend the dynamics of group interaction.

For example, the principle of polarity postulates that centrifugal and centripetal tendencies are simultaneously present in every society, and that each, if unchecked by the other, will exhibit cumulative growth toward its own extreme. Centrifugal tendencies move toward autonomy, independence, or in more extreme cases, toward secession of the parts. Conversely, centripetal tendencies move toward increased participation in the whole by the parts.

Using the two independent variables and this intervening variable, Schermerhorn develops four basic patterns of race relations. These are simplified models, but they do provide the basic variables, indices, and interaction patterns needed to develop some measures of racial intensity and racial mobility in different societies. It should be noted that Schermerhorn has refined and developed his research model with additional variables.[8]

The intervening variable of social context enables us to employ the same basic independent variables suggested by Schermerhorn in different contexts, as in the United States and South Africa, where clearly the centripetal and centrifugal patterns of stratification and interaction are different. The mobility rate of subordinate groups determined by the "enclosure" and "control" variables will be a key factor in assessing the conflict potential. In any white dominance social system, the aspirations of subordinate groups are invariably high since they are influenced by the standards and communications media of the dominant whites; but the "status" and "situs" aspects of stratification limit mobility. Variations in the rate of change in the segregation and stratification pattern may not be as great as is generally supposed. If so, this has very important implications for policy effectiveness, especially in a society committed to an integration policy.

At this point it is necessary to add a second intervening variable to the Schermerhorn model—that of policy influence. Schermerhorn does not make this explicit in his early model, but it is of great importance. Van den Berghe, in his paternalistic-competitive model, refers to government policies and legal systems as "social control variables."[9] The stratification pattern of rewards and the rate of mobility of subordinate groups are theoretically subject to the influence of such government policies as assimilation, integration, or segregation and therefore can influence a centripetal or centrifugal pattern.

There are several criteria for determining the effectiveness of public policy. These are related, of course, to the stratification analysis itself in terms of the changes in patterns of discrimination that can be attributed to public policy. But we have to avoid the pitfalls of a single-factor explanation of change and give some recognition to other variables that affect racial stratification independently of public policy, such as economic development, religious ideas, and even world-wide situations that threaten national security. The general impact of the public-policy variable in relation to these other variables is all that can be established. (I am skeptical about the utility of establishing mathematical percentages in the weighting of these variables. However, the empirical collection of data by modern methods can be very helpful.) In some cases public policy may be predominant whereas in other cases it may be marginal or nonexistent.

First, public policy on discrimination needs to be analyzed problematically and geographically. There are numerous problem areas that can be examined, such as education, employment, political participation, housing, legal protection, compulsory service, religious worship, sports, and cultural observances. The geographic scope may be comprehensive also and include all levels of public instrumentalities. Alternatively, a decision might be made to limit the study to local or national public programs.

These problem areas should be examined in terms of several variables. The mobility variable is of great significance in the Schermerhorn paradigm and is a means of measuring change in terms of opportunity and status in a society. Substantial movement from subordinate to superordinate status economically, socially, and culturally is clearly of importance. Numerous studies on the mobility question have already been made in the United States and South Africa and can provide sources of data for the more precise examination of the effectiveness of public policy. Studies have been made in the United States on race and educational opportunity, but oddly enough little systematic attempt has been made to relate public policy directly to the increased mobility of subordinate groups. Employment mobility studies have been made in South Africa, but again no systematic correlation has been made between the apartheid policy of the government and the changes that have occurred in nonwhite entry into the restricted areas of the economy. Although considerable material exists on this, little meaningful interpretation has been made.

A second variable of effectiveness in public policy is participation in the political life and decision-making process of the society. Here again in the United States considerable work exists on voting-right changes, and some study has been made of the increasing participation of blacks and minorities in the legislative and administrative branches of government. But this material now needs to be studied in terms of the results that can be attributed to public policy. In South Africa participation again has been highly restricted by apartheid laws, but this needs to be viewed in terms of the effectiveness of limitation through public policy.

A third criteria is attitudinal change on the part of dominant whites and subordinate blacks and Africans. Numerous studies have been made of individual and group racial attitudes. The impact of public policy on these attitudes is an important factor in assessing the origins of change in the problem areas of education, employment, and so on.

A fourth criteria for judging policy effectiveness can be established in terms of the violence-stability measures widely employed in social science research such as that of Gurr in America and of Feit in his work on South Africa.[10] This needs to be utilized with discretion, however, since rising levels of violence are not necessarily indications of the failure of a policy. Some violence may call attention to a problem and produce attitudinal changes.

A fifth criteria considers the level of acceptance of international standards of human rights and interjects some universal norms into the process of evaluation. These norms have been established by the United Nations in its several Covenants on Human Rights. Neither the United States nor South Africa has accepted these international norms in official policy. Nevertheless, they constitute certain standards that guide policymakers in the United States and to that extent constitute a criterion for judging effectiveness of policy.

These covenants are methods of critically evaluating the practices of countries and the goals they have set for themselves. Here a certain amount of work has been done by the United Nations Commission on Human Rights and its Subcommission on Prevention of Discrimination and Protection of Minorities, which evaluate the conformity of nations with international standards.[11] Many United Nations documents exist that are critical of South Africa for its failure to comply with these international norms and, in fact, its inclination specifically to reject them.

The criteria for evaluating the effectiveness of government policies is of major importance, and here the UNITAR study does not attempt to establish tests. Instead it raises a number of pertinent questions, points out that different policies are applicable to different situations, and requests further discussion and refinement of criteria by participants.

The question might well be raised at this point: What is the use of bringing under comparative analysis nations with such widely divergent official policies as the United States and South Africa? It is as important to know for South Africa, as elsewhere, to what extent governemnt policy contributes to or fails to achieve its objectives of stratification and segregation. There is much evidence that apartheid breaks down at several points. We may find that the rate of mobility and the conflict level are not substantially different among the various white dominance systems. In any white dominance system there may actually be only a small nonwhite elite that is able to break through discrimination patterns. If this is true, government policy is effective for them while the masses of nonwhites are left behind to become increasingly alienated and violent. This recalls the statement made earlier that liberal analysis and policy have been largely ineffectual in the United States and elsewhere in Western white dominance systems. Obviously South Africa does not conform to international norms. But what is more important is the extent to which other white dominance systems fail to conform as well. A great deal of self-righteousness has characterized the attitude of many liberal social scientists and political leaders toward South Africa and the other deviants from international norms. All Western white dominance systems need to be subjected to an intensive examination of their actual behavior as well as their public statements at this international level of policy.

Much of this may seem obvious. Yet a thorough analysis of the relationship between racial stratification and the public policies of white dominance systems may well lead to greater insights into the nature of race-relation patterns and the effective government policies needed to reduce the amount of racism and conflict in all racially stratified systems. Such a study should begin with the United States, South Africa, Rhodesia, and the Portuguese territories of southern Africa.

From an American perspective, the crisis of the American white dominance system has not yielded to the optimism of liberal diagnosis. Perhaps comparative analysis can lay the basis for more objective analysis and more effective public policies in the future for this society and for its role in connection with white dominance systems in Africa and the rest of the world. A comparative study may well yield results that will contribute to a rational assessment of the extent to which racism deprives a nation of the capacity for objective self-knowledge and social control.

The Racial Factor in American Foreign Policy: A Selected Bibliography of the 1960s

George W. Shepherd, Jr.
Cynthia Kahn
Donald Seegmiller

Introduction

Compiling a selective bibliography on a wide-ranging topic is hazardous, but we hope that this one will produce some significant and useful results. Its shape is determined in large measure by what we have chosen to call race and the concept we have of United States foreign policy. We have used a broad definition of race based upon Michael Banton's view of race as an aspect of intergroup relations stemming from perceptions of hereditary differences. We have presumed that the racial factor cannot be usefully researched in isolation from the wider ethnic and cultural group relations within which it functions. Therefore much material has been included here that would normally be classified as ethnic. We have employed the term "racial factor" here to designate this cultural definition as against the narrower biological view of race so widely employed in previous times.

It is possible to become more precise regarding the role of race in relation to other variables in foreign policy, but this task has only been started and there is still little agreement. Therefore we have chosen to present these materials in undistilled form because they will be more useful to students and researchers.

The concept of foreign policy employed here is one that emphasizes both the domestic inputs as well as the external situations in which United States foreign policy must operate. Theory has been included only where it contributes in some direct way to racial concepts. Admittedly, a preference for systems theory weights the bibliography in that direction. The material on American groups is highly selective, since the amount of literature in this field far exceeds that for the other areas. Africa has the most listings partly because of the abundance of research on plural groups and partly because of the interests of the three authors.

Contents

166

167

I. Theory: Race in International Relations

A. Systems Analysis

Almond, Gabriel, and G. Bingham Powell, Jr. *Comparative Politics: A Developmental Approach.* Boston: Little, Brown and Co., 1966.

Apter, David. "System, Process and the Politics of Economic Development," in *Political Development and Social Change,* ed. Jason L. Finkle and Richard W. Gable. New York: John Wiley, 1966. Pages 441-457.

Blalock, Hubert M. *Toward a Theory of Minority-Group Relations.* New York: John Wiley, 1967.

Claude, Inis L. *National Minorities, an International Problem.* Cambridge: Harvard University Press, 1955.

Crocker, Walter. *The Racial Factor in International Relations.* Canberra, Australia: National University, 1956.

Deutsch, Karl W. *Nationalism and Social Communication: An Inquiry into the Foundations of Nationality,* 2nd ed. Cambridge: M.I.T. Press, 1966.

_____, and William J. Foltz, eds. *Nation-Building.* New York: Atherton Press, 1963.

Edmondson, Locksley. "The Challenges of Race: From Entrenched White Power to Rising Black Power," *International Journal,* vol. 24, no. 4 (Autumn 1969), pp. 693-716.

_____. "The Internationalization of Black Power: Historical and Contemporary Perspectives," *Mawazo,* vol. 1 (December 1968), pp. 16-30.

Gross, Feliks. *World Politics and Tension Areas.* New York: New York University Press, 1966.

Haug, Marie. "Social and Cultural Pluralism as a Concept in Social System Analysis," *American Journal of Sociology,* vol. 73, no. 3 (November 1967).

Hoetink, Harry. "Colonial Psychology and Race," *Journal of Economic History,* vol. 21, no. 4 (December 1961), pp. 629-640.

Hopkins, Terence, and Immanual Wallerstein. "The Comparative Study of National Societies," *Social Science Information,* vol. 6, no. 5 (October 1967), pp. 25-58.

Isaacs, Harold R. "Color in World Affairs," *Foreign Affairs,* vol. 47 (January 1969), pp. 235-250.

Klineberg, Otto. "The Multi-National Society: Some Research Problems," *Social Science Information,* vol. 6, no. 6 (December 1967), pp. 81-102.

Levy, Marion J., Jr. *Modernization and the Structure of Societies: A Setting for International Affairs,* 2 vols. Princeton: Princeton University Press, 1966.

Lieberson, Stanley. "A Societal Theory of Race and Ethnic Relations," *American Sociological Review,* vol. 26, no. 6 (December 1961), pp. 902-909.

Osgood, Charles E. "On the Strategy of Cross-National Research into Subjective Culture," *Social Science Information,* vol. 6, no. 1 (February 1967), pp. 5-37.

Pye, Lucian W. "The Nature of Transitional Politics," in *Political Development and Social Change,* ed. Jason L. Finkle and Richard W. Gable. New York: John Wiley, 1966. Pages 519-630.

Schermerhorn, R. A. *Comparative Ethnic Relations: A Framework for Theory and Research.* New York: Random House, 1970.

———. "Polarity in the Approach to Comparative Research in Ethnic Relations," *Sociology and Social Research,* vol. 51 (January 1967), pp. 235-240.

Shils, Edward. "Color, the Universal Intellectual Community, and the Afro-Asian Intellectual," *Daedalus,* vol. 96, no. 2 (Spring 1967), pp. 279-295.

Smith, M. G. "Social and Cultural Pluralism," *Annals of the New York Academy of Sciences,* vol. 83 (January 1957), p. 779.

Symmons-Symonokwicz, Konstantine. "Nationalist Movements: An Attempt at a Comparative Typology," *Comparative Studies in Society and History,* vol. 7, no. 2 (January 1965), pp. 221-230.

Thompson, Kenneth W., and Joseph E. Black. *Foreign Policies in a World of Change.* New York: Harper and Row, 1963.

Weiner, Myron, ed. *Modernization: The Dynamics of Growth.* New York: Basic Books, 1966.

Willis, Richard H. "Ethnic and National Images: People vs. Nations," *The Public Opinion Quarterly,* vol. 32, no. 2 (Summer 1968), pp. 186-201.

Van den Berghe, Pierre. *Race and Racism: A Comparative Perspective.* New York: John Wiley, 1967.

B. Concept of Race

Alpenfels, Ethel Josephine, ed. *Sense and Nonsense about Race.* New York: Friendship Press, 1946.

Barzun, Jacques. *Race: A Study in Superstition,* rev. ed. New York: Harper and Row, 1965.

Bates, Marston. *Man in Nature.* Englewood Cliffs: Prentice-Hall, 1961.

Benedict, Ruth. *Race: Science and Politics.* New York: Viking Press, 1959.

Berry, Brewton. *Race and Ethnic Relations.* Boston: Houghton Mifflin, 1965.

"Biological Aspects of Race," *International Social Science Journal,* vol. 17, no. 1 (1965), pp. 73-161.

Boyd, William, and Isaac Asimov. *Races and People.* New York: Abelard-Schuman, 1955.

Bunak, Viktor Valerianovich, ed. *Contemporary Raciology and Racism.* Bloomington: Indiana University Research Center in Anthropology, Folklore and Linguistics, 1961.

Bunch, Ralph J. *A World View of Race.* Port Washington, N.Y.: Kennikat Press, 1968.

Cohen, Robert Carl. *The Color of Man.* New York: Random House, 1968.

Cole, Sonia Mary. *Races of Man.* London: British Information Services, 1963.

Coon, Carleton Stevens, and Edward E. Hunt. *The Living Races of Man.* New York: Alfred A. Knopf, 1965.

Count, Earl W., ed. *This Is Race.* New York: Henry Schuman, 1950.

Dordevic, Jovan. "The Views of Contemporary Science on Race and Racism," in Institute for International Politics and Economy, *International Problems* (1968, English ed.), pp. 65-85.

Dunn, L. C., and Theodore Dobzhansky. *Heredity, Race, and Society,* rev. ed. New York: Mentor Books, 1952.

Franklin, John H., ed. *Color and Race.* Boston: Houghton Mifflin, 1968.

Gardiner, Robert K. A. "Race and Color in International Relations," *Daedalus,* vol. 96, no. 2 (Spring 1967), pp. 296-311.

Garn, Stanley M. *Human Races,* 2nd ed. Springfield, Ill.: Charles C. Thomas, 1968.

Garn, Stanley M., ed. *Readings on Race.* Springfield, Ill.: Charles C. Thomas, 1968.

Gergen, Kenneth J. "The Significance of Skin Color in Human Relations," *Daedalus,* vol. 96, no. 2 (Spring 1967), pp. 390-406.

Gossett, Thomas F. *Race: The History of an Idea in America.* Dallas: Southern Methodist University Press, 1963.

Harris, M. "Caste, Class and Minority," *Social Forces,* vol. 37, no. 3 (1958).

Hill, Clifford S., and David Mathews, eds. *Race: A Christian Symposium.* London: Victor Gollancz, 1968.

Hughes, David R. "Race: Reality or Illusions?: A Comment on the 1964 UNESCO Proposals," *Race,* vol. 6 (April 1965), pp. 298-302.

Isaacs, Harold R. "Group Identity and Political Change: The Role of Color and Physical Characteristics," *Daedalus,* vol. 96, no. 2 (Spring 1967), pp. 353-375.

Kuttner, Robert E., ed. *Race and Modern Science: A Collection of Essays by Biologists, Anthropologists, Sociologists and Psychologists.* New York: Social Science Press, 1967.

Lehrman, Robert L. *Race, Evolution, and Mankind.* New York: Basic Books, 1966.

Levi-Strauss, Claude. "Race and History," *The Race Question in Modern Thought.* Paris: UNESCO, 1961.

_____, *Race et histoire.* Paris: Gouthier, 1967.

Linn, L. S. "Verbal Attitudes and Overt Behavior: A Study of Racial Discrimination," *Social Forces,* vol. 43, no. 3 (March 1965), p. 355. Also: L. G. Warner. "Reply with Rejoinder," *Social Forces,* vol. 46, no. 1 (September 1967), pp. 106-107.

Mack, Raymond W., ed. *Race, Class, and Power.* New York: American Book Co., 1963.

Mason, Philip, "Othello and Race Prejudice," *Caribbean Quarterly,* vol. 8, no. 3 (September 1962), pp. 154-162.

Matsuoka, Titsuichi, and Raytha L. Yokley. "Essential Structural Requisites in Race Relations," *Social Forces,* vol. 33, no. 1 (October 1954), pp. 30-35.

Mead, Margaret. "Racial Differences and Cultural Attitudes," *Columbia University Forum,* vol. 10, no. 3 (Fall 1967), pp. 35-36.

Melady, Thomas Patrick. *The Revolution of Color.* New York: Hawthorne Books, 1966.

Montagu, Ashley, ed. *The Concept of Race.* New York: Free Press of Glencoe, 1964.

_____. *The Idea of Race.* Lincoln: University of Nebraska Press, 1965.

_____. *Man's Most Dangerous Myth.* Cleveland: World Publishing Company, 1964.

_____. *Race, Science, and Humanity.* Princeton: Van Nostrand, 1963.

Niebuhr, Reinhold, "The Rising Tide of Color: A Look at the Rebellion Against the White Man's Arrogance," *New Leader,* vol. 44 (January 23, 1961), pp. 16-17.

Noel, Donald L., and Alphonso Pinkney. "Correlates of Prejudice: Some Racial Differences and Similarities," *American Journal of Sociology,* vol. 69, no. 6 (May 1964), pp. 609-622.

Park, Robert Ezra. *Race and Culture.* Glencoe: Free Press, 1950.

Raveau, Francois. "An Outline of the Role of Color in Adaptation Phenomena," *Daedalus,* vol. 96, no. 2 (Spring 1967), pp. 376-389.

Record, Wilson. "American Racial Ideologies and Organizations in Transition," *Phylon,* vol. 26, no. 4 (Winter 1965), pp. 315-329.

Rose, Peter. *The Subject Is Race: Traditional Ideologies and the Teaching of Race Relations.* London: Oxford University Press, 1968.

Rosenblatt, Paul C. "Origins and Effects of Ethnocentrism and Nationalism," *Journal of Conflict Resolution,* vol. 8, no. 2 (June 1964), pp. 131-150.

Schuman, H. "Sociological Racism," *Transaction,* vol. 7 (December 1969), pp. 44-48.

Segall, Marshall, "A Primer on Prejudice," *Transition,* vol. 7, no. 2 (October-November 1967), p. 45.

Shapiro, Harry. *Race Mixture.* Paris: UNESCO, 1953.

Shibutani, Tamotsu, and Kian M. Kwan. *Ethnic Stratification: A Comparative Approach.* New York: Macmillan, 1965.

Simpson, George Eaton, and J. Milton Yinger. *Racial and Cultural Minorities: An Analysis of Prejudice and Discrimination,* 3rd ed. New York: Harper and Brothers, 1965.

Snyder, Louis Leo. *The Idea of Racialism.* Princeton: Van Nostrand, 1962.

Stocking, George W., Jr. *Race, Culture and Evolution—Essays in the History of Anthropology.* New York: Free Press of Glencoe, 1968.

Thompson, Edgar T., and Everett C. Hughes, eds. *Race: Individual and Collective Behavior.* Glencoe: Free Press, 1958.

UNESCO. *The Race Question in Modern Science: Race and Science.* New York: Columbia University Press, 1961.

Van den Berghe, Pierre. *Race and Racism: A Comparative Perspective.* London: John Wiley, 1967.

Walter, Paul A. F., Jr. *Race and Culture Relations.* New York: McGraw-Hill, 1952.

Wirth, Louis. "The Problem of Minority Groups" in *The Science of Man in the World Crisis*, ed. Ralph Linton. New York: Columbia University Press, 1945. Pages 347-372.

II. Area Studies

A. *General*

Banks, Arthur S., and Robert B. Textor. *A Cross-Polity Survey*. Cambridge: M.I.T. Press, 1963.

Banton, Michael. *Race Relations*. New York: Basic Books, 1967.

Barron, Milton Leon, ed. *Minorities in a Changing World*. New York: Alfred A. Knopf, 1967.

Bouscaren, Anthony T. *International Migrations since 1945*. New York: Frederick A. Praeger, 1963.

Burnham, James. "Global Apartheid?" *National Review*, vol. 18, no. 42 (October 18, 1966), p. 1036.

Coleman, A. Lee. "Race Relations and Developmental Change," *Social Forces*, vol. 46, no. 1 (1967), pp. 1-18.

"Color and Race," *Daedalus* (entire issue), vol. 96, no. 2 (Spring 1967).

Connor, Walker. "Self-Determination: The New Phase," *World Politics*, vol. 20, no. 1 (October 1967), pp. 30-53.

DeReuck, Anthony, and Julie Knight, eds. *Symposium on Caste and Race: Comparative Approaches*. Boston: Little, Brown and Co., 1967.

Francia, E. K., "The Ethnic Factor in Nation-Building," *Social Forces*, vol. 46 (1968), pp. 338-346.

Frazier, E. Franklin. *Race and Culture Contacts in the Modern World*. Boston: Beacon Press, 1965.

Freyre, Gilberto. *Racial Factor in Contemporary Politics*. Fernhill, 1966.

Hunter, Guy, ed. *Industrialisation and Race Relations*. New York: Oxford University Press, 1965.

Kitagawa, D. "Race Tension Worldwide," *Christian Century*, vol. 83, no. 40 (October 5, 1966), pp. 1220-1223.

Lichtheim, G. "Race Wars in the Making," *Commentary*, vol. 43, no. 1 (January 1967), pp. 62-66.

Lind, Andrew W., ed. *Race Relations in World Perspective*. Honolulu: University of Hawaii Press, 1955.

MacDonald, Ian A. *Race Relation and Immigration Law*. London: Butterworth and Co., 1969.

Mason, Philip. *Race Relations: A Field of Study Comes of Age*. London: Luzac and Co., 1968.

Mead, Margaret. "The Rights of Primitive Peoples," *Foreign Affairs*, vol. 45, no. 2 (January 1967), pp. 304-318.

Mphahlele, Ezekiel. "Race and Colour at Copenhagen," *Transition,* vol. 5, no. 23 (June 1965), pp. 19-21.

Newman, Jeremiah. *Race: Migration and Integration.* Baltimore: Helicon, 1968.

Research on Racial Relations. Paris: UNESCO, 1966.

Rex, J. "Ubiquitous Shadow of Racism," *Unesco Courier,* vol. 21 (January 1968), pp. 22-25.

Samuelson, Paul A. "Racism as Colonialism," *Newsweek,* vol. 72, no. 1 (July 1, 1968), p. 77.

Segal, Ronald. *The Race War: The World-Wide Clash of White and Non-White.* New York: Viking Press, 1967.

Taft, Donald R., and Richard Robbins. *International Migrations: The Immigrant in the Modern World.* New York: Ronald Press, 1955.

Toynbee, Arnold J. "Is a 'Race War' Shaping Up?" *New York Times Magazine,* vol. 113 (September 29, 1963), p. 26.

Wagley, Charles and Marvin Harris. *Minorities in the New World: Six Case Studies.* New York: Columbia University Press, 1958.

Willis, Richard H. "Ethnic and National Images: People vs. Nations," *Public Opinion Quarterly,* vol. 32, no. 2 (Summer 1968), pp. 186-201.

B. Africa

Ayers, Rita E. "The Racial and Political Problem of the British Eastern African Dependencies." University of California, Berkeley: M. A. thesis, 1932.

Banton, Michael. "Africa South of the Sahara," *International Social Science Journal,* vol. 13, no. 2 (1961), pp. 197-214. (Issue deals with recent research on race relations.)

Barbour, Kenneth M. "North and South in Sudan, a Study in Human Contrasts," *Annals of the Association of American Geographers,* vol. 54, no. 2 (1964), pp. 209-226.

Benedict, Burton. *Mauritius, Problems of a Plural Society.* New York: Frederick A. Praeger, 1967.

Bettison, David G. "Rumor under Conditions of Charismatic Leadership and Racial Political Tension," *African Social Research,* no. 6 (December 1968), pp. 413-462.

Bharati, A. "The Indians in East Africa: A Survey of Problems of Transition and Adaptation," *Sociologus,* vol. 14, no. 2 (1964), pp. 169-177.

"A Black Ruler Tells Why Africa Needs the Whites: Interview with Dr. H. Kamuzu Banda," *U.S. News and World Report,* vol. 64 (May 13, 1968), pp. 64-68.

Blumenfeld, Y. Y. "Tribalism vs. Nationalism in African Development," *Editorial Research Reports.* Washington, D.C.: Congressional Quarterly, 1960.

Brookes, Edgar H. *Apartheid: A Documentary Study of Modern South Africa.* New York: Barnes and Noble, 1968.

Brown, Leon Carl. "Color in North Africa," *Daedalus,* vol. 96, no. 2 (Spring 1967), pp. 464-482

Brown, Robert L. "Social Distance and the Ethiopian Student," *Sociology and Social Research,* vol. 52, no. 1 (October 1967), pp. 101-116.

Brown, William O. "Race Consciousness among South African Natives," *American Journal of Sociology,* vol. 11 (March 1935), pp. 90-97.

Brown, William O., and Hylan Lewis. "Racial Situations and Issues in Africa," in *The United States and Africa,* ed. W. Goldschmidt. New York: Columbia University Press, 1958. Pages 141-163.

Browne, Robert. "East Africa's Displaced Persons," *Africa Today,* vol. 15, no. 2 (April-May 1968), p. 3.

Bull, Theodore, ed. *Rhodesia: Crisis of Color.* Chicago: Quadrangle Books, 1967.

Bunting, Brian. *The Rise of the South African Reich.* New York: Penguin African Library, 1964.

Burrows, Albert H. "A Sociological Perspective of Africa," *Social Studies,* vol. 55 (March 1964), pp. 88-96.

Cable, Vincent. "The Asians of Kenya," *African Affairs,* vol. 68, no. 272 (July 1969), pp. 218-231.

Campbell, Jane. "Multiracialism and Politics in Zanzibar," *Political Science Quarterly,* vol. 77, no. 1 (March 1962), pp. 72-87.

Carstens, Kenneth N. "Churches and Apartheid," *Social Action,* vol. 34 (April 1968), pp. 35-45.

Carstens, Kenneth N. "Terrorism in Southwest Africa," *Christianity and Crisis,* vol. 28 (February 5, 1968), pp. 4-8.

Carter, Gwendolen M. "Multi-Racialism in Africa," *International Affairs* (London), vol. 34, no. 4 (October 1960), pp. 457-463.

Cater, Felice. "The Asian Press in Kenya," *East African Journal,* vol. 6, no. 10 (October 1967), pp. 30-34.

Cohen, Abner. *Custom and Politics in Urban Africa: A Study of Hausa Migrants in Yourba.* Berkeley: University of California Press, 1969.

Conant, Melvin. *Race Issues on the World Scene.* Honolulu: University of Hawaii Press, 1955. Sections entitled, "The African Negro," "Race in Central Africa," and "Race in British East and West Africa," pp. 31-45.

Curtin, Phillip D. *Image of Africa: British Ideas and Action.* Madison: University of Wisconsin Press, 1964.

Da Silva Cunha, J. M. "Political Aspects of the New Africa," *African Affairs,* vol. 63 (October 1964), pp. 270-280.

Davis, John A., ed. *Africa Seen by American Negro Scholars.* New York: American Society of African Culture, 1960.

Delf, George. *Asians in East Africa.* New York: Oxford University Press, 1963.

Dotson, F., and L. Dotson. "Indians and Coloureds in Rhodesia and Nyasaland," *Race,* vol. 5 (July 1963), pp. 61-75.

Dotson, Floyd and Lilian. *The Indian Minority of Zambia, Rhodesia and Malawi.* New Haven: Yale University Press, 1968.

_____. "Nation-Building in Africa," in *Nation Building,* ed. Karl W. Deutsch and William J. Foltz. New York: Atherton Press, 1963.

DuPré, Carole E. *The Luo of Kenya: An Annotated Bibliography.* Washington, D. C.: Institute for Cross-Cultural Research, 1968.

East African Institute of Social and Cultural Affairs.
Tensions in East Africa. Contemporary African Monograph Series, no 3, 1966. Nairobi, Kenya: East African Publishing House. (Papers presented at a seminar on racial and communal tensions, Nairobi, November 26-30, 1964.)

Edmondson, Locksley. "Black Power, Africa and the Caribbean," in *University of East Africa Social Sciences Council, 1968 Conference Proceedings.* Kampala: Makere Institute of Social Research, Paper No. 167.

Feit, E. "Community in a Quandary: The South African Jewish Community and 'Apartheid'," *Race,* vol. 8, no. 4 (April 1967), pp. 395-408.

Feit, E. "Conflict and Cohesion in South Africa: A Theoretical Analysis of the Policy of 'Separate Development' and its Implications," *Economic Development and Cultural Change,* vol. 14, no. 4 (July 1966), pp. 484-496.

Figueredo, Antonia de. "Mozambique's Hidden Racialism," *Venture,* vol. 17 (November 1965), pp. 20-22.

Foot, Hugh. "The Whites in Africa," *Saturday Review,* vol. 47, no. 30 (July 25, 1964), pp. 10-12.

Fordham, Paul, and H. V. Wiltshire. "Some Tests of Prejudice in an East African Adult College," *Race,* vol. 5, no. 2 (October 1963), pp. 70-77.

Franck, Thomas M. *Race and Nationalism: The Struggle for Power in Rhodesia Nyasaland.* New York: Fordham University Press, 1960.

Franck, T. M. "White Settlers and the Independence Movement in Africa South of the Sahara," *Journal of Negro Education,* vol. 30, no. 3 (1961), pp. 223-231.

Frye, William R. *In Whitest Africa: The Dynamics of Apartheid.* Englewood Cliffs, N. J.: Prentice-Hall, 1968.

Ghai, Dharam P. "The Asian Dilemma in East Africa," *East African Journal,* vol. 1 (March 1965), pp. 6-21.

Ghai, Dharam P. *Portrait of a Minority: Asians in East Africa.* London: Oxford University Press, 1965.

Gibbs, James L., ed. *Peoples of Africa.* New York: Holt, Rinehart and Winston, 1965.

Goldthorpe, J. E. "Race Relations in East Africa," *Transition,* vol. 1 (November 1961), pp. 31-36.

Gray, Richard. "Race Relations in Central Africa." *African Affairs,* vol. 62 (October 1963), pp. 333-340.

Gray, Richard. *The Two Nations: Aspects of the Development of Race Relations in the Rhodesias and Nyasaland.* London: Oxford University Press, 1960.

Gupta, Vijaya. "Emergence and Decline of the Concept of Multi-racialism in Kenya," *United Asia,* vol. 20 (July-August 1968), pp. 234-242.

Gupta, Anirudha. "Indians Abroad—in Asia and Africa: The Problem," *African Quarterly,* vol. 7 (January-March 1968), pp. 302-315.

Hall, Richard. *The High Price of Principles: Kaunda and the White South.* London: Hodder and Sloughton, 1969.

Hammond, Richard J. "Race Attitudes and Policies in Portuguese Africa in the 19th and 20th Centuries," *Race,* vol 9, no. 2 (October 1967), pp. 205-216.

Hanna, W. J., and J. Hanna. "The Problem of Ethnicity and Factionalism in Africa Survey Research," *Public Opinion Quarterly,* vol. 30, no. 2 (Summer 1966), pp. 290-294.

Hennings, J. *Some Problems of Multi-Racial Communities in East and Central Africa.* Pittsburgh: Institute of African Affairs, Duquesne University, No. 13, 1963.

Hodson, H. V. "Race Relations in the British Commonwealth," *International Affairs,* vol. 26 (July 1950), pp. 305-315.

Hollingsworth, L. W. *The Asians of East Africa.* London: Macmillan, 1960.

Horrell, Muriel. *A Survey of Race Relations in South Africa, 1965.* Johannesburg: South African Institute of Race Relations, 1966.

Houser, George M. "Cause for Concern," *Africa Today,* vol. 8, no 1 (January 1961), p. 5.

Irvine, Keith. "Southern Africa: The White Fortress," *Current History,* vol. 54, no. 318 (February 1968), p. 72.

Jahoda, G. *White Man: A Study of the Attitudes of Africans to Europeans in Ghana Before Independence.* London: Oxford University Press, 1961.

Kahn, E. J., Jr. *The Separated People: A Look at Contemporary South Africa.* New York: W. W. Norton, 1968.

Keith, Grace. *The Fading Colour Bar.* London: Robert Hale, 1966.

Khuri, F. I. "Kinship, Emigration and Trade Partnership Among the Lebanese of West Africa," *Africa,* vol. 35 (October 1965), pp. 385-395.

Kiano, Gikonyo. "The Federation Issue in Multi-Racial East and Central Africa." University of California, Berkeley: Ph.D. diss., 1956.

Kirk-Greene, A.H.M. "Peoples of Nigeria: The Cultural Background to the Crisis," *African Affairs,* vol. 66, no. 262 (January 1967), pp. 3-11.

Kuper, Hilda. *Uniform of Colour: A Study of Black-White Relationships in Swaziland.* Johannesburg: Witwatersrand University Press, 1947.

Kuper, Leo. *An African Bourgeosie: Race, Class and Politics in South Africa.* New Haven: Yale University Press, 1965.

Kuper, Leo. "The Political Situation of Non-Whites in South Africa," in *Southern Africa and the United States,* ed. William A. Hance. New York: Columbia University Press, 1968.

Kuper, Leo. "Racialism and Integration in South African Society," *Race,* vol. 4, no. 2 (May 1963), pp. 26-31.

Kuper, Leo, and M. G. Smith, eds. *Pluralism in Africa.* Berkeley: University of California Press, 1969.

Laurence, John. *The Seeds of Disaster: A Guide to the Realities, Race Policies and World Wide Propaganda Campaigns of the Republic of South Africa.* New York: Taplinger Publishing Co., 1968.

Legassick, Martin. "Racism and Guerrilla Struggle in Southern Africa," *Africa Today*, vol. 15, no. 1 (February-March 1968), pp. 3-4.

Legum, Colin. "Color and Power in the South African Situation," *Daedalus*, vol. 96, no. 2 (Spring 1967), pp. 483-495.

Legum, Colin. " 'Harambee' in Kenya," *Current History*, vol. 46 (March 1964), pp. 142-147.

Legum, Colin and Margaret. *South Africa: Crisis for the West.* New York: Frederick A. Praeger, 1964.

Lever, Henry. "The Johannesburg Station Explosion and Ethnic Attitudes," *Public Opinion Quarterly*, vol. 33, no. 2 (Summer 1969), pp. 180-189.

———. *Ethnic Attitudes of Johannesburg Youth.* Johannesburg: Witwatersrand University Press, 1968.

Lucan, Lord. "Capricorn Africa Society," *Venture*, vol. 7, no. 9 (February 1956), pp. 6-7.

MacFarlane, L. J. "Justifying Rebellion: Black and White Nationalism in Rhodesia," *Journal of Commonwealth Political Studies*, vol. 6, no. 1 (March 1968), pp. 54-79.

MacLean, Joan C., ed. *Africa: The Racial Issue.* New York: Wilson, 1954.

Magubane, B. "Pluralism and Conflict Situation in Africa: A New Look," *African Social Research*, no. 7 (June 1969), pp. 529-554.

Mair, Lucy P. "Race, Tribalism and Nationalism in Africa," in *Man, Race and Darwin* ed. Philip Mason. London: Oxford University Press, 1960.

Mazrui, Ali. *The Anglo-African Commonwealth: Political Friction and Cultural Fusion.* New York: Pergamon Press, 1967.

———. "Neither Fish nor Foul: A Good Deal of Asian Investment in East Africa Comes from Non-National Settlers," *Ceres*, vol. 2 (March-April 1969), pp. 48-50.

———. "On the Concept We Are All Africans," *American Political Science Review*, vol. 57, no. 1 (March 1963), pp. 88-97.

Markadis, L. "African vs. European in Central Africa," *Journal of International Affairs*, vol. 15, no. 1 (1961), pp. 52-67.

Melady, Thomas P. *The Revolution of Color.* New York: Hawthorne Books, 1966.

———. *The White Man's Future in Black Africa.* New York: Macfadden-Bartell, 1962.

Millin, Sarah Gertrude, comp. *White Africans Are Also People*, 3rd ed. London: Bailey Bros. and Swinfen, 1966.

Moeira, Adriano. "Political Unity and the Status of Peoples," *African Affairs*, vol. 59, no. 236 (July 1960), pp. 249-259.

Mondlane, Eduardo C. "Race Relations and Portuguese Colonial Policy, with Special Reference to Mozambique," *Africa Today*, vol. 15, no. 1 (February-March 1968), pp. 13-18.

Morase, Frank. *The Importance of Being Black: An Asian Looks at Africa.* New York: Macmillan, 1965.

Morris, H. S., Julian Pitt-Rivers, and Ernest Gellner, eds. *The Indians in Uganda: Caste and Sect in a Plural Society*. Chicago: University of Chicago Press, 1968.

Morris, S. "Indians of East Africa: A Study in a Plural Society," *British Journal of Sociology*, vol. 7 (September 1956), pp. 194-211.

Müller, A. L. *Minority Interests: The Political Economy of the Coloured and Indian Communities in South Africa*. Johannesburg: South African Institute of Race Relations, 1968.

Munger, Edwin S. *Afrikaner and African Nationalism: South African Parallels and Parameters*. London: Oxford University Press, 1967.

_____. "Race and National Identification: The Republic of South Africa," in *Expectant Peoples: Nationalism and Development*, ed. Kalman H. Silvert. New York: Random House, 1963.

_____. "Tanganyika for All Tanganyikans, Africans Promote Racial Cooperation," *American University Field Staff Reports*, East African Series, vol. 5, no. 1 (1959).

Nicol, A. "Race Relations in Independent Africa," *World Today*, vol. 19, no. 1 (January 1963), pp. 42-50.

Norton, I. H. "An Inter-Racial Local Council in Tanganyika," *Journal of African Administration* (January 1956), pp. 26-32.

O'Brien, T. P. "The Methods and Aims of a Race Relations Institute," *East African Medical Journal*, vol. 23, no. 12 (December 1946), pp. 361-384.

Ochinsky, L. *The Racial Affinities of the Baganda and Other Bantu Tribes of British East Africa*. Cambridge: Heffer, 1954.

Ogot, B. A. "Racial Consciousness among Africans," *East African Journal* (April 1965), pp. 17-23.

Olorundsa, Victor A. "Nigerian Cultural Nationalism," *African Forum*, vol. 3, no. 1 (Summer 1967), pp. 78-89.

Opara, P.A.U. "Social Distance Attitude of Nigerian Students," *Phylon*, vol. 29, no. 1 (Spring 1968), pp. 13-18.

Perham, Margery. "White Minorities in Africa," *Foreign Affairs*, vol. 37 (July 1959), pp. 637-648.

Prascul, A. "People of Indian Origin in Uganda," *African Quarterly*, vol. 2, no. 4 (1963), pp. 240-250.

Pratt, Cranford. "Multi-Racialism and Local Government in Tanganyika," *Race*, vol. 2, no. 1 (November 1960), pp. 33-49.

Pratt, R. C. "Tribalism and Nationalism in Uganda," *Overseas Quarterly*, vol. 2, no. 3 (1960), pp. 72-80.

Proudfoot, L., and H. S. Wilson. "The Clubs in Crisis: Race Relations in the New West Africa," *American Journal of Sociology*, vol. 66, no. 1 (1961), pp. 317-324.

"Race War Coming in Africa" (interview with Zambia's President Kenneth D. Kaunda), *U.S. News and World Report*, vol. 65 (December 2, 1968), pp. 64-67.

178

Rhoodie, N. J. *Apartheid and Racial Partnership in Southern Africa.* Pretoria, South Africa: H. and R. Academica, 1969.

Richards, Audrey I. "Multi-Tribalism in African Urban Areas," *Civilisations,* vol. 16, no. 3 (1966), pp. 354-360.

Richmond, Anthony H. *The Colour Problem,* rev. ed. Hammondsworth: Penguin Books, 1961.

Roberts, A. D. "The Sub-Imperialism of the Baganda," *Journal of African History,* vol. 3 (1962), pp. 435-450.

Rogers, Cyril. "Study of Race Attitudes in Nigeria," *Rhodes-Livingston Journal,* vol. 26 (1959), pp. 51-64.

_____, and C. Frantz. *Racial Themes in Southern Rhodesia: The Attitudes and Behavior of the White Population.* New Haven: Yale University Press, 1962.

Rothchild, Donald. "African Nationalism and Racial Minorities," *East Africa Journal,* vol. 2 (December 1965), pp. 14-22.

_____. "Kenya's Minorities and the African Crisis over Citizenship," *Race,* vol. 9, no. 4 (April 1968), pp. 421-438.

Sabikhi, Vanita. "The South African Scene," *Africa Quarterly,* (October-December 1966), pp. 206-217.

Sachs, A. *South Africa: The Violence of Apartheid.* 1969.

Scarritt, James R. *Political Change in a Traditional African Clan; A Structural-Functional Analysis of the Nsits of Nigeria.* The Social Science Foundation and Graduate School of International Studies Monograph Series in World Affairs. Denver: University of Denver, 1965.

Schmid, Peter. "Portugal's Last Stand in Mozambique," *Reporter,* vol. 30 (May 21, 1964), pp. 37-40.

Schwarz, Frederick A. O. *Nigeria: The Tribe, the Nation, or the Race—The Politics of Independence.* Cambridge: M.I.T. Press, 1965.

Segal, Aaron. *Massacre in Rwanda.* London: Fabian Research Service, April 1964.

Segal, Ronald, and Ruth First, eds. *Southwest Africa: A Travesty of Trust.* New York: André Deutsch, 1967.

"The Segregated Sudan: Arab Imperialism Invades Black Africa," *Atlas,* vol. 8 (October 1964), pp. 185-187.

Seibal, H. Dieter. "Some Aspects of Inter-Ethnic Relations in Nigeria," *Nigerian Journal of Economic and Social Studies,* vol. 9, no. 2 (July 1967), pp. 217-228.

Seligman, Charles G. *Races of Africa,* 3rd ed. London: Oxford University Press, 1967.

Senghor, L. S. "Negritude and the Germans," *Africa Report* (February 1967), pp. 46-48.

Shepherd, George W., Jr. "The Failure of Sanctions Against Rhodesia and the Effect on African States: A Growing Racial Crisis," *Africa Today,* vol. 15, no. 1 (February-March 1968), pp. 8-12.

_____. "National Integration and the Southern Sudan." *Journal of Modern African Studies,* vol. 4, no. 2 (1966), pp. 193-212.

Smock, Audrey Chapman, "N.C.N.C. and Ethnic Unions in Biafra," *Journal of Modern African Studies*, vol. 7, no. 1 (April 1969), pp. 21-34.

Smythe, H. H. and M. M. "The Non-African Minority in Modern Africa: Social Status," *Sociology and Social Research*, vol. 45 (April 1961), pp. 310-315.

Sofer, Cyril. "Some Aspects of Race Relations in an East African Township." London University: Ph.D. diss., 1953.

Sofer, Cyril. "Working Groups in a Plural Society," *Industrial and Labour Relations Review*, vol. 8 (1964), pp. 68-78.

Southall, Aidan W. "Race and Class in an African Town: Kampala, 1955," *Makerere Sociological Journal*, vol. 2, no. 1 (October 1963), pp. 24-33.

"Southern Sudan: Khartoum Reviews the Race War . . ." *Statist*, vol. 90, no. 4587 (February 1966), pp. 291-292.

Steel, R. W. "The Non-African Populations of British Central and East Africa," *The Advancement of Science*, vol. 19 (July 1962), pp. 113-210.

Stevens, Richard. "Lesotho and Botswana: Challenge to American Policy," *Africa Today*, vol. 14, no. 5 (October-November 1967), p. 4.

Tanner, R.E.S. "Conflict Within Small European Communities in Tanganyika," *Human Organization*, vol. 24 (Winter 1964), pp. 319-327.

_____. "European Leadership in Small Communities in Tanganyika Prior to Independence: A Study of Conflicting Social and Political Interracial Roles," *Race*, vol. 7 (January 1966), pp. 289-302.

Theroux, Paul. "Hating the Asians," *Transition*, vol. 7, no. 2, pp. 46-51.

Thurnwald, Hilde. *Black and White in East Africa. A Study in Social Contact and Adaptation.* London: G. Routledge & Sons, Ltd., 1935.

Troeller, Gordian, and Claude Deffarge. "Slaughter in Africa, Arab Against Black," *Atlas*, vol. 14 (October 1967), pp. 14-19.

Turk, Austin T. "The Futures of South Africa," *Social Forces*, vol. 45, no. 3 (March 1967), pp. 402-412.

United Nations, Dag Hammarskjold Library. *Apartheid—A Selective Bibliography on the Racial Policies of the Government of the Republic of South Africa.* New York: United Nations, 1968.

"The Unwanted Elite of East Africa," *Transaction* (July-August 1966), pp. 37-41.

Van den Berghe, Pierre L. "Language and Nationalism in South Africa," *Race*, vol. 9, no. 1 (July 1967), pp. 37-46.

_____. *Race and Racism: A Comparative Perspective.* New York: John Wiley, 1967.

_____. "Racialism and Assimilation in Africa and the Americas," *Southwestern Journal of Anthropology*, vol. 19, no. 4 (1963), pp. 424-431.

Varma, S. M. *Multi-Racial Society.* New Delhi: Indian Council for Africa, 1963.

Wallerstein, I. "Ethnicity and National Integration in West Africa," *Cahiers d'etudes africaines*, no. 3 (October 1960), pp. 129-139.

Ward, Barbara. "Research on Racial Relations: East Africa," *International Social Sciences Bulletin*, vol. 10 (1958), pp. 372-386.

West, Richard. *The White Tribes of Africa.* New York: Macmillan, 1965.

Willson, F.M.G. "Prospects for Southern Africa," *Current History,* vol. 50, no. 295 (March 1966), p. 165.

Zaidi, Juliet H. *The Asian Community in East Africa: Its Geographical Distribution and Economic and Social Characteristics.* University of Denver: M.A. thesis, 1968.

C. *Middle East*

"Arab Villages in Israel and the West Bank: A Comparison in Economic Growth," *Israel Economist,* vol. 24 (July 1968), pp. 255-262.

Chouraqui, André. *Between East and West; A History of the Jews of North Africa.* Philadelphia: Jewish Publication Society of America, 1968.

Cohen, Erik. "Mixed Marriage in an Israeli Town," *Jewish Journal of Sociology,* vol. 11 (Spring 1969), pp. 41-50.

Cohen, Percy. "Ethnic Group Differences in Israel," *Race,* vol. 9, no. 3 (January 1968), pp. 303-310.

Cottam, Richard W. *Nationalism in Iran.* Pittsburgh: University of Pittsburgh Press, 1964. (Deals with Kurd minority.)

Edmonds, C. J. "The Kurdish War in Iraq: The Constitutional Background," *World Today,* vol. 24 (December 1968), pp. 512-520.

Hourani, Albert H. *Minorities in the Arab World.* New York: Oxford University Press, 1947.

Iatrides, John O. "Cyprus: Anatomy of a Crisis," *Social Science,* vol. 42, no. 4 (October 1967), pp. 213-222.

Landau, Jacob M. *The Arabs in Israel, a Political Study.* London: Oxford University Press, 1969.

Lerner, Daniel. "The Middle East: Human Meaning of Modernization," *Foreign Policy Bulletin,* vol. 38, no. 12 (March 1, 1959), pp. 91-94.

Peretz, Don. "The New Arab Refugees," *Progressive,* vol. 31, no. 12 (December 1967), pp. 29-32.

Rosen, Lawrence. "A Moroccan Jewish Community During the Middle Eastern Crisis," *American Scholar,* vol. 37, no. 3 (Summer 1968), pp. 435-451.

Selzer, Michael. *The Aryanization of the Jewish State.* New York: David White Co., 1967.

Solente, C. "Attitudes israeliennes à l'egard du probleme de la minorité arabe," *Afrique et Asie,* vol. 52, no. 4 (1962), pp. 29-44.

D. *Europe*

Bagley, Christopher. "Migration, Race and Mental Health: A Review of Some Recent Research," *Race,* vol. 9, no. 3 (January 1968), pp. 343-356.

Bell, Robert R. "The Lower-Class Negro Family in the U.S. and Great Britain: Some Comparisons," *Race*, vol. 9, no. 2 (October 1969), pp. 173-181.

Boyle, Sir Edward. "Race Relations: The Limits of Voluntary Action," *Race*, vol. 9, no. 3 (January 1968), pp. 289-302.

Braithwaite, E. R. "The 'Colored Immigrant' in Britain," *Daedalus*, vol. 96, no. 2 (Spring 1967), pp. 496-511.

"Brummagem Tactics: The Party Racialists Have Had Too Long a Run in Exploiting Race as an Electoral Issue," *The Economist*, vol. 214, no. 6338 (February 13, 1965), pp. 638-639.

Buchan, Alastair. "Multicoloured Britain," *International Journal*, vol. 23, no. 4 (Autumn 1968), pp. 520-530.

Burney, Elizabeth. *Black in a White World*. London: *The Economist*, 1968.

Butterworth, Eric. "A Hardening Colour Bar?—The Schools," *New Society* March 16, 1967, p. 382.

Choo, Ng Kwee. *The Chinese in London*. London: Oxford University Press for the Institute of Race Relations, 1968.

Daniel, William Wentworth. *Racial Discrimination in England*. Harmondsworth: Penguin Books, 1968.

Deakin, N. D. "Racial Integration and Whitehall: A Plea for Reorganisation," *Political Quarterly*, vol. 739 (October-December 1968), pp. 415-426.

"Dealing with Hungary's Minorities," *East Europe*, vol. 18 (January 1969), pp. 31-32.

Dickey, Anthony F. "English Law and Incitement to Racial Hatred," *Race*, vol. 9, no. 3 (January 1968), pp. 311-330.

Ennals, David. "Labour's Race Relations Policy," *Venture*, vol. 20 (November 1968), p. 7.

"Federal Union of European Nationalities." Report on the Situation in the Autonomous Provinces of Kosovo and Metohija, March 1966, 10 pages.

Foot, Paul. *Immigration and Race in British Politics*. Baltimore: Penguin Books, 1965.

Great Britain. "Gypsies and Other Travellers: A Report of a Study Carried Out in 1965-66 by the Social Research Section of the Ministry of Housing and Local Government." London: British Information Service, 1967.

Grigg, Mary. *The White Question: A Personal View of Racialism in Britain and America*. London: Martin Secker and Warburg, 1967.

Hepple, Bob. "Ethnic Minorities at Work," *Race*, vol. 10, no. 1 (July 1968), pp. 17-30.

Hepple, Robert. *Race, Jobs and the Law in Britain*. London: 1968.

Hill, Clifford S. *West Indian Migrants and the London Churches*. New York: Oxford University Press, 1963.

Institute of Race Relations. *Colour and Citizenship. A Report on British Race Relations*. London: Oxford University Press, 1968.

Jupp, James. "Immigrant Involvement in British and Australian Politics," *Race*, vol. 10, no. 3 (January 1969), pp. 323-340.

Kosinski, Leszek A. "Changes in the Ethnic Structure in East-Central Europe, 1930-1960," Geographical Review, vol. 59 (July 1969), pp. 388-402.

Kozlov, V. I. "Changes in the Ethnic Composition of Rumania and Bulgaria," Soviet Sociology, vol. 3 (Fall 1964), pp. 26-38.

Lapping, A. "A Hardening Colour Bar?—The Faces," New Society, March 16, 1967, p. 378.

Little, Kenneth. "Some Aspects of Color, Class, and Culture in Britain," Daedalus, vol. 96, no. 2 (Spring 1967), pp. 512-526.

Longaker, Richard P. "The Race Relations Act of 1965: An Evaluation of the Incitement Provision," Race, vol. 11, no. 7 (October 1969), pp. 125-156.

Marsh, Peter. Anatomy of a Strike: Unions, Employers and Punjabi Workers in a Southall Factory. London: Institute of Race Relations, 1967.

Marshall, Roy. "The Law and Race Relations," Political Quarterly, vol. 39, no. 1 (January-March 1968), pp. 70-82.

Mazrui, Ali. The Anglo-African Commonwealth: Political Friction and Cultural Fusion. New York: Pergamon Press, 1967.

Moore, Robert. "Labour and Colour, 1965-68," Venture, vol. 20 (September 1968), pp. 24-29.

Nandy, Dipak. "Immigrants and the Election," Labour Monthly, vol. 46, no. 10 (October 1964), pp. 449-453.

Nash, Dennison. "The Fate of Americans in A Spanish Setting: A Study of Adaptation," Human Organization, vol. 26, no. 3 (Fall 1967), pp. 157-164.

"Not Quite So Easy for Enoch," The Economist, vol. 229 (November 23, 1968), p. 46. (Commenting on some of the provisions of Britain's Race Relations Act and on a bill providing for appeal against decisions of immigration authorities.)

Patterson, S. "A Hardening Colour Bar?—The Jobs," New Society March 16, 1967, p. 380.

Raynor, Lois. "Agency Adoptions of Non-White Children in the United Kingdom: A Quantitative Study," Race, vol. 10, no. 2 (October 1968), pp. 153-162.

Rose, Richard. "Race Problems: U. S. and U. K.," Venture, vol. 17, no. 3 (March 1965), pp. 15-18.

Ruong, Israel. The Lapps in Sweden. Stockholm: Swedish Institute for Cultural Relations with Foreign Countries.

Rusinow, Dennison I. "The Other Albanians: Some Notes on the Yugoslav Kosmet Today," Southeast Europe Series, vol. 12, no. 12 (November 1965).

Shneiderman, S. L. "Poland's Anti-Semitic Maoist Underground," The Reporter, vol. 36, no. 2 (January 26, 1967), pp. 21-23.

Sivanandan, A., and Shelia Bagley. Register of Research on Commonwealth Migrants in Britain. London: Research Publications for the Institute of Race Relations, 1969.

Smith, Stuart S. "The Revival of Anti-Semitism in Poland, " Midstream, vol. 14, no. 2 (February 1968), pp. 3-10.

Street, Harry, Geoffrey Howe, and Geoffrey Bindman. *Anti-Discrimination Legislation—The Street Report.* London: Political and Economic Planning, 1967.

Tajfel, Henri, and John L. Dawson. *Disappointed Quests: Essays by African, Asian and West Indian Students.* London: Oxford University Press, 1965.

Weinstock, S. Alexander. "Motivation and Social Structure in the Study of the Acculturation: A Hungarian Case," *Human Organization,* vol. 23, no. 1 (Spring 1964), pp. 50-52.

Williams, John A. "Black Man in Europe," *Holiday,* vol. 41, no. 1 (January 1967), p. 8.

Wright, Peter L. *The Coloured Worker in British Industry: With Special Reference to the Midlands and North of England.* London: Oxford University Press, 1968.

E. Soviet Union

Armstrong, John A. "The Domestic Roots of Soviet Foreign Policy," *International Affairs,* vol. 41 (January 1965), pp. 37-47.

Avtorkhanov, Abdurankhman. "Denationalization of Soviet Ethnic Minorities," *Studies on the Soviet Union* (n.s.), vol. 4, no. 1 (1964), pp. 74-99.

Bennigsen, Alexandre. "Colonization and Decolonization in the Soviet Union," *Journal of Contemporary History,* vol. 4 (January 1969), pp. 141-151. (The non-Russian people in Siberia and the Muslim territories of Central Asia, the Volga-Ural lands, the Caucasus, and the Crimea.)

Bialer, Seweryn. "How Russians Rule Russia," *Problems of Communism,* vol. 13, no. 5 (September-October 1964), pp. 45-52.

Boychuk, Stephen. "Mongolia and Sino-Soviet Competition," *Ukranian Quarterly,* vol. 23, no. 3 (Autumn 1967), pp. 264-272.

Conquest, Robert, ed. *Soviet Nationalities Policy in Practice.* New York: Frederick A. Praeger, 1967.

Djabaqui, Vassau-Ghiray. "Soviet Nationality Policy and Genocide," *Armenian Review,* vol. 20 (Winter 1967), pp. 45-56.

Doolin, Dennis J. *Territorial Claims in the Sino-Soviet Conflict: Documents and Analysis.* Stanford: Hoover Institute Studies No. 7, 1965.

Fedyshyn, Oleh. "Khrushchev's 'Leap Forward': National Assimilation in the USSR after Stalin," *Southwestern Social Science Quarterly,* vol. 48 (June 1967), pp. 34-43.

Goldhagen, Erick. *Ethnic Minorities in the Soviet Union.* New York: Frederick A. Praeger, 1968.

Lamont, Corliss. *The Peoples of the Soviet Union.* New York: Harcourt, Brace and Co., 1946.

Levin, M. G., and L. P. Potapov, eds. *The Peoples of Siberia.* Chicago: University of Chicago Press, 1964.

"Nationalities and Nationalism in the USSR," *Problems of Communism*, vol. 16, no. 2 (September-October 1967), p. 131.

Naulko, V. I. "The Present Ethnic Composition of the Population of the Ukrainian SSR," *Soviet Sociology*, vol. 3 (Summer 1964), pp. 12-23.

Rothenberg, Joshua. "How Many Jews Are There in the Soviet Union?" *Jewish Social Studies*, vol. 29, no. 4 (October 1967), pp. 234-240.

Shultz, Harold J. "Search for Utopia: The Exodus of Russian Mennonites to Canada, 1917-1927," *Journal of Church and State*, vol. 11, no. 3 (Autumn 1969), pp. 487-512.

Tsamerian, I. P., and S. L. Ronin. *Equality of Rights Between Races and Nationalism in the USSR*. Paris: UNESCO, 1962.

F. Asia

Abulkhanov, Rustem. "Birth of Nations: The Social Importance of Central Asia's Socialist Industrialization," in *Industrialisation and Race Relations*, ed. Guy Hunter. New York: Oxford University Press, 1965. Pages 161-176.

Berreman, Gerald D. "Caste and Community Development," *Human Organization*, vol. 22, no. 1 (Spring 1963), pp. 90-94.

Berreman, Gerald D. "Caste in India and in the United States," *American Journal of Sociology*, vol. 66, no. 2 (September 1960), pp. 120-127.

Boychuk, Stephen. "Mongolia and Sino-Soviet Competition," *Ukrainian Quarterly*, vol. 23, no. 3 (Autumn 1967), pp. 264-272.

Chandra, Sri. "Stereotypes of University Students Toward Different Ethnic Groups," *Journal of Social Psychology*, vol. 71 (February 1967), pp. 87-94.

DeKingston, Charles. "China: The Yellow Peril on the Wane," *Eastern World*, vol. 21 (September-October 1967), pp. 7-8.

De Vos, George, and Hiroshi Wagatsuma. *Japan's Invisible Race*. Berkeley: University of California Press, 1966.

Dey, Mukul K. "A Comparative Study of the Population Trends of the Races of Ceylon," *Population Review*, vol. 9 (January-July 1965), pp. 48-54.

Di Bona, Joseph. "Fair Communities and Foul Cities: The Ethnic Factor in Urban Community Development, the Indian Case," *Indian Journal of Social Work*, vol. 30 (April 1969), pp. 23-32.

Eglar, Zekiye. *A Punjabi Village in Pakistan*. New York: Columbia University Press, 1960.

Farmer, B. H. "The Social Basis of Nationalism in Ceylon," *Journal of Asian Studies*, vol. 24, no. 3 (May 1965), pp. 431-439.

Fitzgerald, C. P. "China in Asia," *Current History*, vol. 53, no. 307 (March 1967), pp. 129-134.

Fitzgerald, Stephen. "Erring Compatriots: The Overseas Chinese," *Far Eastern Economic Review*, vol. 59 (March 28, 1968), pp. 618-620.

Funnell, Victor C. "Social Stratifications," *Problems of Communism*, vol. 17, no. 2 (March-April 1968), pp. 14-20.

185

Gorme, K. K. "Ceylon's Dilemma," *United Asia,* vol. 20 (March-April 1968), pp. 77-86.

Irschick, Eugene F. *Politics and Social Conflict in South India: The Non-Brahman Movement and Tamil Separatism, 1916-1929.* Berkeley: University of California Press, 1969.

Kearney, Robert N. *Communalism and Language in the Politics of Ceylon.* Durham: Duke University Press, 1967.

Kolmas, Josef. "The Minority Nationalities in China," *Bulletin of the Atomic Scientists,* vol. 22, no. 6 (June 1966), pp. 71-74.

Krishna, K. B. *The Problem of Minorities in India.* London: George Allen, 1939.

Lew, Hilary. "People of the World," *Free China Review,* vol. 17, no. 5 (May 1967), pp. 33-38.

Mason, Philip, ed. *India and Ceylon: Unity and Diversity.* New York: Oxford University Press, 1967.

Mitchell, Richard H. *The Korean Minority in Japan.* Berkeley: University of California Press, 1967.

Moseley, George. "China's Fresh Approach to the National Minorities Question," *China Quarterly,* no. 24 (October-December 1965), pp. 15-27.

Newell, William H. "Some Problems of Integrating Minorities into Japanese Society," *Journal of Asian and African Studies,* vol. 2, nos. 3-4 (July-October 1967), pp. 212-229.

Nicholson, Norman K. "Political Aspects of Indian Food Policy," *Pacific Affairs,* vol. 41, no. 1 (Spring 1968), pp. 34-50.

Pauker, Guy J. *The Future Role of the United States in Asia and the Pacific.* Los Angeles: RAND Corporation, 1968.

Quigg, Philip. "Japan in Neutral," *Foreign Affairs,* vol. 44, no. 2 (January 1966), pp. 253-263.

Raj, Hilda. "Persistence of Caste in Southern India: An Analytic Study of the Hindu and Christian Nadars." American University: Ph.D. diss., 1958.

Roucek, Joseph S. "Racial Elements in the Sino-Russian Dispute," *Contemporary Review,* vol. 210, no. 1213 (February 1967), pp. 77-84.

Rowe, William L., ed. "Contours of Culture Change in South Asia," *Human Organization* (entire issue), vol. 22, no. 1 (Spring 1963).

Rowland, John. *A History of Sino-Indian Relations: Hostile Co-Existence.* Princeton: Van Nostrand, 1967.

Stockwin, Harvey. "Crisis in Malaysia," *Far Eastern Economic Review,* vol. 49, no. 4 (July 22, 1965), pp. 187-188, and "Malaysia Approaches," *Far Eastern Economic Review,* vol. 49, no. 6 (August 5, 1965), pp. 252-254.

Ter-Grigoryan, A. "Minority Nationalities in China," *New Times* (Moscow), October 9, 1968, pp. 14-15.

Van Der Kroef, Justin M. "Philippine Communism and the Chinese," *China Quarterly,* no. 30 (April-June 1967), pp. 115-148.

Wagner, Edward W. *Korean Minority in Japan: 1904-1950.* Honolulu: Institute of Pacific Relations, 1951.

Watso, Vincent C. *Communal Politics in India and the United States: A Comparative Analysis.* Atlanta: Georgia State College, 1965.

Weightman, George H. "The Philippine Chinese Image of the Filipino," *Pacific Affairs,* vol. 40, nos. 3, 4 (Fall, Winter 1967-68), pp. 315-323.

Wikeley, J. M. *Punjabi Musalamans.* Lahore: Pakistan National Publishers.

Willmott, William E. *The Chinese in Cambodia.* Vancouver: Publication Centre, University of British Columbia, 1967.

Wood, Arthur L. "Political Radicalism in Changing Sinhalese Villages," *Human Organization,* vol. 23, no. 2 (Summer 1964), pp. 199-207.

Wriggins, W. Howard. "Impediments to Unity in New Nations: The Case of Ceylon," in *Political Development and Social Change,* ed. Jason L. Finkle and Richard W. Gable. New York: John Wiley, 1966. Pages 563-572.

Yarwood, A. I. "The Overseas Indians: A Problem in Indian and Imperial Politics at the End of World War I," *Australian Journal of Politics and History,* vol. 14, no. 2 (August 1968), pp. 204-218.

G. Southeast Asia

Benda, Harry J. "Political Elites in Colonial Southeast Asia: An Historical Analysis," *Comparative Studies in Society and History,* vol. 7, no. 3 (April 1965), pp. 233-251.

Connor, Walker. "Ethnology and the Peace of South Asia," *World Politics,* vol. 22, no. 1 (October 1969), pp. 51-86.

Cowgill, Donald O. "Social Distance in Thailand," *Sociology and Social Research,* vol. 52 (July 1968), pp. 363-376. (Deals with attitudes of students toward 28 national and religious categories.)

Davies, Derek. "Malaysian Economy: The Racial Balance Sheet," *Far Eastern Economic Review,* vol. 65 (July 10, 1969), pp. 119-123.

Davies, Derek. "Racial Tension in Malaysia," *Far Eastern Economic Review,* vol. 64 (June 26, 1969), p. 700.

Edmonds, Juliet. "Religion, Intermarriage and Assimilation: The Chinese in Malaya," *Race,* vol. 10, no. 1 (July 1968), pp. 57-68.

Embree, John F., and Lillian O. Dotson. *Bibliography of the People and Cultures of Mainland Southeast Asia.* New Haven: Yale University Press, 1950.

Fraser, Thomas. *Rusembilan: A Maylay Fishing Village in Southern Thailand.* Ithaca: Cornell University Press, 1960.

Heiss, Jerold. "Factors Related to Immigrant Assimilation: The Early Post-Migration Situation," *Human Organization,* vol. 26, no. 4 (Winter 1967), pp. 265-272.

Hunter, Guy. *Southeast Asia—Race, Culture and Nation.* New York: Oxford University Press, 1966.

Kelly, R. A. "The Politics of Racial Equality," *New Zealand Journal of Public Administration,* vol. 24, no. 2 (March 1962), pp. 23-36.

Kunstadter, Peter, ed. *Southeast Asian Tribes, Minorities, and Nations.* Princeton: Princeton University Press, 1967.

LeBar, Frank M., Gerald C. Hickey, and John K. Musgrave, eds. *Ethnic Groups of Mainland Southeast Asia.* New Haven: Human Relations Area Files Press, 1964.

Mangrai, Sao Saimong. *The Shan States and the British Annexation,* Southeast Asia Program Data, Paper No. 57. Ithaca: Cornell University Department of Asian Studies, n.d.

McGee, T. G. "Down—But Not Out," *Far Eastern Economic Review,* vol. 64 (June 5, 1969), pp. 566-568. (Deals with ethnic-group relations in Malaysia and recent parliamentary elections.)

Milne, R. S., and K. J. Ratman. "Patterns and Peculiarities of Ethnic Voting in Sabah, 1967," *Asian Survey,* vol. 9, no. 5 (May 1969), pp. 373-381. (Deals with Malaysia.)

Mitchell, Edward J. "Some Econometrics of the Huk Rebellion," *American Political Science Review,* vol. 63, no. 4 (December 1969), pp. 1159-1172.

Moerman, Michael. "Ethnic Identification in Complex Civilization: Who are the Lue?" *American Anthropologist,* vol. 67, no. 5, pt. 1 (October 1965), pp. 1215-1230.

Peck, Cornelius J. "Nationalism, Race, and Developments in the Philippine Law of Citizenship," *Journal of Asian and African Studies,* vol. 2, nos. 1, 2 (January, April 1967), pp. 125-146.

Pilling, Arnold R. "An Australian Aboriginal Minority: The Tiwi See Themselves as a Dominant Majority," *Phylon,* vol. 26, no. 4 (Winter 1965), pp. 305-314.

Poole, Peter A. "Thailand's Vietnamese Minority," *Asian Survey,* vol. 7, no. 12 (December 1967), pp. 886-895.

Purcell, Victor W.W.S. *The Chinese in Southeast Asia.* London: Oxford University Press, 1965.

Rabushka, Alvin. "Integration in a Multi-Racial Institution: Ethnic Attitudes among Chinese and Malay Students at the University of Malaya," *Race,* vol. 11, no. 1 (July 1969), pp. 53-63.

"The Race Trouble in Malaysia," *Statist,* vol. 187, no. 4553 (June 11, 1965), pp. 1603-1604.

Sandhu, Kernial Singh. "A Note on the Migration Policies of India and Malaya," *International Studies,* vol. 9, no. 1 (July 1967), pp. 65-86.

Skinner, William, ed. *Local Ethnic and National Loyalties in Village Indonesia.* New Haven: Yale University Cultural Report Series, 1959.

Taft, R. "Ethnic Stereotypes, Attitudes, and Familiarity: Australia," *Journal of Social Psychology,* vol. 49 (1959), pp. 177-186.

Thompson, Virginia McLean, and Richard Adloff. *Minority Problems in Southeast Asia.* Stanford: Stanford University Press, 1955.

Western, J. S. "The Australian Aboriginal: What White Australians Know and Think About Him—A Preliminary Survey," *Race,* vol. 10, no. 4 (April 1969), pp. 411-434.

Willmott, D. E. *The Chinese of Semarang: A Changing Minority Community in Indonesia.* Ithaca: Cornell University Press, 1960.

Wilson, John. "Interaction Analysis: A Supplementary Fieldwork Technique Used in the Study of Leadership in a 'New-Style' Australian Aboriginal Community," *Human Organization,* vol. 21, no. 4 (Winter 1962-63), pp. 290-294.

H. Latin America

Avila, Fernando Bastos. *Immigration in Latin America.* Washington, D.C.: Pan American Union, 1964.

Bahadoorsingh, Krishna. *Trinidad Electoral Politics: The Persistence of the Race Factor.* London: Institute of Race Relations, 1968.

Bastide, Roger. "Race Relations in Brazil," *International Social Science Bulletin,* vol. 9, no. 4 (1957), pp. 495-512.

Beals, Ralph L. "Social Stratification in Latin America," in *Contemporary Cultures and Societies of Latin America,* ed. Dwight B. Heath and Richard N. Adams. New York: Random House, 1965. Pages 342-360.

Biesanz, John. "Cultural and Economic Factors in Panamanian Race Relations," in *Readings in Latin American Social Organizations and Institutions,* ed. Olen E. Leonard and Charles P. Loomis. East Lansing: Michigan State College Press, 1953.

Borah, Woodrow. "Race and Class in Mexico," *Pacific Historical Review,* vol. 23, no. 4 (November 1954), pp. 331-342.

Bray, Donald W. "The Political Emergence of Arab-Chileans, 1952-1958," *Journal of Inter-American Studies,* vol. 4, no. 4 (October 1962), pp. 557-562.

Clissold, Stephen. "The Indian Problem in Latin America: Changing Attitudes in the Andean Republics," *Race,* vol. 7, no. 1 (July 1965), pp. 47-58.

Cobo, Juan. "Genocide on the Amazon," *New Times* (Moscow), no. 16 (April 24, 1968), pp. 21-22.

Comas, Juan. "Latin America," *International Social Science Journal* (issue entitled "Recent Research on Racial Relations"), vol. 13, no. 2 (1961), pp. 271-299.

Coulthard, G. R. "The French West Indian Background of Negritude," *Caribbean Quarterly,* vol. 7, no. 3 (December 1961), pp. 128-136.

Coulthard, G. R. *Race and Colour in Caribbean Literature.* New York: Oxford University Press, 1962.

Cumberland, Charles C. "The Sonora Chinese and the Mexican Revolution," *Hispanic American Historical Review,* vol. 40, no. 2 (May 1960), pp. 191-211.

De Azevedo, Thales. "Race and Class," in *Social Change in Brazil.* University of Florida School of Inter-American Studies Latin American Monograph Series, No. 22, December 1962. Gainesville: University of Florida Press, 1963.

Dodge, Peter. "Comparative Racial Systems in the Greater Caribbean," *Social and Economic Studies,* vol. 16 (September 1967), pp. 249-261.

"The Extermination of Indians in Brazil," *Bulletin of the International Commission of Jurists,* September 1968, pp. 18-24.

Ferguson, J. H. *Latin America: The Balance of Race Redressed.* New York: Oxford University Press, 1961.

Fernandes, Florestan. *The Negro in Brazilian Society,* ed. Phyllis B. Eveleth, trans. Jacqueline D. Skiles, A. Brund, and Arthur Rothwell. New York: Columbia University Press, 1969.

Fernandes, Florestan. "The Weight of the Past," *Daedalus,* vol. 96, no. 2 (Spring 1967), pp. 560-579.

Fretz, Joseph Winfield. *Immigrant Group Settlements in Paraguay.* North Newton, Kansas: Bethel College Press, 1962.

Freyre, Gilberto. "Ethnic Democracy: the Brazilian Example," *Americas,* vol. 15 (December 1963), pp. 1-6.

Freyre, Gilberto. *The Masters and the Slaves.* New York: Alfred A. Knopf, 1946.

Furer-Haimendorf, Christof von. "Mexico's Racial Mixture," *New Society,* vol. 1 (October 1964).

Garibay, Angel Maria. "The Mexican Indian," *The Month,* vol. 33 (February 1965).

Germani, Gino. "The Transition to a Mass Democracy in Argentina," in *Contemporary Cultures and Societies of Latin America,* ed. Dwight B. Heath and Richard N. Adams. New York: Random House, 1965. Pages 454-472.

Gillin, John. "Race Relations Without Conflict: A Guatemalan Town," *American Journal of Sociology,* vol. 53, no. 5 (March 1948), pp. 337-343.

Gordon, M. W. "Race Patterns and Prejudice in Puerto Rico, " *American Sociological Review,* vol. 14 (April 1949), pp. 294-301.

Halperin, Ernst. "Racism and Communism in British Guiana," *Journal of Inter-American Studies,* vol. 7 (January 1965), pp. 95-134.

Harris, Marvin. *Patterns of Race in the Americas.* New York: Walker and Co., 1964.

Heath, Dwight B., and Richard N. Adams, eds. *Contemporary Cultures and Societies of Latin America.* New York: Random House, 1965.

Hoetink, Harry. *Two Variants in Caribbean Race Relations: A Contribution to the Sociology of Segmented Societies.* New York: Oxford University Press, 1967.

Hopkins, Jack W. "Socio-Backgrounds of Peruvian Government Executives," *International Review of Administrative Sciences,* vol. 33, no. 3 (1967), p. 231.

Hopper, Janice H. *Indians of Brazil in the Twentieth Century.* Washington, D.C.: Institute for Cross-Cultural Research, 1967.

Irie, Toraji. "The History of Japanese Migration to Peru," *Hispanic American Historical Review,* vol. 31, pt. 1, no. 3 (August 1951), pp. 437-452, and pt. 2, no. 4 (November 1951), pp. 648-664.

Iutaka, Sugiyama. "Social Mobility and Differential Occupational Opportunities in Brazil," *Human Organization,* vol. 26, no. 2 (Summer 1966), pp. 126-130.

Kubler, George. *The Indian Caste of Peru, 1795-1940.* Washington, D.C., 1952.

Lambert, Jacques. *Latin America: Social Structure and Political Institutions,* trans. Helen Katel. Berkeley: University of California Press, 1967.

"Latin American Integration, the Guerrilla Movements and Human Rights," *International Commission of Jurists Bulletin,* vol. 2 (December 1967), pp. 34-42.

Lowenthal, David. "Race and Color in the West Indies," *Daedalus,* vol. 96, no. 2 (Spring 1967), pp. 580-626.

Maier, Joseph. "The Problem of Color in Foreign Relations," in *Politics of Change in Latin America,* ed. Joseph Maier and Richard W. Weatherhead. New York: Frederick A. Praeger, 1964. Pages 207-216.

Manchester, Alan K. "Racial Democracy in Brazil," *South Atlantic Quarterly,* vol. 64, no. 1 (Winter 1965), pp. 27-35.

Mazzarelli, Marcella. "Intercommunity Relations in British Honduras," *Human Organization,* vol. 26, no. 4 (Winter 1967), pp. 222-229.

Mendieta y Nunez, Lucio. "Racial and Cultural Tension in Latin America," *International Social Science Bulletin,* vol. 4, no. 3 (1952), pp. 442-451.

Metall, R. A., and M. Paranhos da Silva. "Equality of Opportunity in a Multi-Racial Society: Brazil," *International Labour Review,* vol. 43 (May 1966), pp. 477-508.

Metraux, F. "Lights and Shadows in the Racial Landscape of Latin America," *UNESCO Courier* (October 1960), pp. 21-23.

Mitchell, Sir Harold P. *Contemporary Politics and Economics in the Caribbean.* Athens: Ohio University Press, 1968.

Mörner, Magnus. "The History of Race Relations in Latin America: Some Comments on the State of Research," *Latin American Research Review,* vol. 1, no. 3 (Summer 1966), pp. 17-44.

_____. "Race and Class In Twentieth Century Latin America," *Cahiers d'histoire mondiale,* vol. 8, no. 2 (Spring 1964), pp. 298-304.

_____. *Race Mixture in the History of Latin America.* Boston: Little, Brown and Co., 1967.

Morse, Richard. "Negro-White Relations in Latin America," *Reports and Speeches of the Ninth Yale Conference on the Teaching of Social Sciences.* New Haven, 1964. Multigraph.

Newman, Peter Kenneth. *British Guiana: Problems of Cohesion in an Integrated Society.* London: Oxford University Press, 1964.

Niehoff, Arthur and Juanita. *East Indians in the West Indies.* Milwaukee: Public Museum, Publication No. 61, 1960.

Normano, Joao F., and Antonello Gerbi. *The Japanese in South America: An Introductory Survey, with Special Reference to Peru.* New York: John Day, 1943.

Pearse, Andrew. "The Indians of the Andes," in *Latin America and the Caribbean, A Handbook.* New York and Washington, D.C.: Frederick A. Praeger, 1968. Pages 690-703.

Pierson, Donald. *Negroes in Brazil.* Chicago: University of Chicago Press, 1942.

Pike, Fredrick B. "Aspects of Class Relations in Chile, 1958-1960," *Hispanic American Historical Review,* vol. 43, no. 1 (February 1963), pp. 14-33.

Pitt-Rivers, Julian. "Mestizo or Ladino?" *Race,* vol. 10, no. 4 (April 1969), pp. 463-477.

_____. "Race, Color, and Class in Central America and the Andes," *Daedalus,* vol. 96, no. 2 (Spring 1967), pp. 542-559.

_____. "Who Are the Indians?" *Encounter,* vol. 25, no. 3 (September 1965), pp. 41-49.

Reed, Nelson. *The Caste War of Yucatan.* Stanford: Stanford University Press, 1964.

Roberts, Robert E. "A Comparison of Ethnic Relations in Two Guatemalan Communities," *Acta America,* vol. 6, no. 3-4 (1948), pp. 139-151.

Rothman, Stanley, and Frank Jay Moreno. "Chileans and Americans: Some Observations," *South Atlantic Quarterly,* vol. 63, no. 3 (Summer 1964), pp. 261-266.

Russell-Wood, A.J.R. "Class, Creed, and Colour in Colonial Bahia: A Study in Prejudice," *Race,* vol. 9, no. 2 (October 1967), pp. 133-158.

_____. "Race and Class in Brazil, 1937-1967, a Reassessment: A Review," *Race,* vol. 10, no. 2 (October 1968), pp. 185-191.

Salz, Beate. "Indianismo," *Social Research,* vol. 2, no. 4 (November 1944), pp. 441-469.

Sayers, Raymond. *The Negro in Brazilian Literature.* New York: Hispanic Institute in the U.S., 1956.

Smith, Thomas L. "The Racial Composition of the Population of Columbia," *Journal of Inter-American Studies,* vol. 8, no. 2 (April 1966), pp. 213-235.

Speckman, J. D. "The Indian Group in the Segmented Society of Surinam," *Caribbean Studies,* vol. 3, no. 1 (April 1962), pp. 3-18.

Stewart, Watt. *Chinese Bondage in Peru: A History of the Chinese Coolie in Peru, 1849-1874.* Durham: Duke University Press, 1951.

Stokes, William S. "Social Classes in Latin America," in *Government and Politics in Latin America,* ed. P. C. Snow. New York: Holt, Rinehart and Winston, 1967. Pages 51-70.

Tannenbaum, Frank. *Slave and Citizen: The Negro in the Americas.* New York: Alfred A. Knopf, 1947.

_____. *Ten Keys to Latin America.* New York: Random House, 1966.

Thompson, Era Bell. "Surinam: Multi-Racial Paradise at the Crossroads," *Ebony,* vol. 22, no. 4 (February 1967), pp. 112-116.

Wagley, Charles. "On the Concept of Social Race in the Americas," in *Contemporary Cultures and Societies of Latin America,* ed. Dwight B. Heath and Richard N. Adams. New York: Random House, 1965. Pages 531-544.

Wagley, Charles, ed. *Race and Class in Rural Brazil.* New York: UNESCO, 1952.

Wagley, Charles and Marvin Harris. *Minorities in the New World: Six Case Studies.* New York: Columbia University Press, 1958.

Willems, Emilio. "Racial Attitudes in Brazil," *American Journal of Sociology,* vol. 54 (March 1949), pp. 402-408.

Williams, Eric. "The Contemporary Pattern of Race Relations in the Caribbean," *Phylon,* vol. 16, no. 4 (1955), pp. 367-379.

Zelinsky, Wilbur. "The Historical Geography of the Negro Population of Latin America," *Journal of Negro History,* vol. 34 (April 1949), pp. 153-221.

I. Canada

Bourassa, Guy. "Canada 1967: In Search of a New Equilibrium," *African Forum,* vol. 3, no. 1 (Summer 1967), pp. 59-77.

Drew, Benjamin. *A North-Side View of Slavery. The Refugee; or, The Narratives of Fugitive Slaves in Canada Related by Themselves with an Account of the History and Condition of the Colored Population of Upper Canada.* New York: Negro University Press, 1968.

Lubka, Nancy. "Ferment in Nova Scotia," *Queen's Quarterly,* vol. 76 (Summer 1969), pp. 213-228. (Deals with race relations in Nova Scotia.)

III. American Ethnic Studies

A. General

Adamic, Louis. *A Nation of Nations.* New York: Harper and Brothers, 1945.

Aho, William R. "Ethnic Mobility in Northeastern United States: An Analysis of Census Data," *Sociological Quarterly,* vol. 10, no. 4 (Fall 1969), pp. 512-526.

Banton, Michael. *Race Relations.* New York: Basic Books, 1967.

Berry, Brewton. *Race and Ethnic Relations.* Boston: Houghton Mifflin, 1965.

Boskin, J. *Urban Racial Violence in the Twentieth Century.* Glencoe: Macmillan, 1969.

Brown, Francis J., and Joseph S. Roucek, eds. *One America: The History, Contributions, and Present Problems of our Racial and National Minorities,* rev. ed. New York: Prentice-Hall, 1945.

Carter, Mark Benham. "Measures Against Discrimination: The North American Scene," *Race,* vol. 9, no. 1 (July 1967), pp. 1-26.

Clemence, Theodore G. "Residential Segregation in the Mid-Sixties," *Demography,* vol. 4, no. 2 (1967), pp. 562-568.

Curry, Jesse E. *Race Tensions and the Police.* Springfield, Ill.: Charles C. Thomas, 1962.

Fairchild, Henry Pratt. *Race and Nationality as Factors in American Life.* New York: Ronald Press, 1947.

Fairlie, Henry. "Angry Blacks, Guilty Whites, Threatened Jews," *Interplay,* vol. 3, no. 1 (June-July 1969), pp. 25-28.

Fendrich, J. M. "Perceived Reference Group Support: Racial Attitudes and Overt Behavior," *American Sociological Review,* December 1967, p. 960.

Gittler, Joseph B. *Understanding Minority Groups.* New York: John Wiley, 1956.

Glock, Charles Y., and Ellen Siegelman, eds. *Prejudice U.S.A.* New York: Frederick A. Praeger, 1969.

Gordon, Milton M. *Assimilation in American Life.* New York: Oxford University Press, 1964.

_____. "Recent Trends in the Study of Minority and Race Relations," *The Annals,* vol. 350 (November 1963), pp. 148-156.

Grigg, Mary. *The White Question: A Personal View of Racialism in Britain and America.* London: Martin Secker and Warburg, 1967.

Handlin, Oscar, ed. *Children of the Uprooted.* New York: George Braziller, 1966.

Handlin, Oscar. *The Uprooted: The Epic Story of the Great Migrations That Made the American People.* Boston: Little, Brown and Co., 1951.

Hansen, Marcus Lee. *The Immigrant in American History.* New York: Harper and Row, 1964.

Harris, Marvin. "Race Relations Research Aspices and Results in the United States," *Social Science Information,* vol. 1, no. 1 (April 1962), pp. 28-51.

Himes, Joseph S. "The Functions of Racial Conflict," *Social Forces,* vol. 45 (September 1966), pp. 1-10.

Hutchinson, E. P. *Immigrants and Their Children.* New York: John Wiley, 1956.

Lieberson, Stanley, and A. R. Silverman. "The Precipitants and Underlying Conditions of Race Riots," *American Sociological Review,* vol. 30 (December 1965), pp. 887-898.

Mason, Philip. "The Revolt Against Western Values," *Daedalus,* vol. 96, no. 2 (Spring 1967), pp. 328-352.

McKenna, Marian C. "The Melting Pot: Comparative Observations in the United States and Canada," *Sociology and Social Research,* vol. 53 (July 1969), pp. 433-447.

Messner, Stephen D., ed. *Minority Groups and Housing: A Selected Bibliography, 1950-1967.* Storrs: University of Connecticut, Center for Real Estate and Urban Economic Studies, 1968.

Miller, Roger R., ed. *Race, Research and Reason: Social Work Perspectives.* New York: National Association of Social Workers, 1969.

Molotch, Harvey. "Racial Integration in a Transition Community," *American Sociological Review,* vol. 34, no. 6 (December 1969), pp. 878-893.

Palisi, B. J. "Ethnic Patterns of Friendship," *Phylon,* vol. 27, no. 3 (Fall 1966), pp. 217-225.

Robertson, L. S., et al. "Race, Status and Medical Care," *Phylon,* vol. 28, no. 4 (Winter 1967), pp. 353-360.

Rose, Arnold M. *Minority Problems: A Textbook of Readings in Intergroup Relations.* New York: Harper and Row, 1965.

Rose, Peter I. *They and We: Racial and Ethnic Relations in the United States.* New York: Random House, 1964.

Rose, Richard. "Race Problems: U.S. and U.K.," *Venture,* vol. 17, no. 3 (March 1965), pp. 15-18.

Schermerhorn, Richard A. *These Our People: Minorities in American Culture.* Boston: D. C. Heath, 1949.

Schrieke, M. *Alien Americans: A Study of Race Relations.* New York: Viking Press, 1936.

Segal, Bernard E., ed. *Racial and Ethnic Relations.* New York: Thomas Crowell, 1966.

Simpson, George Eaton, and J. Milton Yinger. *Racial and Cultural Minorities: An Analysis of Prejudice and Discrimination,* 3rd ed. New York: Harper and Brothers, 1965.

Singer, J. David. "Soviet and American Foreign Policy Attitudes: Content Analysis of Elite Articulations," *Journal of Conflict Resolution,* vol. 8, no. 4 (December 1964), pp. 424-485.

Smith, Timothy L. "New Approaches to the History of Immigration in 20th Century America," *American Historical Review,* vol. 71, no. 4 (July 1966), p. 1237.

"Steam for the Melting Pot," *Fortune,* vol. 26, no. 9 (September 1942), p. 75.

"Studies in Race and Culture," *Phylon,* vol. 26, no. 4 (Winter 1965), pp. 401-407.

Suttles, Gerald D. *The Social Order of the Slum; Ethnicity and Territory in the Inner City.* Chicago: University of Chicago Press, 1968.

United States, Social Security Administration. *Not Just Some of Us: A Limited Bibliography on Minority Group Relations.* Prepared by the Special Staff for Employee Management Relations and Equal Employment Opportunity, Office of Administration. Baltimore, 1968.

Van der Zanden, James W. *American Minority Relations: The Sociology of Race and Ethnic Groups.* New York: Ronald Press, 1963.

Wiley, Norbert F. "The Ethnic Mobility Trap and Stratification Theory," *Social Problems,* vol. 15, no. 2 (Fall 1967), pp. 147-159.

Wills, Garry. *The Second Civil War: Arming for Armageddon.* New York: New American Library, 1968.

Yinger, John Milton. *A Minority Group in American Society.* New York: McGraw-Hill, 1965.

_____. "Recent Developments in Minority and Race Relations," *The Annals,* vol. 378 (July 1968), pp. 130-145.

B. *Black Americans*

Adams, Russell L. *Great Negroes Past and Present.* Chicago: Afro-American Publishing Co., 1964.

Adler, Franklin Hugh. "Black Power," *Socialist Register,* 1968, pp. 87-109.

Allen, Irving L. "Selecting an Economic Probability Sample of Negro House-holds in a City," *Journal of Negro Education,* vol. 38 (Winter 1969), pp. 4-13.

Allen, James Egert. *The Negro in New York: A Historical-Biographical Evaluation from 1626.* New York: Exposition Press, 1964.

Aptheker, Herbert, ed. *A Documentary History of the Negro People in the United States.* Vol. 2: *From the Reconstruction Era to 1910.* New York: Citadel Press, 1964.

_____. *Essays in the History of the American Negro.* New York: International Publishers, 1945.

_____. *To Be Free: Studies in American Negro History.* New York: International Publishers, 1948.

Bennett, Lerone, Jr. *Confrontation: Black and White.* Baltimore: Penguin Books, 1965.

Berremen, Gerald D. "Caste in India and in the United States," *American Journal of Sociology,* vol. 66, no. 2 (September 1960), pp. 120-127.

Billingsley, Andrew. *Black Families in White America.* Englewood Cliffs, N.J.: Prentice-Hall, 1968.

Blauner, Robert. "Internal Colonialism and Ghetto Revolt," *Social Problems,* vol. 16 (Spring 1969), pp. 393-408. (Explores the thesis that white-black relations in America are essentially those of colonizer and colonized.)

Blaustein, Albert P., and Robert L. Zangrando, eds. *Civil Rights and the American Negro; A Documentary History.* New York: Trident Press, 1968.

Bloch, Herman D. *The Circle of Discrimination: An Economic and Social Study of the Black Man in New York.* New York: New York University Press, 1969.

Booker, Simeon. *Black Man's America.* Englewood Cliffs, N.J.: Prentice-Hall, 1964.

Bowles, Chester. *Africa's Challenge to the United States.* Berkeley: University of California Press, 1956.

Brink, William, and Louis Harris. *Black and White: A Study of U.S. Racial Attitudes Today.* New York: Simon and Schuster, 1967.

_____. *The Negro Revolution in America.* New York: Simon and Schuster, 1964.

Carothers, Leslie A. *The Public Accommodations Law of 1964: Arguments, Issues and Attitudes in a Legal Debate.* Northampton, Mass., Smith College Library, 1968.

Carter, Mark Benham. "Measures Against Discrimination: The North American Scene," *Race,* vol. 9, no. 1 (July 1967), pp. 1-26.

Chick, C. A., Sr. "The American Negroes' Changing Attitude Toward Africa," *Journal of Negro Education,* vol. 31, no. 4 (Fall 1962), pp. 531-535.

Clark, Kenneth. *Dark Ghetto.* New York: Harper and Row, 1965.

Clark, E. John Henrik, ed. *Harlem, a Community in Transition.* New York: Citadel Press, 1964.

_____, and Robert S. Browne. "The American Negro's Impact," *Africa Today,* vol. 14, no. 1 (December-January 1966-67), pp. 16-18.

Collins, Herbert. "The Sociology of Emancipation," *Phylon,* vol. 26, no. 2 (Summer 1965), pp. 148-161.

Daniel, Johnnie. "Negro Political Behavior and Community Political and Socioeconomic Structural Forces," *Social Forces,* vol. 47, no. 3 (March 1969), pp. 274-288.

Davis, John A. "The American Negro and Africa," *Jewish Frontier,* vol. 31 (March 1964), pp. 11-15.

Delany, Martin Robison. *The Condition, Elevation, Emigration, and Destiny of the Colored People of the United States.* New York: Arno Press, 1968 (first printed in 1852).

Drake, St. Clair. *The American Dream and the Negro: One Hundred Years of Freedom?* Chicago: Roosevelt University Division of Continuing Education and Extension, 1963.

Drake, St. Clair. "The American Negro's Relation to Africa," *Africa Today,* vol. 14, no. 6 (December-January 1967-68), pp. 12-14.

Durham, Philip, and Everett L. Jones. *The Negro Cowboys.* New York: Dodd, Mead, 1965.

Edmondson, Locksley. "Black Power: A View from the Outside," *Africa Today,* vol. 14, no. 6 (December-January 1967-68), pp. 6-9.

_____, and Martin Kilson. "The American Dilemma in a Changing World: The Rise of Africa and the Negro American," *Daedalus,* vol. 94, no. 4 (Fall 1965), pp. 1055-1084.

Essien-Udom, E. U. *Black Nationalism: A Search for an Identity in America.* New York: Dell Publishing Co., 1964.

Farmer, James. *Freedom—When?* New York: Random House, 1966.

Frazier, E. Franklin. *The Negro Church in America.* New York: Schocken Books, 1963.

Garvey, A. Jacques. *Garvey and Garveyism.* Jamaica: A. Jacques Garvey, 1963.

Glenn, Norval D. "The Role of White Resistance and Facilitation in the Negro Struggle for Equality," *Phylon,* vol. 26, no. 2 (Summer 1965), pp. 105-116.

Grossack, Martin M., ed. *Mental Health and Segregation.* New York: Springer Publishing Co., 1963.

Handlin, Oscar. *The Newcomers: Negroes and Puerto Ricans in a Changing Metropolis.* Cambridge: Harvard University Press, 1959.

Hannerz, Ulf. "The Rhetoric of Soul: Identification in Negro Society," *Race,* vol. 9, no. 4 (April 1968), pp. 453-468.

Hansen, Asael T. "Teaching about Caste in Intra-Caste and in Cross-Caste Situations, United States," *Human Organization,* vol. 19, no. 2 (Summer 1960), pp. 77-81.

Hart, Richard. "The Life and Resurrection of Marcus Garvey," *Race,* vol. 9, no. 2 (October 1967), pp. 217-238.

Heer, David, "Intermarriage and Racial Amalgamation in the United States," *Eugenics Quarterly,* vol. 14 (June 1967), pp. 112-120.

197

Hernton, Calvin C. *Sex and Racism in America.* New York: Doubleday, 1965.

Hill, Roy L. *Rhetoric of Racial Revolt.* Denver: Golden Bell Press, 1964.

Hofstetter, C. Richard. "Political Disengagement and the Death of Martin Luther King," *Public Opinion Quarterly,* vol. 33 (Summer 1969), pp. 160-173.

Holzner, L., et al. "The Negro in the American City: A Review," *South Africa Geographical Journal,* vol. 50 (1968), pp. 73-88.

Hough, Joseph C., Jr. *Black Power and White Protestants: A Christian Response to the New Negro Pluralism.* Oxford University Press, 1968.

Howe, Russell Warren. "Brown Britain and Black America," *Statist,* vol. 187, no. 4548 (May 7, 1965), pp. 1250-1252.

Isaacs, Harold R. *The New World of Negro Americans.* New York: John Day, 1963.

Jeanpierre, W. A. "African Negritude—Black American Soul," *Africa Today,* vol. 14, no. 6 (December-January 1967-68), pp. 10-11.

Jones, Ira G. "Trollope, Carlyle, and Mill on the Negro: An Episode in the History of Ideas," *Journal of Negro History,* vol. 7, no. 3 (July 1967), pp. 185-199.

Killian, Lewis M. *The Impossible Revolution? Black Power and the American Dream.* New York: Random House, 1968.

Lee, Ulysses. "The Draft and the Negro," *Current History,* vol. 55, no. 323 (July 1968), pp. 28-33.

Leggett, John C. "Working Class Consciousness, Race and Political Choice," *American Journal of Sociology,* vol. 69, no. 2 (September 1963), pp. 171-176.

LeMelle, Tilden. "The Ideology of Blackness African-American Style," *Africa Today,* vol. 14, no. 6 (December-January 1967-68), pp. 2-4.

Lincoln, C. Eric. "Color and Group Identity in the United States," *Daedalus,* vol. 96, no. 2 (Spring 1967), pp. 527-541.

Lincoln, C. Eric. *My Face Is Black.* Boston: Beacon Press, 1964.

Marshall, Ray. *The Negro and Organized Labor.* New York: John Wiley, 1965.

Martin, James G. "Racial Ethnocentrism and Judgment of Beauty," *Journal of Social Psychology,* vol. 63 (February 1964), pp. 59-64.

Marx, Gary T. *Protest and Prejudice: A Study of Belief in the Black Community.* New York: Harper and Row, 1967.

McPherson, James M. *The Negro's Civil War.* New York: Pantheon Books, 1965.

_____. *The Struggle for Equality: Abolitionists and the Negro in the Civil War and Reconstruction.* Princeton: Princeton University Press, 1964.

Meier, August. *Negro Thought in America, 1880-1915: Racial Ideologies in the Age of Booker T. Washington.* Ann Arbor: University of Michigan Press, 1963.

Meyer, Philip. "Aftermath of Martyrdom: Negro Militancy and Martin Luther King," *Public Opinion Quarterly,* vol. 33 (Summer 1969), pp. 160-173.

Moynihan, Daniel P., Paul Barton, et al. *The Negro Family: The Case for National Action* (The Moynihan Report). U.S. Department of Labor, Office of Policy Planning and Research. Washington, D.C.: U.S. Government Printing Office, 1965.

Nagenda, John. "Pride or Prejudice? Relationships between Africans and American Negroes," *Race,* vol. 9, no. 2 (October 1967), pp. 159-172.

National Advisory Commission on Civil Disorders (The Kerner Commission Report). New York: Grosset and Dunlap, 1968.

Northrup, Herbert R. "Intra-Plant Mobility of Negroes: Do Negro Employees Have Opportunities for Promotion or Transfers to Better Positions?" *Wharton Quarterly,* vol. 2 (Summer 1968), pp. 2-9.

Orbell, John M., and Kenneth S. Sherrill. "Racial Attitudes and the Metropolitan Context: A Structural Analysis," *Public Opinion Quarterly,* vol. 33, no. 1 (Spring 1969), pp. 46-54.

Pettigrew, Thomas F., and Daniel C. Thompson, eds. "Negro American Personality," *Journal of Social Issues* (entire issue), vol. 20, no. 2 (April 1964).

Pinkney, Alphonso. *Black Americans.* Englewood Cliffs, N.J.: Prentice-Hall, 1969.

Quarles, Benjamin. *The Negro in the Making of America.* New York: Collier Books, 1964.

Racism and White Christians: A Resource Study by Students at the Chicago Theological Seminary. Chicago: Chicago Theological Seminary, 1968.

Record, Wilson. *Race and Radicalism: The NAACP and the Communist Party in Conflict.* Ithaca: Cornell University Press, 1964.

Rollins, Charlemae Hill. *They Showed the Way: Forty American Negro Leaders.* New York: Thomas Crowell, 1964.

Rose, Arnold. *The Negro in America* (condensed version of Gunnar Myrdal's *An American Dilemma*). Foreword by Gunnar Myrdal. New York: Harper and Row, 1964.

Rose, Harold M. "The Origin and Pattern of Development of Urban Black Social Areas," *Journal of Geography,* vol. 68 (September 1969), pp. 326-332.

Scott, Benjamin. *The Coming of the Black Man.* Boston: Beacon Press, 1969.

Segal, Bernard E., ed. *Racial and Ethnic Relations: Selected Readings.* New York: Thomas Crowell, 1966.

Taeuber, Karl and Alma. *Negroes in Cities.* Chicago: Aldine Press, 1965.

Vander, Harry Joseph. *The Political and Economic Progress of the American Negro,* 1940-1963. Dubuque, Iowa: W. C. Brown Book Co., 1968.

Washington, Joseph R. *Black and White Power Subreption.* Boston: Beacon Press, 1969.

Weaver, Robert C. *Negro Labor: A National Problem.* New York: Harcourt, Brace and Co., 1946.

Wish, Harvey, ed. *The Negro Since Emancipation.* Englewood Cliffs, N.J.: Prentice-Hall, 1964.

Work, Monroe N. *A Bibliography of the Negro in Africa and America.* New York: H. W. Wilson Co., 1928.

Wright, Nathan, Jr. *Black Power and Urban Unrest.* New York: Hawthorne Books, 1967.

Youmans, E. Grant, S. E. Gringsby, and H. King. "Social Change, Generation, and Race," *Rural Sociology,* vol. 34, no. 3 (September 1969), pp. 305-312.

Zinn, Howard. *SNCC: The New Abolitionists.* Boston: Beacon Press, 1964.

C. *Japanese-Americans*

Grodzins, Morton. *Americans Betrayed: Politics and the Japanese Evacuation.* Chicago: University of Chicago Press, 1949.

Gulick, Sidney L. *The American Japanese Problem; A Study of the Racial Relations of East and West.* New York: Charles Scribner's Sons, 1914.

Ichihashi, Yamoto. *Japanese in the United States.* Stanford: Stanford University Press, 1932.

Kitano, Harry H. *Japanese Americans: The Evolution of a Subculture.* Englewood Cliffs, N.J.: Prentice-Hall, 1969.

Lind, Andrew W. *Hawaii's Japanese, an Experiment in Democracy.* Princeton: Princeton University Press, 1946.

McKenzie, R. D. *Oriental Exclusion, the Effect of American Immigration Laws, Regulations, and Judicial Decisions upon the Chinese and Japanese on the American Pacific Coast.* Chicago: Chicago University Press, 1928.

McWilliams, Carey. *Prejudice, Japanese-Americans: Symbol of Racial Intolerance.* Boston: Little, Brown and Co., 1944.

Smith, Bradford. *Americans from Japan.* Philadelphia: J. B. Lippincott, 1948.

Ten Brock, Jacobus, Edward N. Barnhart, and Floyd W. Matson. *Prejudice, War and the Constitution.* Berkeley: University of California Press, 1954.

Thomas, Dorothy Swaine. *The Salvage: Japanese-American Evacuation and Resettlement.* Berkeley: University of California Press, 1952.

D. *Chinese-Americans*

Barnett, Milton L. "Cantonese Economic Adaptation in the United States," *Human Organization,* vol. 19, no. 1 (1960), pp. 40-46.

Barth, Gunther. *Bitter Strength: A History of the Chinese in the United States, 1850-1870.* Cambridge: Harvard University Press, 1964.

Cowan, Robert Ernest, and Boutwell Dunlap. *Bibliography of the Chinese Question in the United States.* San Francisco: A. M. Robertson, 1909.

Fallers, L. A., ed. *Immigrants and Associations.* New York: Mouton, 1967.

Fong, Stanley L. M. "Assimilation of Chinese in America: Changes in Orientation and Social Perception," *American Journal of Sociology,* vol. 71 (November 1965), pp. 265-273.

Kwan, Kian Moon. "Assimilation of the Chinese in the United States: An Exploratory Study in California." University of California, Berkeley: Ph.D. diss., 1958.

Leo, Calvin. *Chinatown U.S.A.* Garden City: Doubleday, 1965.

Lee, Rose Hum. *The Chinese in the United States of America.* Hong Kong: Hong Kong University Press, 1960.

McKenzie, R. D. *Oriental Exclusion, the Effect of American Immigration Laws, Regulations, and Judicial Decisions upon the Chinese and Japanese on the American Pacific Coast.* Chicago: Chicago University Press, 1928.

Riggs, Fred W. *Pressures on Congress: A Study of the Repeal of Chinese Exclusion.* New York: King's Crown Press, 1950.

Sung, Betty Lee. *Mountain of Gold: The Story of the Chinese in America.* New York: Macmillan, 1967.

Yuan, D. Y. "Division of Labor Between Native-Born and Foreign-Born Chinese in the U.S.: A Study of Their Traditional Employments," *Phylon,* vol. 30 (Summer 1969), pp. 30: 160-169.

E. European Immigrants

Bagley, Christopher. "Migration, Race and Mental Health: A Review of Some Recent Research," *Race,* vol. 9, no. 3 (January 1968), pp. 343-356.

Bean, Louis H. *How To Predict Elections.* New York: Alfred A. Knopf, 1948.

Dore, Grazia. "Some Social and Historical Aspects of Italian Emigration to America," *Journal of Social History,* vol. 2, no. 2 (Winter 1968), pp. 95-122.

Galitzi, Christine Avghi. *A Study of Assimilation among the Roumanians in the United States.* New York: Columbia University Press, 1929.

Gerson, Louis L. *The Hyphenate in Recent American Politics and Diplomacy.* Lawrence: University of Kansas Press, 1964.

_____. *Woodrow Wilson and the Rebirth of Poland, 1914-1920.* New Haven: Yale University Press, 1953.

Gleason, Philip. "An Immigrant Group's Interest in Progressive Reform: A Case of the German-American Catholics," *American Historical Review,* vol. 73, no. 2 (December 1967), p. 367.

Guterman, Stanley. "The Americanization of Norwegian Immigrants: A Study of Historical Sociology," *Sociology and Social Research.* vol. 52, no. 3 (April 1968), pp. 252-270.

Lippmann, Walter. *Isolation and Alliances: An American Speaks to the British.* Boston: Little, Brown and Co., 1952.

Marchikian, George Magar. *Song of America.* New York: McGraw-Hill, 1956.

Nam, Charles B. "Nationality Groups and Social Stratification in America," *Social Forces,* vol. 37, no. 4 (May 1959), pp. 328-333.

Roucek, Joseph S. "The Image of the Slav in U.S. History and in Immigration Policy," *American Journal of Economics and Sociology,* vol. 28 (January 1969), pp. 29-48.

Vecoli, Rudolph J. "Prelates and Peasants: Italian Immigrants and the Catholic Church," *Journal of Social History,* vol. 2, no. 3 (Spring 1969), pp. 217-268.

Vrga, Djuro J., and Frank J. Fahey. "Structural Sources of Ethnic Factionalism," *Social Science,* vol. 44, no. 1 (January 1969), pp. 12-19. (Deals with Serb-Americans.)

Wittke, Carl Frederick. *The Irish in America.* Baton Rouge: Louisiana State University Press, 1956.

_____. *Refugees of Revolution: The German Forty-Eighters in America.* Philadelphia: University of Pennsylvania Press, 1952.

F. Jewish-Americans

Bernheimer, Charles S., ed. *The Russian Jew in the United States.* Philadelphia: J. C. Winston Co., 1905.

Berkson, Isaac B. *Theories of Americanization: A Critical Study with Special Reference to the Jewish Group.* New York: Columbia Teachers College, 1920.

Bisgyer, Maurice. *Challenge and Encounter: Behind the Scenes in the Struggle for Jewish Survival.* New York: Crown Publishers, 1967.

Brown, Heywood and George Britt. *Christians Only, a Study in Prejudice.* New York: Vanguard Press, 1931.

Davis-DuBois, Rachel, ed. *The Jews in American Life.* New York: Thomas Nelson, 1935.

Fuchs, Lawrence. *The Political Behavior of American Jews.* Glencoe: Free Press, 1956.

Gilbert, Arthur. *A Jew in Christian America.* New York: Sheed Ward, 1966.

Glazer, Nathan. *American Judaism.* Chicago: University of Chicago Press, 1957.

Hero, Alfred O., Jr. "Southern Jews, Race Relations, and Foreign Policy," *Jewish Social Studies,* vol. 27 (October 1965), pp. 213-235.

Janowsky, Oscar I., ed. *The American Jew.* New York: Harper and Brothers, 1942.

Kertzer, Morris N. *Today's American Jew.* New York: McGraw-Hill, 1967.

Kogan, L. A. "Jewish Conception of Negroes in the North," *Phylon,* vol. 28, no. 4 (Winter 1967), p. 376.

Liskofsky, Sidney. *Eliminating Intolerance and Discrimination Based on Religion or Belief: The U.N. Role.* New York: American Jewish Committee Institute of Human Relations, February 1968.

McWilliams, Carey. *A Mask for Privilege: Anti-Semitism in America.* Boston: Little, Brown and Co., 1948.

Ringer, Benjamin. *The Edge of Friendliness: A Study of Jewish-Gentile Relations.* New York: Basic Books, 1967.

Rosenberg, Stuart E. *The Search for Jewish Identity in America.* New York: Doubleday, 1965.

Sachar, Abram Leon. *A History of the Jews.* New York: Alfred A. Knopf, 1964.
Sklare, Marshall, and Joseph Greenblum. *Jewish Identity on the Suburban Frontier.* New York: Basic Books, 1967.

G. *Puerto Ricans*

Handlin, Oscar. *The Newcomers: Negroes and Puerto Ricans in a Changing Metropolis.* Cambridge: Harvard University Press, 1959.
Lewis, Oscar. *La Vida: A Puerto Rican Family in the Culture of Poverty—San Juan and New York.* New York: Random House, 1966.
———. *A Study of Slum Culture: Backgrounds for La Vida.* New York: Random House, 1968.
Mills, C. Wright, Clarence Senior, and Rose Kohn Goldsen. *The Puerto Rican Journey: New York's Newest Migrants.* New York: Harper and Brothers, 1950.
Padilla, Elena. *Up from Puerto Rico.* New York: Columbia University Press, 1958.
Rand, Christopher. *The Puerto Ricans.* New York: Oxford University Press, 1958.
Senior, Clarence. *The Puerto Ricans: Strangers—Then Neighbors.* Chicago: Quadrangle Books, 1965.
Sexton, Patricia C. *Spanish Harlem: Anatomy of Poverty.* New York: Harper and Row, 1965.
Sternau, Herbert, comp. *Puerto Rico and the Puerto Ricans: An Outline of Basic Facts for Speakers, Educators, Civic and Religious Leaders.* New York: Council of Spanish-American Organizations and American Jewish Committee, 1958.
Steward, Julian. *The People of Puerto Rico.* Urbana: University of Illinois Press, 1966.
Thomas, Piri. *Down These Mean Streets.* New York: Alfred A. Knopf, 1967.

H. *Cubans*

Alexander, T. "Those Amazing Cuban Emigrés," *Fortune,* vol. 74 (October 1966), pp. 144-149.
"Cuba and U.S. Agreement on the Refugees," *International Legal Materials,* vol. 4 (November 1965), pp. 1118-1127.
"An Exposé of the Insidious File: 'Three Faces of Cuba'." Published by The Truth About Cuba Committee, 1963.
Johnson, K. "Ebullient Ybor," *Travel,* vol. 127 (February 1967), pp. 52-53.
Micocci, A. A. "New Life for Cuban Exiles," *American Education,* vol. 1, no. 3 (March 1965), pp. 29-32.

Plank, John, ed. *Cuba and the United States: Long Range Perspectives, Essays.* Washington, D.C.: Brookings Institution, 1967.

United States., Senate Committee on the Judiciary Subcommittee to Investigate Problems Connected with Refugees and Escapees. "Refugees and Escapees: Report." Washington, D.C.: Government Printing Office, 1964.

Wine, James. "The Refugee Problem Is Greater Than Ever," *American Council on Judaism,* vol. 21 (Summer 1967), pp. 1-6.

Yearley, C. K. "Cubans in Miami," *Commonweal,* vol. 83 (March 11, 1966), p. 651.

I. Mexican-Americans

Berma, John H. *Spanish-Speaking Groups in the United States.* Durham: Duke University Press, 1954.

Gamio, Manuel. *The Mexican Immigrant, His Life-Story; Autobiographic Documents.* Chicago: University of Chicago Press, 1931.

———. *Mexican Immigration to the United States.* Chicago: University of Chicago Press, 1930.

Griffith, Beatrice Winston. *American Me.* Boston: Houghton Mifflin, 1948.

Heller, Celia S. *Mexican American Youth: Forgotten Youth at the Crossroads.* New York: Random House, 1966.

Helm, June, ed. *Spanish-Speaking People in the United States—Proceedings of the 1968 Annual Spring Meeting of the American Ethnological Society.* Seattle and London: University of Washington Press, 1969.

Kibbe, Pauline R. *Latin Americans in Texas.* Albuquerque: University of New Mexico Press, 1946.

Madsen, William. *Mexican-Americans of South Texas.* New York: Holt, Rinehart and Winston, 1964.

McWilliams, Carey. *North from Mexico: The Spanish-Speaking People of the United States.* Philadelphia: J. B. Lippincott, 1949.

Mexicans in the United States: A Bibliography. Washington, D.C.: Pan American Union, 1942.

Mittelbach, Frank G., and Grace Marshall. *The Burdened Poverty.* Los Angeles: Division of Research, Graduate School of Business Administration, University of California, 1966.

Moore, Joan W., and Frank G. Mittelbach. *Residential Segregation in the Urban Southwest.* Los Angeles: Division of Research, Graduate School of Business Administration. University of California, 1966.

"Northern Colorado Conference on Problems of the Spanish-Speaking People." Greeley, Colorado: Colorado State College, 1942. Mimeograph.

Penalosa, Fernando, and E. C. McDonagh, "Social Mobility in a Mexican-American Community," *Social Forces,* vol. 44 (June 1966), pp. 498-505.

Robinson, Cecil. *With the Ears of Strangers: The Mexican in American Literature.* Tucson: University of Arizona Press, 1963.

Rubel, Arthur J. *Mexican-Americans in a Texas City.* Austin: University of Texas Press, 1966.

Samora, Julian, and Richard A. Lamanna. *Mexican-Americans in a Midwest Metropolis: A Study of East Chicago.* Los Angeles: University of California Press, 1967.

Saunders, Lyle, comp. *A Guide to Materials Bearing on Cultural Relations in New Mexico.* Albuquerque: University of New Mexico Press, 1944.

Taylor, Paul Schuster. *An American-Mexican Frontier, Nueces County, Texas.* Chapel Hill: University of North Carolina Press, 1934.

_____. *Mexican Labor in the United States.* Vols. 1-2, nos. 1-10. Berkeley: University of California Press, 1928-1934.

Tuck, Ruth D. *Not with the Fist: Mexican-Americans in a Southwest City.* New York: Harcourt, Brace and Co., 1946.

Valdes, Daniel T. *The Spanish-Speaking People of the Southwest.* Denver: Works Program Administration, 1938.

United States, Commission on Civil Rights. *The Mexican American.* Washington, D.C., Government Printing Office, 1968.

J. American Indians

Ablon, Joan. "American Indian Relocation: Problems of Dependency and Management in the City," *Phylon,* vol. 26 (Winter 1965), pp. 362-371.

Adair, John, and Evon Vogt. "Navaho and Zuni Veterans: A Study of Contrasting Modes of Culture Change," *American Anthropologist,* vol. 51, no. 4 (October-December 1949), pp. 547-560.

"Another American Dilemma: American Indians," *Social Action,* vol. 32 (May 1966), pp. 7-26.

Bruner, Edward M. "Assimilation among Fort Berthold Indians," *American Indian,* vol. 6, no. 4 (Summer 1953), pp. 21-29.

Bryde, John Francis. *The Sioux Indian Student: A Study of Scholastic Failure and Personality Conflict.* Pine Ridge, South Dakota: Holy Rosary Mission, 1966.

Cohen, H., and Philip M. Maugh. "The Indian: The Forgotten American," *Harvard Law Review,* vol. 81 (June 1968), pp. 1818-1858.

Dozier, Edward P., George E. Simpson, and Milton Yinger. "The Integration of Americans of Indian Descent," *The Annals,* vol. 311 (May 1957), pp. 158-165.

Farb, Peter. *Man's Rise to Civilization as Shown by the Indians of North America from Primeval Times to the Coming of the Industrial State.* New York: Dutton, 1968.

Haas, Theodore H. "The American Indian in Recent Perspective," *Race Relations,* vol. 5, nos. 3, 4 (December 1947, January 1948), pp. 51-59.

LaFarge, Oliver. "Assimilation—The Indian View," *New Mexico Quarterly*, vol. 26, no. 1 (Spring 1956), pp. 5-13.

Prodipto, Roy. "The Measurement of Assimilation: The Spokane Indians," *American Journal of Sociology*, vol. 67 (March 1962), pp. 541-551.

Steiner, Stan. *The New Indian*. New York: Harper and Row, 1968.

————. "Political Awakening on the Reservation—Our Emergent Indian Voting Bloc," *New Leader*, vol. 48 (June 21, 1965), pp. 16-18.

Underhill, Ruth M. *Red Man's America*. Chicago: University of Chicago Press, 1953

Voget, Fred. "Acculturation at Caughanawaga: A Note on the Native-Modified Group," *American Anthropologist*, vol. 53, no. 1 (January-March 1951), pp. 220-380.

Vogt, Evon Z. "The Acculturation of American Indians," *The Annals*, vol. 311 (May 1957) pp. 137-146.

————. "Navaho Veterans, a Study of Changing Values," *Papers of the Peabody Museum of American Archaeology and Ethnology* (Harvard University), vol. 41, no. 1 (1951).

White, Robert A. "American Indian Crisis," *Social Order*, vol. 11 (May 1961), pp. 201-211.

IV. Race and United States Institutions

A. Foreign-Policy Processes

Bowles, Chester. *Africa's Challenge to the United States*. Berkeley: University of California, 1956.

Cefkin, Leo. "United States Policy Toward the Rhodesian Rebellion," *Africa Today*, vol. 14, no. 5 (October-November 1968), pp. 14-17.

Dulles, Eleanor Lansing. *American Foreign Policy in the Making*. New York: Harper and Row, 1968.

Emerson, Rupert. "Dilemmas of American Policy on Africa," *Transition*, vol. 5, no. 2 (1966), pp. 11-16.

Frankel, Joseph. *The Making of Foreign Policy*. New York: Oxford University Press, 1963.

Furniss, Edgar S., Jr. *American Military Policy*. New York: Rinehart, 1957.

Haviland, H. Field, Jr., ed. *The Formulation and Administration of United States Foreign Policy*. Washington, D.C.: Brookings Institution, 1960.

Hutchinson, Edward P. "The New Immigration," *The Annals*, vol. 367 (September 1966), pp. 1-3.

Lerche, Charles O. *Foreign Policy of the American People*, 3rd ed. Englewood Cliffs, N.J.: Prentice-Hall, 1967.

London, Kurt, and Kent Ives. *How Foreign Policy Is Made*. Princeton: Van Nostrand, 1949.

Marcum, John. "Southern Africa and United States Policy: A Consideration of Alternatives," *Africa Today,* vol. 14, no. 5 (October-November 1968), pp. 5-13.

Marshall, Burke. *Federalism and Civil Rights.* New York: Columbia University Press, 1964.

McKenzie, R. D. *Oriental Exclusion, the Effect of American Immigration Laws, Regulations, and Judicial Decisions upon the Chinese and Japanese on the American Pacific Coast.* Chicago: Chicago University Press, 1928.

Morrow, Everett Frederic. *Black Man in the White House: A Diary of the Eisenhower Years by the Administrative Officer for Special Projects, the White House, 1955-61.* New York: Coward-McCann, 1963.

Rostow, W. W. *The United States in the World Arena.* New York: Harper and Row, 1960.

Sapin, Burton M. *The Making of United States Foreign Policy.* New York: Frederick A. Praeger, 1966.

Stevens, Richard. "Lesotho and Botswana: Challenge to American Policy," *Africa Today,* vol. 14, no. 5 (October-November 1967), p. 4.

Westerfield, Holt Bradford. *The Instruments of America's Foreign Policy.* New York: Thomas Y. Crowell, 1962.

Wolf, Charles, Jr. *United States Policy and the Third World.* Boston: Little, Brown and Co., 1967.

B. Military

Bogart, Leo. "The Army and Its Negro Soldiers," *Reporter,* vol. 11, no. 12 (December 30, 1954), pp. 8-11.

_____, ed. *Social Research and the Desegregation of the U.S. Army: Two Original 1951 Field Reports.* Chicago: Markham Publishing Co., 1969.

Chapman, Bruce K. *The Wrong Man in Uniform: Our Unfair and Obsolete Draft and How We Can Replace It.* New York: Trident Press, 1967.

Dalfiume, Richard M. *Desegregation of the U.S. Armed Forces: Fighting on Two Fronts, 1939-1953.* Columbia: University of Missouri Press, 1969.

Davenport, R. K. "Implications of Military Selection and Classification in Relation to Universal Military Training," *Journal of Negro Education,* vol. 15 (Fall 1946), pp. 585-594.

Davis, B. J. "On the Use of Negro Troops in Wall Street's Aggression Against the Korean People," *Political Affairs,* October 1950, pp. 47-57.

Davis, P. C. "The Negro in the Armed Services," *Virginia Quarterly Review,* vol. 24 (September 1948), pp. 499-520.

Foreman, Paul B. "The Implications of Project Clear," *Phylon,* vol. 16 (Third Quarter 1955), pp. 263-274.

Integration in the Armed Service: A Progress Report. U.S. Office of the Assistant Secretary of Defense (Manpower and Personnel), Office of the

Civilian Assistant. Washington, D.C.: Government Printing Office, January 1, 1955.

Johnson, Jesse J. *Ebony Brass: An Autobiography of Negro Frustration amid Aspiration.* New York: William and Frederick Press, 1967.

Lee, Irvin H. *Negro Medal of Honor Men.* New York: Dodd, Mead, 1967.

Mandelbaum, David Goodman. *Soldier Groups and Negro Soldiers.* Berkeley: University of California Press, 1952.

Mitchell, Clarence. "The Status of Racial Integration in the Armed Services," *Journal of Negro Education,* vol. 23 (Summer 1954), pp. 203-213.

Moskos, C. C. "Racial Integration in the Armed Forces," *American Journal of Sociology,* vol. 72, no. 2 (September 1966), pp. 132-148.

Mulzac, Hugh. *A Star To Steer By.* New York: International Publishers, 1963.

"Negroes in Uniform," *The Economist,* vol. 158 (May 6, 1950), pp. 999-1000.

Nichols, Lee. *Breakthrough on the Color Front.* New York: Random House, 1954.

Puner, Morton. "Integration in the Army: Armed Forces Have Led the Way in Desegregation Over the Past Ten Years and Their Example Has Helped Correct Europe's Image of the U.S.," *New Leader,* vol. 42 (January 12, 1959), pp. 10-14.

Reddick, L. D. "The Relative Status of the Negro in the American Armed Forces," *Journal of Negro Education,* vol. 22 (Summer 1953), pp. 380-387.

Roberts, H. W. "The Impact of Military Service upon the Racial Attitudes of Negro Servicemen in World War II," *Social Problems,* vol. 1 (October 1953), pp. 65-69.

Schoenfeld, Seymour J. *The Negro in the Armed Forces, His Value and Status, Past, Present and Potential.* Washington, D.C.: Associated Publishers, 1945.

Spore, John B., and Robert I. Cocklin. "Our Negro Soldiers: Korea Has Proved Segregation Doesn't Pay in Battle; After Years of Official Sidestepping It's on Its Way Out." *Reporter,* vol. 6, no. 2 (January 22, 1952), pp. 6-9.

Stillman, Richard Joseph. *Integration of the Negro in the U.S. Armed Forces.* New York: Frederick A. Praeger, 1968.

Stillman, Richard. "Negroes in the Armed Forces," *Phylon,* vol. 30 (Summer 1969), pp. 139-159.

Whittemore, I. C. "An Uncontrolled Experiment in Race Relations," *Journal of Educational Sociology,* vol. 22 (May 1949), pp. 590-597.

Williams, George W. *A History of the Negro Troops in the War of the Rebellion, 1861-65;* (preceded by a review of the military services of Negroes in ancient and modern times). New York: Bergman Publishers, 1968.

Wilson, Joseph T. *The Black Phalanx.* New York: Arno Press, 1968.

C. *Business, Industry, and Labor*

Blumer, Herbert. "Industrialisation and Race Relations," *Industrialisation and Race Relations,* ed. Guy Hunter. New York: Oxford University Press, 1965. Pages 220-253.

"Business and Race: Nation's Biggest Firms Now Committed to Helping Solve the Racial Crisis," *Wall Street Journal,* vol. 171 (June 11 and June 14, 1968), p. 1.

Cross, Theodore L. *Black Capitalism: Strategy for Business in the Ghetto.* New York: Atheneum, 1969.

"Discrimination in Employment and in Housing: Private Enforcement Provisions of the Civil Rights Act of 1964 and 1968," *Harvard Law Review,* vol. 82 (February 1969), pp. 834-863.

Edmonson, Munro S., and David R. Norsworthy. "Industry and Race in the Southern United States," in *Industrialisation and Race Relations,* ed. Guy Hunter. New York: Oxford University Press, 1965.

Ferman, Louis A. *The Negro and Equal Employment Opportunities: A Review of Management Experience in Twenty Companies.* New York: Frederick A. Praeger, 1968.

Ferman, Louis A., ed. *Negroes and Jobs: A Book of Readings.* Ann Arbor: University of Michigan Press.

Ginzberg, Eli, ed. *Business Leadership and the Negro Crisis.* New York: McGraw-Hill, 1968.

Gourlay, Jack G. *The Negro Salaried Worker.* New York: American Management Association, 1965.

Hadad, William F., and Douglas G. Pugh, eds. *Black Economic Development.* Englewood Cliffs, N.J.: Prentice-Hall, 1969.

Haynes, George E. *The Negro at Work in New York City.* New York: Arno Press, 1968.

Helper, Rose. *Racial Policies and Practices of Real Estate Brokers.* Minneapolis: University of Minnesota Press, 1969.

Hiestand, Dale L. *Economic Growth and Employment for Minorities.* New York: Columbia University Press, 1964.

Hutchinson, John E. "The AFL-CIO and the Negro," in *Employment, Race, and Poverty,* ed. A. M. Ross and Herbert Hill. New York: Harcourt Brace, and World, 1967.

Lekachman, Robert. "Business Must Lead the Way," *Dun's Review,* vol. 91, no. 4 (April 1968), p. 11.

Marshall, F. Roy, and V. M. Briggs, Jr. *The Negro and Apprenticeship.* Baltimore: Johns Hopkins Press, 1967.

Marshall, Ray. "Industrialisation and Race Relations in the Southern United States," in *Industrialisation and Race Relations,* ed. Guy Hunter. New York: Oxford University Press, 1965. Pages 61-96.

_____. *The Negro and Organized Labor.* New York: John Wiley, 1965.

Peterson, William, ed. *American Social Patterns: Studies of Race Relations, Popular Heroes, Voting Union Democracy and Government Bureaucracy.* Garden City: Doubleday, 1956.

Price, Daniel O. "Occupational Changes among Whites and Non-Whites, with Projections for 1970," *Social Science Quarterly,* vol. 49 (December 1968), pp. 563-572.

Ross, A. M. and Herbert Hill, eds. *Employment, Race and Poverty.* New York: Harcourt Brace, and World, 1967.

Rowan, Richard L. "Negro Employment in the Basic Steel Industry," *Industry and Labor Relations Review,* vol. 23 (October 1969).

Scruggs, Ramon S. "The Ethnic Challenge: Business Can't Be Done as Usual," *Public Relations Journal,* vol. 24, no. 1 (January 1968), pp. 19-20.

"A Special Issue on Business and the Urban Crisis," *Fortune,* vol. 72 (January 1968), pp. 1-234.

Taeuber, Karl E. "The Effect of Income Redistribution on Racial Residential Segregation," *Urban Affairs Quarterly,* vol. 4 (September 1968), pp. 5-14.

Trooboff, Benjamin M. "Employment Opportunity for Negroes in the Health Related Occupations," *Journal of Negro Education,* vol. 38 (Winter 1969), pp. 22-31.

Weaver, Robert C. *Negro Labor: A National Problem.* New York: Harcourt, Brace and Co., 1946.

D. Pressure Groups and Public Opinion

Bailey, Thomas A. *The Man in the Street: The Impact of American Public Opinion on Foreign Policy.* Magnolia, Mass: Peter Smith, 1964.

Clarke, John Henrik, and Robert S. Browne. "The American Negro's Impact," *Africa Today,* vol. 14, no. 1 (December-January 1966-67), pp. 16-18.

Cohen, Bernard C. *The Influence of Non-Governmental Groups on Foreign Policy-Making.* Boston: World Peace Foundation, 1959.

Cohen, Bernard C. *The Press and Foreign Policy.* Princeton: Princeton University Press, 1963.

Coombs, Philip H. *The Fourth Dimension of Foreign Policy: Educational and Cultural Affairs.* New York: Harper and Row, 1964.

Fitzpatrick, Joseph. "Cultural Pluralism and Religious Identification: A Review," *Sociological Analysis,* vol. 25, no. 2 (Summer 1964), pp. 129-134.

Free, Lloyd, and Hadley Cantril. *The Political Beliefs of Americans: A Study of Public Opinion.* New Brunswick: Rutgers University Press, 1967.

Fuchs, Lawrence H., ed. *American Ethnic Politics.* New York and London: Harper and Row, 1968.

Gosnell, Harold F. *Negro Politicians: The Rise of Negro Politics in Chicago.* Chicago: University of Chicago Press, 1967.

Hero, Alfred O., Jr. *The Southerner and World Affairs.* Baton Rouge: Louisiana State University Press, 1965.

Hohenberg, John. *Between Two Worlds: Policy, Press, and Public Opinion in Asian-American Relations.* New York: Frederick A. Praeger, 1967.

Hooker, J. R. "The Negro-American Press and Africa in the Nineteen-Thirties," *Canadian Journal of African Studies,* no. 1 (March 1967), pp. 43-50.

Key, Vladimer O., Jr. *Public Opinion and American Democracy.* New York: Alfred A. Knopf, 1961.

Lamanna, Richard A., and John B. Stephenson. "Religious Prejudice and Intended Voting Behavior," *Sociological Analysis,* vol. 25, no. 2 (Summer 1964), pp. 121-125.

Leonard, Edward A. "Non-Violence and Violence in American Racial Protest, 1942-1967," *Rocky Mountain Social Science Journal,* vol. 5, no. 1 (April 1969), pp. 10-22.

Lubell, Samuel. *The Future of American Politics,* 2nd ed., rev. New York: Doubleday Anchor, 1955.

Mack, Raymond W. "Riot, Revolt, or Responsible Revolution: Of Reference Groups and Racism," *Sociological Quarterly,* vol. 10, no. 2 (Spring 1969), pp. 147-156.

Oldham, J. H. *Christianity and the Race Problem.* New York: George H. Doran, 1924.

"Public Opinion and Foreign Policy," *Intercom,* vol. 8, no. 2 (March-April 1966), pp. 25-72.

Rischin, Moses. *Our Own Kind: Voting by Race, Creed or National Origin.* Santa Barbara: Center for the Study of Democratic Institutions, 1960.

Rosenau, James N. *The Attentive Public and Foreign Policy: A Theory of Growth, Some New Evidence.* Princeton: Woodrow Wilson School of Public and International Affairs. Research Monograph No. 31, March 1968.

————. *Public Opinion and Foreign Policy.* New York: Random House, 1961.

Schevitz, J. M. "Do-Gooder as Status Striver," *Phylon,* vol. 28, no. 4 (Winter 1967), pp. 386-398.

Sindler, Allan P. "Negroes, Ethnic Groups and American Politics," *Current History,* vol. 55 (October 1968), p. 207.

Steele, Archibald T. *The American People and China.* New York: McGraw-Hill, 1966.

Stone, Charles Sumner, Jr. *Black Political Power in America.* New York: Bobbs-Merrill, 1968.

Tobias, Henry J., and Charles E. Woodhouse, eds. *Minorities and Politics.* Albuquerque: University of New Mexico Press, 1969.

Turner, Julius. *Party and Constituency: Pressures on Congress.* Baltimore: Johns Hopkins Press, 1951.

Von Eschen, Donald, Jerome Kirk, and Maurice Pinardi. "The Disintegration of the Negro Non-Violent Movement," *Journal of Peace Research,* no. 3 (1969), pp. 215-234.

E. Education

Beggs, David W., and S. Kern Alexander. *Integration and Education.* Chicago: Rand McNally, 1969.

Bolner, James. "Defining Racial Imbalance in Public Educational Institutions," *Journal of Negro Education,* vol. 37 (Spring 1968), pp. 114-126.

Campbell, Ernest Q. "Negroes, Education, and the Southern States," *Social Forces,* vol. 47, no. 3 (March 1969), pp. 253-265.

Dye, Thomas R. "Urban School Segregation: A Comparative Analysis," *Urban Affairs Quarterly,* vol. 4 (December 1968), pp. 141-165.

Edwards, Thomas B. and Frederick M. Wirt, eds. *School Desegregation in the North: The Challenge and the Experience.* San Francisco: Chandler Publishing Co., 1967.

Journal of Social Issues, vol. 25, no. 3 (Summer 1969). Entire issue devoted to "Motivation and Academic Achievement of Negro Americans."

Levine, Daniel U., and Robert J. Havighurst. "Negro Population Growth and Enrollment in the Public Schools: A Case Study and Its Implications," *Education and Urban Society,* vol. 1 (November 1968), pp. 21-46.

"Race and Equality in American Education," *Journal of Negro Education,* vol. 37 (Summer 1968), pp. 185-358.

Sorkin, Alan L. "Education, Migration and Negro Unemployment," *Social Forces,* vol. 47, no. 3 (March 1969), pp. 265-274.

"The Wall of Racial Separation: The Role of Private and Parochial Schools in Racial Integration," *New York University Law Review,* vol. 43 (May 1968), pp. 514-540.

Weinberg, Meyer. *Integrated Education: A Reader.* Beverly Hills: Glencoe Press, 1968.

Wise, Arthur E. *Rich Schools, Poor Schools: The Promise of Equal Educational Opportunity.* Chicago: University of Chicago Press, 1968.

V. Foreign Views of United States Race Problems

Beals, Carleton, et al. *What the South Americans Think of Us.* New York: Medill McBride, 1945.

Beneyto, J. "Opinión pública y política exterior," *Revista de estudios políticos,* vols. 117-118 (May-August 1961), pp. 183-189.

Buchanan, W., and Hadley Cantril. *How Nations See Each Other.* Urbana: University of Illinois Press, 1953.

Coelho, C. V. *Changing Images of America: A Study of Indian Students' Perceptions.* New York: Free Press, 1958.

Crocker, Walter Russel. *The Racial Factor in International Relations.* Canberra: Australian National University, 1956.

European Opinions of Race Relations in America. Washington, D.C.: USIA Research and Reference Service, World Survey Series, June 1964.

Isaacs, Harold R. "American Race Relations and the United States Image in World Affairs," *Journal of Human Relations,* vol. 10 (Winter-Spring 1962), pp. 266-280.

Isaacs, Harold R. "World Affairs and U.S. Race Relations: A Note on Little Rock," *Public Opinion Quarterly,* vol. 22, no. 3 (Fall 1958), pp. 364-370.

Merrill, John C. *Gringo: The American as Seen by Mexican Journalists.* Gainesville: University of Florida Press, 1963.

Merritt, Richard L., and D. J. Puchala, eds. *Western European Perspectives on International Affairs: Public Opinion Studies and Evaluations.* New York: Frederick A. Praeger, 1967.

New Delhi Reactions to the Mississippi Segregation Crisis. Washington, D.C.: USIA Research and Reference Service, November 29, 1962.

Radler, Don H. *El Gringo: The Yankee Image in Latin America.* Philadelphia: Chilton Co., 1962.

Schwarz, Henry G. "America Faces Asia: The Problem of Image Projection," *Journal of Politics,* vol. 26, no. 3 (August 1964), pp. 532-549.

Vigil, Antonio S. *The Ugly Angle: An Analysis of White Extremism in Latin American Relations.* New York: Exposition Press, 1967. (Deals with foreign opinion of U.S.)

VI. The Race Factor in American Foreign Policy

Bowles, Chester. *Africa's Challenge to the United States.* Berkeley and Los Angeles: University of California Press, 1956.

Browne, Robert S. *Race Relations in International Affairs.* Washington: Public Affairs Press, 1961.

Bunche, Ralph J. "The International Implications of Racial Tensions," *Yale Political Quarterly,* vol. 3 (August 1963), p. 13.

Cefkin, Leo. "United States Policy Toward the Rhodesian Rebellion," *Africa Today,* vol. 14, no. 5 (October-November 1968), pp. 14-17.

Davis, John A. "The American Negro and Africa," *Jewish Frontier,* vol. 31 (March 1964), pp. 11-15.

Emerson, Rupert. *Africa and United States Policy.* Englewood Cliffs, N.J.: Prentice-Hall, 1967.

_____. "Dilemmas of American Policy on Africa," *Transition,* vol. 5, no. 2 (1966), pp. 11-16.

_____, and Martin Kilson. "The American Dilemma in a Changing World: The Rise of Africa and the Negro American," *Daedalus,* vol. 94, no. 4 (Fall 1965), pp. 1055-1084.

Ferkiss, Victor C. "U.S. Policy in Southern Africa," in *Southern Africa in Transition,* ed. John A. Davis and James K. Baker. New York: Frederick A. Praeger for the American Society of African Culture, 1966.

Fuchs, Lawrence H. "Minority Groups and Foreign Policy," *American Political Science Quarterly,* vol. 74 (June 1959), pp. 161-176.

Gerson, Louis L. *The Hyphenate in Recent American Politics and Diplomacy.* Lawrence: University of Kansas Press, 1964.

Gonze, Collin, George M. Houser, and Perry M. Sturges. *South African Crisis and United States Policy.* New York: American Committee on Africa, 1962.

Hero, Alfred O., Jr. "American Negroes and United States Foreign Policy: 1937-1967," *Journal of Conflict Resolution,* vol. 8, no. 2 (June 1969), pp. 220-251.

Houser, George M. "What the U.S. Can Do About Apartheid," *Africa Today,* vol. 13, no. 3 (March 1966), p. 4.

Isaacs, Harold R. *Images of Asia: American Views of China and India.* New York: Capricorn Books, 1962. Published originally as *Scratches on Our Minds.* New York: John Day, 1958.

Legum, Colin. "Color and World Politics: The Challenge of Southern Africa to the United States," *Motive,* vol. 28 (April 1968), pp. 12-20.

Legum, Colin, et al. "Racism in Southern Africa: Challenge to U.S. Policy," *Social Action,* vol. 34 (April 1968), pp. 5-47.

———, and Margaret Legum. *South Africa: Crisis for the West.* New York: Frederick A. Praeger, 1964.

Lincoln, C. Eric. "The Race Problem and International Relations," *New South,* vol. 21, no. 4 (Fall 1966), pp. 2-14.

Marcum, John. "Southern Africa and United States Policy: A Consideration of Alternatives," *Africa Today,* vol. 14, no. 5 (October-November 1968), pp. 5-13.

Middleton, Drew. *America's Stake in Asia.* Philadelphia: J. B. Lippincott, 1968.

Nielsen, Waldemar A. *African Battleline: American Policy Choices in Southern Africa.* New York: Harper and Row for the Council on Foreign Relations, 1965.

Pauker, Guy J. *The Future Role of the United States in Asia and the Pacific.* Los Angeles: RAND Corporation, 1968.

Pike, Frederick B. *Chile and the United States, 1880-1962: The Emergence of Chile's Social Crisis and the Challenge to the United States Diplomacy.* South Bend: University of Notre Dame Press, 1963.

Rosenau, James, ed. *International Aspects of Civil Strife.* Princeton: Princeton University Press, 1964.

Segal, Ronald, and Ruth First, eds. *A Travesty of Trust: South West Africa.* New York: André Deutsch, 1967.

Taft, Donald R., and Richard Robbins. *International Migrations: The Immigrant in the Modern World.* New York: Ronald Press, 1955.

Walshe, A. P. "Black American Thought and African Political Attitudes in South Africa," *Review of Politics,* vol. 32, no. 1 (January 1970), pp. 51-77.

Weisbord, R. "Africa, Africans and the Afro-American: Images and Identities in Transition," *Race,* vol. 10 (January 1969), pp. 305-321.

Zartman, I. William. "Problems in American Policy Toward Africa," *Motive,* vol. 26 (January 1966), pp. 48-50.

VII.   Race, National Minorities, Human Rights, and the United Nations

Azcarate y Florez, Pablo de. *Protection of National Minorities.* New York: Carnegie Endowment for International Peace, 1967.

Cabrones, José A. "Human Rights and Non-Intervention in the Inter-American System (in the Decade since the Founding of the OAS)," *Michigan Law Review,* vol. 65 (April 1967), pp. 1147-1182.

"Changing Dimensions in Human Rights," *Social Action,* vol. 30 (October 1963), pp. 1-36.

Connor, Walker. "Self-Determination: The New Phase, *World Politics,* vol. 20, no. 1 (October 1967), pp. 30-53.

Economic and Social Consequences of Racial Discrimination. Paris: UNESCO, 1962.

Friedman, Julian R. "Background Paper B: Prepared for the UN Human Rights Seminar on Apartheid." Brasilia, Brazil, August 5-September 5, 1966.

Gardner, Richard N. "A Costly Anachronism (Argument for the Ratification by the U.S. of the U.N. Conventions on Human Rights)," *American Bar Association Journal,* vol. 53 (October 1967), pp. 907-910.

Gerber, William. "Human Rights Protection,"*Editorial Research Reports,* April 3, 1968, pp. 243-260.

Green, James Frederick. *The United Nations and Human Rights.* Washington, D.C.: Brookings Institution, 1956.

Human Rights. A Study Guide for the International Year for Human Rights, 1968. New York: Heinemann Educational Books, 1967.

Leclercq, Jacques. "Human Rights and the Social Order"; Albert Verdoot, "The Present Significance of the Universal Declaration of Human Rights"; Karel Rimanque, "Human Rights: Legal Implications in a Historical and Philosophical Context," *World Justice,* vol. 7 (December 1965), pp. 147-193.

Luard, Evan, ed. *The International Protection of Human Rights.* New York: Frederick A. Praeger, 1967.

Malhotra, Ram C. "Apartheid and the United Nations," *The Annals* vol. 354 (July 1964), pp. 135-144.

Mason, Philip. "Race Relations and Human Rights," *Race,* vol. 10, no. 1 (July 1968), pp. 1-16.

McDougal, Myres S., and Gerhard Bebr. "Human Rights in the U.N." *American Journal of International Law,* vol. 58 (July 1964), pp. 603-641.

Newman, Frank C. "The New International Tribunal on Racial Discrimination," *California Law Review* (November 1968), pp. 1559-68.

Patterson, William L., ed. *We Charge Genocide: The Historic Petition to the United Nations for Relief from a Crime of the United States Government Against Negro People.* New York: Civil Rights Congress, 1952.

"Racism at the U.N.," *New Republic,* vol. 151, no. 26 (December 26, 1964), pp. 9-10.

Radojkovic, Milos. "The Protection of Minorities under International Law," *International Affairs,* vol. 20 (February 20, 1969), pp. 25-27 (to be continued).

Robinson, Nehemiah. *The Genocide Convention: Its Origins and Interpretations.* 1949.

Rowe, Edward T. "The Emerging Anti-Colonial Consensus in the United Nations," *Journal of Conflict Resolution,* vol. 8, no. 3 (September 1964), pp. 209-230.

Schwelb, Egan. *Human Rights and the International Community: The Roots and Growth of the Universal Declaration of Human Rights, 1948-1963.* New York: Quadrangle Books, 1964.

"Symposium on the International Law of Human Rights," *Howard Law Journal,* vol. 2 (Spring 1965), pp. 257-623.

Twitchett, Kenneth J. "The Racial Issue at the United Nations: A Study of the African States' Reaction to the American-Belgian Congo Rescue Operation of November 1964," *International Relations,* vol. 2 (October 1965), pp. 830-846.

UNESCO. *Meeting of Experts on Educational Methods Designed to Combat Racial Prejudice.* Paris: UNESCO, 1968 (ED/MD/4).

United Nations. *Apartheid: A Selective Bibliography on the Racial Policies of the Government of the Republic of South Africa.* New York: United Nations Secretariat, May 15, 1968.

United Nations Commission on Human Rights, Subcommittee on Prevention of Discrimination and Protection of Minorities. *Special Study of Racial Discrimination in the Political, Economic, Social and Cultural Spheres,* June 24, 1969 (E/CN.4/Sub.2/301); July 25, 1968 (E/CN.4/Sub.2/288).

United Nations General Assembly. "Measures Taken within the U.N. in the Field of Human Rights." New York: United Nations Secretariat, 1967.

United Nations General Assembly. *Yearbook on Human Rights,* 1964. New York: United Nations Secretariat, 1964.

United Nations Seminar on Human Rights in Developing Countries. Kabul, Afganistan, May 12-25, 1964, organized by the United Nations in cooperation with the Afganistan government. New York: United Nations Secretariat, 1964.

United Nations Seminar on the Multi-National Society. Ljubljana, Yugoslavia, August 21, 1965, organized by the United Nations and the Yugoslav government, New York: United Nations Printing Office, 1965.

Van Dyke, Vernon. *Human Rights, the United States, and World Community.* New York: Oxford University Press, 1970.

Verdoodt, A. "Ethnic and Linguistic Minorities and the United Nations," *World Justice,* vol. 11, no. 1 (September 1969), pp. 66-75.

Werck, Victor. "The Minority Problem and Modern International Law," *World Justice,* vol. 7 (September 1965), pp. 7-21.

Wilkins, Roy. "Implementing Human Rights: The New Understanding, New Attitudes, and New Will," *Department of State Bulletin,* vol. 58 (May 20, 1968), pp. 661-663.

Notes

Notes

Chapter 1
The Study of Race in American Foreign
Policy and International Relations

1. Gunnar Myrdal, in noting the absence of American research on race and foreign policy, calls it "a conspiracy of silence." "The Role and Reality of Race," speech to the Foreign Policy Association, May 28, 1968, mimeographed.

2. Gabriel Almond, *The American People and Foreign Policy* (New York: Frederick A. Praeger, 1960), pp. xxix-xxx.

3. Almond notes this lack of attention in the social science journals. *Ibid.*, p. 155.

4. *Ibid.*, p. xxx.

5. *Ibid.*

6. It is a striking fact that culture and pluralism receive very scanty treatment in the writings of leading international-relations theorists and American foreign-policy texts. Race is mentioned only as a colonial problem or an issue at the United Nations. Hans Morgenthau, in his discussion of "national character," is an exception, but not even his discussion of national morale suggests the importance of race or pluralism. Felix Gross, in his *World Politics and Tension Areas*, is concerned with ethnic groups, but does not consider race separately.

7. Especially Ashley Montagu and Jacques Barzun.

8. Peter Rose has a good discussion of this in the last chapter of *They and We* (New York: Random House, 1964), pp. 150-161.

9. Otto Klineberg, *Race and Psychology* (Paris: UNESCO, 1951), p. 440.

10. Rose, p. 8.

11. Harold D. Lasswell and Daniel Lerner, eds., *The World Revolution and Elites: Studies in Coercive Ideological Movements* (Cambridge: M.I.T. Press, 1965), p. 94.

12. Anderson, von der Mehden, and Young in their study *Issues of Political Development,* (Englewood Cliffs, N.J.: Prentice-Hall, 1967), point out the significance of racial attitudes in creating cultural stereotypes. "Although race is today largely discredited as a scientific concept, the dynamics of cultural pluralism rest upon subjective human sentiment not the detachment of the scientific laboratory" (p. 21).

13. Pierre van den Berghe, *Race and Racism: A Comparative Perspective* (New York: John Wiley, 1967), p. 22.

14. See Tamotsu Shibutani and Kian M. Kwan, *Ethnic Stratification: A Comparative Approach* (New York: Macmillan, 1965).

15. Anderson, von der Mehden, and Young, p. 26.

16. One method of measuring plurality and race in nations is to be found in Arthur S. Banks and Robert B. Textor, *A Cross Polity Survey* (Cambridge: M.I.T. Press, 1963).

17. Maurice East, "International Political Systems: An Approach Revisited" (Denver: Graduate School of International Studies, February 1968), mimeographed. I am indebted to Professor East for his lucid distinction between an approach and a theory.

18. See Eugene Lerner, "Pathological Nazi Stereotypes Found in Recent German Technical Journals," *Journal of Psychology* vol. 13 (1942), and Frederick Schuman, *The Nazis Dictatorship,* 2nd ed. (New York: Alfred A. Knopf, 1939).

19. This survey was published by the Social Science Research Council as Bulletin 62, 1950.

20. Daniel Katz and Kenneth Braly found strong racial and ethnic stereotypes in one hundred Princeton University students, such as Germans are scientific, Italians are artistic, Negroes are superstitious, English are sportsmanlike, and Jews are shrewd. "Racial Stereotypes of One Hundred College Students," *Journal of Abnormal and Social Psychology,* vol. 28 (1933).

21. See Gabriel Almond and Sidney Verba, *The Civic Culture* (Princeton: Princeton University Press, 1963).

22. R. A. Schermerhorn, "Polarity in the Approach to Comparative Research in Ethnic Relations," *Sociology and Social Research,* vol. 48 (January 1964), p. 237. See also the diagram reproduced below, in Peter Rose's essay.

23. Louis H. Bean, *How to Predict Elections* (New York: Alfred A. Knopf, 1948).

24. Bailey lists eight major factors. The fourth is hyphenated Americans, of which he says, "When wars, revolutions and persecutions have convulsed the homeland, Irish-hyphen-Americans, German-hyphen-Americans, Polish-hyphen-Americans, Jewish-hyphen-Americans, and others have brought pressure on the Washington government to shape foreign policy interests." *A Diplomatic History of the American People,* 6th ed. (New York: Appleton, Century Crofts, 1958), p. 5.

25. Both Bean and Gerson leave this impression. They ignore many other causes such as ideology, geography, and economics.

26. Hans Morgenthau, *Politics among Nations,* 4th ed. (New York: Alfred A. Knopf, 1967).

27. In *Defense of the National Interest,* Morgenthau's major work in the foreign-policy field, his national-interest idea does not allow for multinational interests.

28. Paul Seabury takes this position in "Race in American Foreign Policy," (Denver: Graduate School of International Studies, 1967), mimeographed.

29. Lawrence Fuchs is one of the exceptions. In his study of the role of the Jewish-American he maintains that cultural identity is legitimate and even desirable. See *The Behavior of American Jews* (Glencoe: Free Press, 1956).

30. See Myres S. McDougal and Gerhard Bebr, "Human Rights in the U.N." *American Journal of International Law,* vol. 58 (July 1964), pp. 603-641.

31. Roy Wilkins, "Implementing Human Rights, New Understanding, New Attitudes and New Will," *Department of State Bulletin,* vol. 58, (May 20, 1968), pp. 661-663. Also Richard Gardner, "A Costly Anachronism" (argument for the ratification by the United States of UN conventions on human rights), *American Bar Association Journal,* vol. 53, (October 1967), pp. 907-910.

32. See William Casey Morey, *Diplomatic Episodes* (New York: Longmans

Green, 1926). Also E. H. Carr, The Twenty Years' Crisis, 2nd ed. (New York: St. Martin's Press, 1946), and *Nationalism and After* (New York: Macmillan, 1945).

33. See Michael Edwardes, *High Noon of Empire, India under Curzon,* (London: Eyre and Spottiswoode, 1965).

34. See Fanon's *Toward the African Revolution* (New York: Grove Press, 1967), especially his chapter on "Race and Culture."

35. Ali Mazrui, the African political scientist, gives suggestive subjects in his article, "From Social Darwinism to Current Theories of Modernization: A Tradition of Analysis," *World Politics,* vol. 21 (October 1968), pp. 69-84. Also see Philip Curtin, *The Image of Africa, British Ideas and Action, 1780-1850* (Madison: University of Wisconsin Press, 1964).

36. Lincoln's article, "The Problem of Race in International Relations," *New South,* vol. 21 (Fall 1966), pp. 2-14, was originally given as a paper to a GSIS symposium in Spring 1966.

37. Karl Kaiser, in his article "The Interaction of Regional Sub-Systems," *World Politics,* vol. 21 (October 1968), p. 86, makes the distinction between the historical sociology systems work of Hoffman and Aran as contrasted with the quantitative systems theory of Basten and Kaplan.

38. David Easton's concept of a political system used here is found in his book, *A Systems Analysis of Political Life* (New York: John Wiley, 1965), p. 27.

39. See pp. 31-33 for his comparative models.

40. This has been fully elaborated by Peter Rose, Chapter Two below.

41. Van den Berghe uses the United States as one of the cases in his comparative study (pp. 77-96).

42. See Dankwart A. Rustow, *A World of Nations* (Washington, D.C.: Brookings Institution, 1967), pp. 244-253.

43. Samuel P. Huntington, *Political Order and Changing Societies* (New Haven: Yale University Press, 1960), esp. chap. 1.

44. See Joseph La Polombara, "Macro Theories and Micro Applications," *Comparative Politics,* vol. 1 (April 1968), pp. 61-62.

45. Michael Lofchie, "Political Theory and African Politics," *Journal of Modern African Studies,* vol. 6 (May 1968), p. 14. J. S. Furnivall is generally credited with first outlining the concept of cultural pluralism in his *Colonial Policy and Practice* (Cambridge: Cambridge University Press, 1948). Also see M. G. Smith, "Social and Cultural Pluralism," *Annals of the New York Academy of Sciences,* vol. 83 (January 20, 1960).

46. The pioneering work of Anderson, von der Mehden, and Young has already been noted.

47. *American Journal of Sociology,* vol. 73 (November 1967), p. 299.

48. Banks and Textor (p. 302) define this as "effective allocation of power to functionally autonomous legislative, executive and judicial organs." The data indicate that the greater the degree of pluralism, the less horizontal power distribution.

49. It is interesting to compare the Haug classifications with Anderson, von der Mehden, and Young, pp. 80-81, although they use different variables and

methods. Results are roughly similar, though Equador and Congo-Kinshasa come out with lower ratings for the Wisconsin team than for Haug.

50. Haug, pp. 303-304.

51. Franz Fanon, *Toward the African Revolution* (New York: Monthly Review Press, 1967). See especially "West Indians and Africans" and "Racism and Culture."

52. Stokely Carmichael and Charles Hamilton, *Black Power* (New York: Vintage Books, 1967). "Black people in the United States have a colonial relationship to the larger society, a relationship characterized by institutional racism" (p. 6).

53. Remarks on the panel, "Black America and Black Africa," African Studies Association meeting, Los Angeles, October 1968.

54. Kaiser, pp. 99-100.

55. See Karl Deutsch, *The Nerves of Government,* (London: Free Press of Glencoe, 1963), and *Arms Control and the Atlantic Alliance,* (New York: John Wiley, 1967).

56. Joseph Nye, *Pan-Africanism and East African Integration,* (Cambridge: Harvard University Press, 1965).

57. See Larry Bowman, "The Subordinate State System of Southern Africa," *International Studies Journal,* vol. 12 (September 1968); I. William Zartman, "The Subordinate State System of Africa," *International Organization* (Summer 1967); and George W. Shepherd, Jr., *Non-Aligned Africa: An International Subsystem,* to be published by Van Nostrand.

58. Herbert Spiro does this in his *World Politics: The Global System* (Homewood, Ill.: Dorsey Press, 1966), but he does not stress or develop ideas about plural factors.

59. Rosenau defines an issue-area as: (1) a cluster of values, the allocation or potential allocation of which (2) leads the affected or potentially affected actors to differ so greatly over (a) the way in which values should be allocated or (b) the horizontal levels at which allocations would be authorized that (3) they engage in distinctive behavior designed to mobilize support for the attainment of their particular values. "Pre-Theories and Theories of Foreign Policy," in R. B. Farrel, ed., *Approaches to Comparative and International Politics* (Evanston: Northwestern University Press, 1966), p. 31.

60. James Rosenau, *Domestic Sources of Foreign Policy,* (New York: Free Press, 1967), pp. 30, 36.

61. *Ibid.,* p. 49.

62. See Bowman, "The Subordinate State System of Southern Africa." Also in the same issue of *International Studies Journal* (September 1968), Patrick McGowan in his "Africa and Nonalignment: A Comparative Study of Foreign Policy" develops a concept of nonalignment as interaction with the communist world that totally ignores the ethnic and racial variables. This narrow perspective distorts what otherwise would be an interesting approach.

Chapter 2
The Development of Race Studies

1. See William Stanton, *The Leopards' Spots: Scientific Attitudes Toward Race in America, 1815-59* (Chicago: University Chicago Press, 1960).

2. Jacques Barzun, *Race: A Study in Modern Superstition* (London: Metheun, 1938), p. 159.

3. *Ibid.,* p. 162.

4. See Ruth Benedict, *Race, Science & Politics* (New York: The Viking Press, 1943, rev. ed.) chap. 3. Also S. L. Washburn, p. 524; and Gustav Retizus, "The Development of Race Measurements and Classifications," in *Source Book in Anthropology,* ed. Alfred L. Kroeber and Thomas T. Waterman, rev. ed. (New York: Harcourt, Brace, 1931), pp. 94-102.

5. See, for example, Juan Comas, "Scientific Racism Again?", *Current Anthropology,* vol. 2 (October 1961), pp. 303-340. See also Benedict, esp. chap. 7; and Pierre L. van den Berghe, *Race and Racism* (New York: John Wiley, 1967), esp. pp. 1-18.

6. See UNESCO, *The Race Question in Modern Science* (New York: Whiteside and William Morrow, 1956).

7. See George E. Simpson and J. Milton Yinger, *Racial and Cultural Minorities* (New York: Harper and Row, 1965), pp. 41-48.

8. Franz Boas, *Aryans and Non-Aryans* New York: Information and Service Associates, 1934, p. 11.

9. Theodosius Dobzhansky, "Comment," *Current Anthropology,* vol. 2 (October 1961), p. 31.

10. *Ibid.,* p. 317.

11. Manning Nash, "Race and the Ideology of Race," *Current Anthropology,* vol. 3 (June, 1962), p. 285.

12. Marvin Harris, "Race," *International Encyclopedia of the Social Sciences* (New York: Macmillan, 1968), XIII, 263.

13. *Ibid.* See also Bruce K. Eckland, "Genetics and Sociology: A Reconsideration," *American Sociological Review,* vol. 32 (April 1967), pp. 173-194.

14. Harris, p. 264.

15. H. Hoetink, *The Two Variants of Caribbean Race Relations* (New York: Oxford University Press, 1967), p. 120; and Michael Banton, *Race Relations* (New York: Basic Books, 1968), pp. 54-62.

16. See C. Wright Mills, "The Professional Ideology of Social Pathologists," *American Journal of Sociology,* vol. 49 (September 1943), pp. 165-180.

17. William Graham Sumner, *Folkways* (Boston: Ginn, 1906), p. 13.

18. *Ibid.,* p. 238.

19. See E. B. Reuter, "Racial Theory," *American Journal of Sociology,* vol. 50 (May 1945), pp. 452-461.

20. William I. Thomas, "The Psychology of Race Prejudice," *American Journal of Sociology,* vol. 9 (March 1904), 593-611.

21. Thomas, *Source Book of Social Origins,* p. 156.

22. Sigmund Freud, *Group Psychology and the Analysis of the Ego* (New York: Boni and Liveright, 1950), p. 55.

23. See E. Digby Baltzell, *The Protestant Establishment* (New York: Random House, 1964), p. 104.

24. See Robert E. Park and Ernest W. Burgess, *Introduction to the Science of Sociology* (Chicago: University of Chicago Press, 1924), p. 578. Italics added.

25. See, for example, Robert E. Park, "The Nature of Race Relations," in *Race Relations and the Race Problem,* ed. Edgar T. Thompson (Durham: North Carolina University Press, 1939), pp. 3-45. Italics added.

26. See Reuter, "Racial Theory," pp. 452-461. See also Herbert Blumer, "Reflections on a Theory of Race Relations," in *Race Relations in World Perspective,* ed. Andrew W. Lind (Honolulu: University of Hawaii Press, 1955), pp. 3-21.

27. See Brewton Berry, "The Concept of Race in Sociology Textbooks," *Social Forces,* vol. 18 (1940), p. 11; and Chester L. Hunt, "The Treatment of 'Race' in Beginning Sociology Textbooks," *Sociology and Social Research,* vol. 35 (March-April 1951), pp. 1277-1284.

28. Donald Young, *American Minority Peoples* (New York: Harper, 1932), p. xiii.

29. Louis Wirth, "The Problem of Minority Groups," in *The Science of Man in the World Crisis,* ed. Ralph Linton (New York: Columbia University Press, 1945), p. 347.

30. *Ibid.,* p. 348.

31. *Ibid.*

32. See, for example, E. K. Francis, "The Nature of Ethnic Groups," *American Journal of Sociology,* vol. 52 (March, 1947), pp. 393-400.

33. See Louis Wirth, *The Ghetto* (Chicago: University of Chicago Press, 1928).

34. Reuter, p. 455.

35. *Ibid.*

36. Robert E. Park, "Our Racial Frontier on the Pacific," *Survey Graphic,* vol. 9 (May 1926), p. 196.

37. For synopses and critiques of "race relations cycles" see Brewton Berry, *Race and Ethnic Relations* (Boston: Houghton, Mifflin, 1965), chap. 6; van den Berghe, *Race and Racism,* pp. 25-34; and Banton, *Race Relations,* chap. 4.

38. See Robert E. Park, "Racial Assimilation in Secondary Groups with Particular Reference to the Negro," *Publications of the American Sociological Society,* vol. 8 (1913), pp. 66-83; Robert E. Park, "Human Migration and the Marginal Man," *American Journal of Sociology,* vol. 33 (May 1928), pp. 881-893; and Everett V. Stonequist, *The Marginal Man,* (New York: Scribners, 1937). See also Robert E. Park, "The Concept of Social Distance," *Journal of Applied Sociology,* vol. 8 (1924), pp. 339-344; and the following by Emory S. Bogardus: "Measuring Social Distance," *Journal of Applied Sociology,* vol. 9 (1925), pp. 299-308; "Social Distance: A Measuring Stock," *Survey,* vol. 56 (May 1926), pp. 169-170; and *Immigration and Race Attitudes* (New York: Heath, 1928).

39. See John Dollard, *Caste and Class in a Southern Town* (New Haven: Yale University Press, 1937); Gunnar Myrdal, *An American Dilemma* (New York: Harper, 1944); Bruno Bettelheim and Morris Janowitz, *The Dynamics of Prejudice* (New York: Harper, 1950), and their restudy, *Social Change and Prejudice* (New York: Free Press of Glencoe, 1964); Melvin M. Tumin, *Desegregation* (Princeton: Princeton University Press, 1961); Robin M. Williams, Jr., *Strangers Next Door* (Englewood Cliffs: Prentice-Hall, 1964); Kenneth B. Clark, *Dark Ghetto* (New York: Harper and Row, 1965); Gary T. Marx, *Protest and Prejudice* (New York: Harper and Row, 1967); and Elliot Liebow, *Tally's Corner: A Study of Negro Streetcorner Men* (Boston: Little, Brown, 1967). And see the brief discussion of such work by Hoetink in his *The Two Variants in Caribbean Race Relations*, pp. 62-67.

40. Personal correspondence with Everett C. Hughes, December 9, 1965.

41. Louis Wirth, "Problems and Orientations of Research in Race Relations in the United States," *British Journal of Sociology*, vol. 1 (1930), pp. 118-119.

42. Everett C. Hughes and Helen MacGill Hughes, *Where Peoples Meet* (Glencoe: Free Press, 1952), pp. 8-9. See also Hoetink's discussion of "sociologistic visions" and prevalent optimism in his *Two Variants on Caribbean Race Relations*, pp. 86-90.

43. See Richard Christie and Marie Jahoda, eds., *Studies in the Scope and Method of "The Authoritarian Personality"* (Glencoe: Free Press, 1954); John P. Davis, ed., *The American Negro Reference Book* (Englewood Cliffs: Prentice-Hall, 1966); Milton M. Gordon, "Recent Trends in the Study of Minority and Race Relations," *The Annals* vol. 350 (November 1963), pp. 148-156; John Harding, Bernard Kutner, Harold Proshansky, and Isidor Chien, "Prejudice and Ethnic Relations," in *Handbook of Social Psychology*, II, ed. Gardner Lindsey (Cambridge: Addison-Wesley, 1954), pp. 1021-1061; Otto Klineberg, *Tensions Affecting International Understanding: A Survey of Research* (New York: Social Science Research Council, Bulletin 62, 1950); Raymond W. Mack, "Race Relations," *Social Problems: A Modern Approach*, ed. Howard S. Becker (New York: John Wiley, 1966), pp. 317-358; Elizabeth W. Miller, *The Negro in America: A Research Guide* (Bloomington: Indiana University Press, 1965); Theodore M. Newcomb, "Social Psychology and Group Processes," in *Annual Review of Psychology*, ed. Calvin P. Stone and Donald W. Taylor (Stanford: Annual Reviews, 1953), pp. 183-214; Arnold M. Rose, *Studies in the Reduction of Prejudice* (Chicago: American Council on Race Relations, 1947); Peter I. Rose, *Joint Newsletter on Desegregation* (1961), *Joint Newsletter on Intergroup Relations* (1962), *Research Bulletin on Intergroup Relations* (1963 and 1964), all published in New York: Anti-Defamation League for the Society for the Study of Social Problems and the Society for the Psychological Study of Social Issues; Melford E. Spiro, "The Acculturation of American Ethnic Groups," *American Anthropologist*, vol. 57 (December 1955), pp. 1240-1252; Edward A. Suchman, John P. Dean, and Robin M. Williams, Jr., *Desegregation: Some Propositions and Research Suggestions* (New York: Anti-Defamation League,

1958); Melvin M. Tumin, *Segregation and Desegregation: A Digest of Research* (New York: Anti-Defamation League, 1957), and *Supplement: Segregation and Desegregation* (by the same publisher, 1960); Melvin M. Tumin, *An Inventory and Appraisal of Research on American Anti-Semitism* (New York: Freedom Books, 1961); Melvin M. Tumin, *Research Annual on Intergroup Relations—1965* (New York: Frederick A. Praeger, 1966); Erwin K. Welsch, *The Negro in the United States* (Bloomington: Indiana University Press, 1915); Robin M. Williams, Jr., *The Reduction of Intergroup Tensions: A Survey of Research on Problems of Ethnic, Racial and Religious Group Relations* (New York: Social Science Research Council, Bulletin 57, 1947); and Robin M. Williams, Jr., "Racial and Cultural Relations," in *Review of Sociology: Analysis of a Decade,* ed. Joseph B. Gittler (New York: John Wiley, 1957), pp. 433-464.

44. Gordon W. Allport, *The Nature of Prejudice* (Cambridge: Addison-Wesley, 1954); Brewton Berry, *Race and Ethnic Relations,* 3rd ed. (Boston: Houghton Mifflin, 1965); Ina C. Brown, *Race Relations in a Democracy* (New York: Harper, 1949); E. Franklin Frazier, *Race and Culture Contacts in the Modern World* (New York: Alfred A. Knopf, 1957); Eugene L. Hartley, *Problems in Prejudice* (New York: King's Crown Press, 1946); Charles F. Marden and Gladys Meyer, *Minorities in American Society,* 2nd ed. (New York: American Book Company, 1962); Edward C. McDonagh and Eugene S. Richards, *Ethnic Relations in the United States* (New York: Appleton-Century-Crofts, 1953); Arnold and Caroline Rose, *America Divided* (New York: Alfred A. Knopf, 1953); Peter I. Rose, *They and We: Racial and Ethnic Relations in the United States* (New York: Random House, 1964); R. A. Schermerhorn, *These Our People* (Boston: Heath, 1949); Tamotsu Shibutani and Kian M. Kwan, *Ethnic Stratification: A Comparative Approach* (New York: Macmillan, 1965); George E. Simpson and J. Milton Yinger, *Racial and Cultural Minorities,* 3rd ed. (New York: Harper and Row, 1965); Pierre L. van den Berghe, *Race and Racism* (New York: John Wiley, 1967); James W. Vander Zanden, *American Minority Relations,* 2nd ed. (New York: Ronald Press, 1966); Charles Wagley and Marvin Harris, *Minorities in the New World* (New York: Columbia University Press, 1958); Paul A. F. Walter, Jr., *Race and Culture Relations* (New York: McGraw-Hill, 1952). Also see the following "readers": Milton Barron, *Minorities in a Changing World* (New York: Alfred A. Knopf, 1967); Francis J. Brown and Joseph C. Roucek, *One America,* 2nd ed. (Englewood Cliffs: Prentice-Hall, 1945); Raymond W. Mack, *Race, Class and Power* (New York: American Book Co., 1963); Talcott Parsons and Kenneth Clark, *The Negro American* (Boston: Houghton Mifflin, 1966); Earl Raab, *American Race Relations* (Garden City: Doubleday, 1962); Arnold and Caroline Rose, *Minority Problems* (New York: Harper and Row, 1965); Bernard E. Segal, *Racial and Ethnic Relations* (New York: Crowell, 1966); Marshall Sklare, *The Jews: Social Patterns of an American Group* (Glencoe: Free Press, 1958); Edgar T. Thompson and Everett C. Hughes, *Race: Individual and Collective Behavior* (Glencoe: Free Press, 1958).

45. See Peter I. Rose, *The Subject Is Race: Traditional Ideologies and the Teaching of Race Relations* (New York: Oxford University Press, 1968), esp. chaps. 7, 8, and 9.

46. A very important exception to this trend is found in Hubert Blalock's *Toward a Theory of Minority-Group Relations* (New York: John Wiley, 1967).

47. *Ibid.*, p. 15. See also Melvin M. Tumin, "The Functionalist Approach to Social Problems," *Social Problems*, vol. 12 (Spring 1965), pp. 379-388.

48. Shibutani and Kwan, loc.

49. *Ibid.*, chap. 4.

50. See also Donald L. Noel, "A Theory of the Origin of Ethnic Stratification," *Social Problems*, vol. 16 (Fall 1968), pp. 157-172.

51. *Ibid.*, p. 572.

52. *Ibid.*, p. 573.

53. Donald Noel says that "Ethnic stratification is a system of stratification wherein some relatively fixed group membership (e.g. race, religion or nationality) is utilized as a major criterion for acquiring social positions with their attendant differential rewards" (p. 157).

54. Ibid.

55. See Edward T. Hall, *The Silent Language* (Garden City: Doubleday, 1959).

56. Shibutani and Kwan, p. 574.

57. *Ibid.*, p. 575.

58. *Ibid.*

59. Park, "Our Racial Frontier on the Pacific," p. 196.

60. The comment appears in Schermerhorn's newest work, "Comparative Ethnic Relations" (Random House, in press). Professor Schermerhorn has given me permission to quote from his manuscript.

61. See, for example, Gabriel A. Almond, "A Functional Approach to Comparative Politics," in *The Politics of Developing Areas*, ed. Gabriel A. Almond and James J. Coleman (Princeton: Princeton University Press, 1960), chap. 1.

62. One other book Schermerhorn might have mentioned is Michael Banton's *Race Relations* (New York: Macmillan, 1967). He may have decided not to do so because it is far more difficult to pigeonhole than, say, van den Berghe's. Banton's book is a potpourri: part text, part treatise, part description, part analysis. It is built, in large measure, upon an earlier work, *White and Coloured* (1959), some of his previously published journal papers, and the excellent Munro Lectures he delivered at Edinburgh in 1966. Though not divided as such, the result is the presentation of several "books" in one, each of which fits rather fortuitously into one or another of Schermerhorn's categories.

63. *Race and Racism*, p. 9.

64. *Ibid.*, pp. 9-10.

65. *Ibid.*, p. 11.

66. *Ibid.*, p. 14.

67. *Ibid.*, pp. 14-15.

68. *Ibid.*, pp. 17-18.

69. *Ibid.*, p. 18.

70. I am not certain that the use of the term *Herrenvolk* is appropriate here given its earlier connotation with regard to the self-description of Nazi officials about their societies.

71. See Karl Mannheim, "The Democratization of Culture," in *Essays on the Sociology of Culture* (London: Routledge and Kegan Paul, 1962), pp. 171-246. This essay and the dichotomy discussed in it was brought to my attention by Professor H. Hoetink.

72. *Ibid.,* p. 26.

73. *Ibid.,* pp. 31-33.

74. See, for example, Milton M. Gordon, *Assimilation in American Life* (New York: Oxford University Press, 1964). And see discussion of the uses of the term "pluralism" by Schermerhorn below.

75. See J. S. Furnivall, *Colonial Policy and Practice* (Cambridge: Eng. University Press, 1948); J. H. Boeke, *Economics and Economic Policy of Dual Societies* (New York: 1953; M. G. Smith, "Social and Cultural Pluralism in the Caribbean," *The Annals* vol. 83 (1960), pp. 763-777, and *The Plural Society in the British West Indies* (Berkeley: University of California Press, 1965).

76. Van den Berghe, pp. 34-35.

77. Robert Bierstedt has described this phenomenon in terms of the development of "societal groups." See Robert Bierstedt, "The Sociology of Majorities," *American Sociological Review,* vol. 13 (December 1948), pp. 700-710.

78. See also M. G. Smith, *The Plural Society in the British West Indies* (Berkeley: University of California Press, 1965).

79. Van den Berghe, pp. 122-126.

80. *Ibid.,* p. 126.

81. *Ibid.,* p. 132.

82. *Ibid.,* p. 135.

83. See, for example, Rose, *They and We.*

84. Van den Berghe, pp. 136-138.

85. *Ibid.,* p. 139. See also his article, "Dialectic and Functionalism: Toward a Theoretical Synthesis," *American Sociological Review,* vol. 28 (1963), pp. 695-705.

86. Three notable exceptions to this generalization are Milton M. Gordon, Robert K. Merton, and, especially, Robin M. Williams, Jr., although even their theoretical work on the subject has been confined to the American scene.

87. Banton, *Race Relations,* p. 63.

88. *Ibid.,* p. 64.

89. See Richard A. Schermerhorn, "Toward a General Theory of Minority Groups," *Phylon,* vol. 25 (1964), pp. 238-246.

90. Richard A. Schermerhorn, "Polarity in the Approach to Comparative Research in Ethnic Relations," *Sociology and Social Research,* vol. 51 (January 1967), pp. 235-240.

91. Elsewhere Schermerhorn defines an ethnic group as follows: "a collectivity within a larger society having real or putative common ancestry, memories of a shared historical past, and a cultural focus on one or more symbolic elements defined as the epitome of their peoplehood." The statement appears in his "Comparative Ethnic Relations," chap. 1 (manuscript p. 13).

92. A dominant group is defined by Schermerhorn as "that collectivity within a society which has prominent authority to function both as guardians and sustainers of the controlling value-system, and as prime allocators of rewards in the society." Such dominant groups might be restricted elites, majorities, or an ethnic group, according to his description. See "Comparative Ethnic Relations," p. 13.

93. Schermerhorn, "Polarity in the Approach to Comparative Research in Ethnic Relations," p. 238.

94. Having served as consulting editor on the new Schermerhorn book for Random House, I was able to watch a series of ideas and working typologies grow into a treatise with far-reaching implications. I feel the book is destined to become a primary source for those concerned with examining racial and ethnic relations from a comparative perspective.

95. See, for example, Kingsley Davis, "A Conceptual Analysis of Stratification," *American Sociological Review,* vol. 7 (1942), pp. 309-321; Kingsley Davis and Wilbert E. Moore, "Some Principles of Stratification," *American Sociological Review,* vol. 10 (1945), pp. 242-249; and Melvin M. Tumin, "Some Principles of Stratification: A Critical Analysis," *American Sociological Review,* vol. 18 (1953), pp. 387-394.

96. See also Robin M. Williams, Jr., "Some Further Comments on Chronic Controversies," *American Journal of Sociology,* vol. 71 (1966), pp. 717-721.

97. Schermerhorn, "Comparative Ethnic Relations," manuscript p. 41.

98. See full statement in Georg Simmel, *Conflict,* trans. Kurt Wolff (New York: Free Press, Macmillan, 1955), p. 13; also Lewis A. Coser, *The Functions of Social Conflict* (Glencoe: Free Press, 1956.

99. Gerhard Lenski, *Power and Privilege: A Theory of Social Stratification* (New York: McGraw-Hill, 1966), p. 17.

100. Schermerhorn, "Comparative Ethnic Relations," p. 41.

101. *Ibid.,* pp. 66-67 *passim.*

102. Wirth, "The Problem of Minority Groups," pp. 354-363.

103. See Rose, *They and We,* pp. 131-146. In the early printings Type 3 was called "Avoidance," not "Separatism"; now the latter term is being used (see 7th printing).

104. Two modifications include substituting the word "Incorporation" for "Amalgamation" in Type A and "Autonomy" for "Federalism" in Type B.

105. Again, see Hoetink, *The Two Variants on Caribbean Race Relations,* and Sidney Greenfield's *English Rustics in a Black Skin.* In the latter volume, a study of family life in Barbados, Greenfield stresses the dual perspectives he used, structural-functional and cultural-historical.

106. Schermerhorn manuscript, pp. 17-18.

107. See Schermerhorn manuscript, p. 377. See also Gabriel Almond and Sidney Verba, *The Civic Culture* (Princeton: Princeton University Press, 1963); William Buchanan and Hadley Cantril, *How Nations See Each Other* (Urbana: University of Illinois Press, 1953); Stein Rokkan, "International Action to Advance Comparative Research: The Role of UNESCO," in *Comparing Nations*

ed. R. L. Merritt and Stein Rokkan (New Haven: Yale University Press, 1966); Beatrice Whiting, ed., *Six Cultures* (New York: John Wiley, 1963); and Donald T. Campbell and Robert A. LeVine, "A Proposal for Comparative Cross-Cultural Research on Ethnocentrism," *Journal of Conflict Resolution*, vol. 5 (March 1961), pp. 82-108.

Chapter 3
Race in International Politics:
A Dialogue in Five Parts

1. For example, see Robert S. Browne, *Race Relations in International Affairs* (Washington, D.C.: Public Affairs Press, 1961); Robert K.A. Gardiner, "Race and Color in International Relations," *Daedalus*, vol. 96 (Spring 1967), pp. 296-311; Harold R. Isaacs, "Color in World Affairs," *Foreign Affairs*, vol. 47 (January 1969), pp. 235-250; and Ronald Segal, *The Race War* (New York: Viking Press, 1967).

2. Milton Rokeach, *Beliefs, Attitudes and Values: A Theory of Organization and Change* (San Francisco: Jossey-Bass, 1968), chap. 3.

3. President Kenneth D. Kaunda of Zambia "was unable to continue his speech for almost a minute after he spoke of the 'duplicity and contradiction in the policy of those who profess to be the foremost advocates of freedom, liberty and rule of law'." *New York Times*, September 17, 1968, p. 8.

4. The only two texts to list a substantial number of entries under race in the index were W. W. Kulski, *International Politics in a Revolutionary Age*, 2nd ed. (Philadelphia: J. B. Lippincott, 1968); and Norman J. Padelford and George A. Lincoln, *The Dynamics of International Politics*, 2nd ed. (New York: Macmillan, 1962). A few paragraphs on the subject were found in Hans J. Morgenthau, *Politics among Nations*, 4th ed. (New York: Alfred A. Knopf, 1967); Harold and Margaret Sprout, *Foundations of International Politics* (Princeton: Van Nostrand, 1962); and John G. Stoessinger, *The Might of Nations*, rev. ed. (New York: Random House, 1965). The indexes of the following five texts listed no entry whatsoever equivalent to race: Ivo D. Duchacek, *Conflict and Cooperation among Nations* (New York: Holt, Rinehart and Winston, 1960); K. J. Holsti, *International Politics* (Englewood Cliffs: Prentice-Hall, 1967); A.F.K. Organski, *World Politics*, 2nd ed. (New York: Alfred A. Knopf, 1968); Charles P. Schleicher, *International Relations* (Englewood Cliffs: Prentice-Hall, 1962); and Vernon Van Dyke, *International Politics*, 2nd ed. (New York: Appleton-Century-Crofts, 1966).

5. Arnold J. Toynbee, "Is a 'Race War' Shaping Up?" *New York Times Magazine*, September 29, 1963.

6. A useful point of departure with respect to this literature is the new *International Encyclopedia of the Social Sciences* (New York: Macmillan and Free Press, 1968). In particular see the bibliographies in vol. 13, pp. 267-268, 276-277, and 282.

7. James N. Rosenau, "Moral Fervor, Systematic Analysis, and Scientific Consciousness in Foreign Policy Research," in Austin Ranney, ed., *Political Science and Public Policy* (Chicago: Markham, 1968), pp. 197-236.

8. In *Foreign Affairs* alone, for example, the reader will find in virtually every issue a couple of articles that probe specific situations in which racial factors are considered to be important.

9. James N. Rosenau, "Toward the Study of National-International Linkages," in James N. Rosenau, ed., *Linkage Politics: Essays on the Convergence of National and International Systems* (New York: Free Press, 1969), chap. 3.

10. James N. Rosenau, "Pre-Theories and Theories of Foreign Policy," in R. Barry Farrell, ed., *Approaches to Comparative and International Politics* (Evanston: Northwestern University Press, 1966), pp. 71-88.

11. For a succinct summary of this model, see Robert C. North, "Research Pluralism and the International Elephant," *International Studies Quarterly*, vol. 11 (December 1967), pp. 394-416.

12. Morton A. Kaplan, *System and Process in International Politics* (New York: John Wiley, 1957).

13. Richard C. Snyder, H. W. Bruck, Burton Sapin, *Foreign Policy Decision Making: An Approach to the Study of International Politics* (New York: Free Press, 1962), pp. 14-185.

14. Karl W. Deutsch, "External Influences on the Internal Behavior of States," in Farrell, pp. 5-26.

15. Louis Hartz, *The Founding of New Societies* (New York: Harcourt, Brace and World, 1964). But this exception is cast so fully in historical terms that its application beyond the phenomena investigated is extremely limited.

16. For a poignant set of data in this regard, see E. John Hevi, *An African Student in China* (London: Pall Mall Press, 1965).

17. Harold R. Isaacs, "Group Identity and Political Change: The Role of Color and Physical Characteristics," *Daedalus*, Spring 1967, p. 363.

18. *Ibid.*, p. 364.

19. See note 2.

20. See E. Franklin Frazier, *Black Bourgeoisie* (Glencoe: Free Press, 1957).

21. This is how Rokeach uncovered the findings cited in note 2.

22. Peter F. Drucker, "A Warning to the Rich, White World," *Harper's*, December 1968, p. 67.

23. A good example in this regard is provided by the current U.S. efforts to get food and medical supplies into Biafra.

24. See J. David Singer, "The Level-of-Analysis Problem in International Relations," *World Politics*, vol. 14 (October 1961), pp. 77-92.

25. The useful distinction between system- and subsystem-dominant systems is developed at greater length in Kaplan, pp. 16-17.

26. See James N. Rosenau, "Comparative Foreign Policy: Fad, Fantasy, or Field?" *International Studies Quarterly*, vol. 12 (September 1968), pp. 296-329.

27. For an example of a convincing model at this level of abstraction, see Kaplan, chap. 2.

28. Rosenau, "Moral Fervor, Systematic Analysis, and Scientific Consciousness in Foreign Policy Research."

29. For listings of other forms of conflict behavior, see Rudolph J. Rummel, "The Relationship between National Attributes and Foreign Conflict Behavior," in J. David Singer, ed., *Quantitative International Politics: Insights and Evidence* (New York: Free Press, 1968), pp. 187-214 and Charles A. McClelland and Gary D. Hoggard, "Conflict Patterns in the Interactions among Nations," in James N. Rosenau ed., *International Politics and Foreign Policy: A Reader in Research and Theory* Rev. Ed., (New York: Free Press, 1969), pp. 711-724.

30. Rosenau, "Pre-Theories and Theories of Foreign Policy," pp. 42-48.

31. For a more elaborate discussion of how individual tendencies are altered by the requirements of office, see James N. Rosenau, "Private Preferences and Political Responsibilities: The Relative Potency of Individual and Role Variables in the Behavior of U.S. Senators," in Singer, pp. 17-50.

32. Other examples of the requirements built into top policymaking roles can be found in the attitudes and behavior of the role occupants with respect to other top policymakers, the bureaucracy, domestic groups, and the general public.

33. For an incisive discussion of the impact that different governmental structures can have on policy content, see Kenneth N. Waltz, *Foreign Policy and Democratic Politics: The American and British Experience* (Boston: Little, Brown and Co., 1967).

34. See Jack Sawyer, "Dimensions of Nations: Size, Wealth, and Politics," *American Journal of Sociology,* vol. 73 (September 1967), pp. 145-172; and R. J. Rummel, "Some Dimensions in the Foreign Behavior of Nations," *Journal of Peace Research,* no. 3 (1966), pp. 201-224.

35. Actually the ensuing analysis deviates slightly from this format. In several instances it seemed appropriate either to encompass more than one comparison in a single hypothesis or to hypothesize about the interaction between a race-susceptible variable and the nonracial extreme of a race-susceptible variable in another cluster—with the result that thirty-four formal hypotheses are presented.

36. *New York Times,* March 8, 1963.

37. *Ibid.,* April 22, 1968.

38. *Ibid.,* December 8, 1968, p. 2. Subsequently, in the General Assembly, the proposal was defeated, falling eleven short of the necessary two-thirds majority for adoption. See *New York Times,* December 14, 1968, p. 11.

39. *Ibid.,* October 14, 1968, p. 15.

40. Rosenau, "Private Preferences and Political Responsibilities: The Relative Potency of Individual and Role Variables in the Behavior of U.S. Senators," pp. 28-50.

41. The reaction to Senator Ellender's aforementioned (p. 30) venture into African politics, for example, was of this order, albeit there is no evidence as to whether the outcry subsequently curbed similar predispositions on the part of like-minded senators.

42. Marshall R. Singer, "Weak States in a Power-Full World" (mimeograph), chap. 4, p. 39.

43. For an analysis of the vote on this resolution, see *New York Times,* December 21, 1966.

44. See Howard J. Taubenfeld, *Race, Peace, Law, and Southern Africa* (New York: Association of the Bar of the City of New York, 1966), pp. 36-79; and Vernon Van Dyke, "Violations of Human Rights as Threats to the Peace" (mimeograph 1968).

45. Morton A. Kaplan, "Intervention in Internal War: Some Systemic Sources," in James N. Rosenau ed., *International Aspects of Civil Strife* (Princeton: Princeton University Press, 1964), pp. 92-121.

46. For an account of one such protest in Lisbon, see *New York Times,* January 2, 1969, p. 1.

47. Most notably see Rudolph J. Rummel, "Dimensions of Conflict Behavior within and between Nations," *General Systems: Yearbook of the Society for General Systems Research,* vol. 3 (1963), 1-50; and Raymond Tanter, "Dimensions of Conflict Behavior within and between Nations" (Bloomington: Indiana University, Ph.D. diss., 1964).

48. For evidence that foreign criticism mounts as racial tensions increase see William Parente, "A Comparative Analysis of American Racial Conflict in the Communist Press" (Washington: American Political Science Association, mimeograph, 1968).

49. In Singer, pp. 213-214.

50. *Pakistan Affairs* (issued by the Embassy of Pakistan, Washington, D.C.); *The Bulletin* (issued by the Press and Information Office of the German Federal Government); and *News from South Africa* (issued by the Information Service of South Africa, New York).

Chapter 4
**Research Problems on Race in
Intranational and International Relations**

1. Walter White's autobiography is called *A Man Named White* (New York: Viking Press, 1948).

2. See Chapter One above, Table 1.1.

3. Carolyn Ware, "Ethnic Communities," *Encyclopedia of the Social Sciences,* 1st ed. (New York: Macmillan, 1931), V, 607-613.

4. I wrote an essay on this when I was a graduate student at Harvard, in 1942.

5. Harold Isaacs, *Emergent Americans: A Report on "Crossroads Africa"* (New York: John Day, 1961).

6. Norman Podhoretz, *Making It* (New York: Random House, 1967).

Chapter 5
Comparative Policy in White Dominance Systems:
A Framework of Analysis

1. Gabriel Almond speaks of the importance of the systems concept, "The emerging analytical framework in contemporary political theory is the concept of system whether it is employed at the level of sub-national, regional, or structural units, such as communities, legislative bodies or committees, at the level of the international political system." "Political Theory and Political Science," *American Political Science Review,* December 1966, p. 876.

2. *Ibid.,* p. 877.

3. "Guidelines for a Study of the Effectiveness of Policies and Measures against Discrimination," United Nations (A/Conf.32/11), February 29, 1968, prepared for the International Conference on Human Rights in Teheran.

4. *Ibid.,* p. 5.

5. See Roger Bastide, "Color, Racism and Christianity," *Daedalus,* Spring 1967, pp. 312-328.

6. Badi Foster, "Racial Aspects and Implications of Arab-African Relations," paper delivered to I.S.A. Convention, San Francisco, 1969; André Beteille, "Race and Descent as Social Categories in India," *Daedalus,* Spring 1967, pp. 444-464.

7. R. A. Schermerhorn, "Polarity in the Approach to Comparative Research in Ethnic Relations," *Sociology and Social Research,* January 1964, p. 237. See also above, Chapter Two.

8. See his *Comparative Ethnic Relations: A Framework for Theory and Research* (New York: Random House, 1970).

9. Pierre van den Berghe, *Race and Racism: A Comparative Perspective* (New York: John Wiley, 1967), p. 33.

10. See Ted Robert Gurr in *Violence in America,* ed. H. D. Davis and T. R. Gurr (New York: Signet, 1969); Edward Feit, "Urban Revolt in South Africa," *Journal of Modern African Studies,* April 1970, vol. 8, no. 1, pp. 37-54.

11. See "Special Study of Racial Discrimination in the Political, Economic, Social and Cultural Spheres," Hernan Santa Cruz, reporter (E/CN4,Sub.2/301), June 24, 1969.

Index

About the Contributors

George W. Shepherd, Jr. received his B.A. from the University of Michigan in 1949 and his Ph.D. from the University of London in 1952. He taught political science at Brooklyn College and St. Olaf College. Since 1961 he has been at the University of Denver as a professor of international relations. In 1964-65, Professor Shepherd was a Rockefeller Foundation Visiting Professor at Khartoum. He is currently associated with the Graduate School of International Studies, University of Denver, is director of the Center on International Race Relations, and is editor of *Africa Today*. Among his publications are *They Wait in Darkness* (Day, 1956) and *Politics of African Nationalism: Challenge to American Policy* (Praeger, 1962).

Tilden J. LeMelle, co-editor of this volume, received his B.A. in 1953 and M.A. in 1958 from Xavier University and his Ph.D. in international relations and African politics in 1965 from the University of Denver. Professor LeMelle has taught at Grambling College, Northern Illinois University, and Fordham University. Currently he is a visiting professor at the Graduate School of International Studies, University of Denver, and is associate director of the Center on International Race Relations. He was a Hudson Institute scholar in 1967, a U.S. Office of Education lecturer in 1968, and received a Social Science Foundation research grant in 1968. Professor LeMelle has published a number of articles on African politics and with his brother co-authored *The Black College* (1969).

Peter Rose is a professor of anthropology and sociology at Smith College. In 1954 he received his B.A. and in 1957 his M.A. from Syracuse and in 1959 his Ph.D. from Cornell. He taught at Goucher College before going to Smith in 1960 and was a Fulbright lecturer at the University of Leicester in 1964-65. Professor Rose edited *The Study of Society* (Random House, 1968) and authored *The Subject Is Race* (Oxford University Press, 1968).

James Rosenau has been a professor of political science at Rutgers University since 1949. He received his B.A. from Bard College in 1948, an M.A. from Johns Hopkins in 1949 and from Princeton in 1952, and his Ph.D. from Princeton in 1957. His publications include: *International Politics and Foreign Policy,* editor (1969), *Public Opinion and Foreign Policy* (1961), *National Leadership and Foreign Policy* (1963), and *Contending Approaches to International Politics,* editor (1969).

Karl Deutsch received his doctorate in political science from Charles University, Pargue, in 1938 and his Ph.D. from Harvard in 1951. He has taught at Massachusetts Institute of Technology and Yale and has been professor of government at Harvard since 1967. Professor Deutsch was a Guggenheim Fellow in 1954 and a lecturer at Fletcher School of Law and Diplomacy, 1955-1960. Among his publications are *Nationalism and Social Communication* (M.I.T. Press, 1966) and *Arms Control and the Atlantic Alliance* (John Wiley, 1967).